PENGUIN BOOKS

ACTION PARK

Andy Mulvihill is the son of Action Park founder Gene Mulvihill. At the park, Andy worked testing rides and as a lifeguard before moving into a managerial role. He is currently the CEO of Crystal Springs Resort Real Estate.

Jake Rossen is a senior staff writer at *Mental Floss*. His byline has appeared in *The New York Times*, *Playboy*, *The Village Voice*, ESPN.com, and *Maxim*, among other outlets. He is also the author of *Superman vs. Hollywood*, which examines the life of the Man of Steel from 1940s radio dramas to big-budget features.

ACTION PARK

Fast Times, Wild Rides, and the
Untold Story of America's
Most Dangerous Amusement Park

Andy Mulvihill

with Jake Rossen

PENGUIN BOOKS

PENGUIN BOOKS
An imprint of Penguin Random House LLC
penguinrandomhouse.com

All photos courtesy of the author.

LIBRARY OF CONGRESS CATALOGING-IN-PUBLICATION DATA
Names: Mulvihill, Andy, author. | Rossen, Jake, author.
Title: Action Park : fast times, wild rides, and the untold story
    of America's most dangerous amusement park / Andy Mulvihill
    with Jake Rossen.
Description: New York : Penguin Books, 2020.
Identifiers: LCCN 2020011878 (print) | LCCN 2020011879 (ebook) |
    ISBN 9780143134510 (trade paperback) | ISBN 9780525506294 (ebook)
Subjects: LCSH: Action Park (Vernon, N.J.)—History. | New Jersey—
    Social life and customs—20th century.
Classification: LCC GV1853.3.N52 A476 2020 (print) |
    LCC GV1853.3.N52 (ebook) | DDC 791.06/874976—dc23
LC record available at https://lccn.loc.gov/2020011878
LC ebook record available at https://lccn.loc.gov/2020011879

Printed in the United States of America
10 9 8 7 6 5 4 3 2 1

Book design by Daniel Lagin

For Gene

Contents

ACTION PARK

The Cannonball Loop, open only sporadically over the years due to its uncanny ability to maim our guests.

PROLOGUE

My knees will not stop trembling.

I'm standing some sixty feet in the air at the mouth of an enclosed water slide, padded hockey equipment cinched tightly to my arms, legs, and torso. The artificial bulk is intended to protect my adolescent body against whatever trauma is waiting at the other end. Leaning precariously against a dirt-strewn hill in an empty parking lot, the blue tube resembles a giant drinking straw with a knot inexplicably tied at the bottom.

The hope is that, if I jump in, my momentum will push me through the improbable three-hundred-and-sixty degree vertical turn at the far end and out the other side. It feels like the kind of thing NASA would force astronauts to do to assess their fitness for space. I envision a doctor using a penlight to look at my unfocused pupils in the aftermath, offering a dismissive shake of his head at my poor judgment.

As he wraps my head in bandages, I will tell him it was not my idea. It was my father's.

According to my older sister, Julie, I'm the first human to make the attempt. Prior to this, someone had tied off the ankles and sleeves of an old janitorial jumpsuit, stuffed it with sand, and fabricated a head out of a plastic grocery bag. The makeshift dummy cleared the loop but emerged decapitated.

"We haven't told Mom you're doing this," she says, by way of encouragement.

Today, a mechanical engineer would use computer software to calculate the exact pitch of the chute required for riders to make it through successfully. An army of lawyers would pour over the injury statistics for comparable attractions and demand changes based on risk mitigation. A feasibility expert would evaluate plans and antici- pate logistical issues.

This being 1980, none of that happened. Instead, my father drew the slide on a cocktail napkin and hired some local welders, who had just been laid off from a nearby car factory, to cobble it together. On windy days, it wobbles back and forth, perilously unanchored to its temporary location in the lot.

"Looks feasible," he said.

I peer into the opening. The smell of the industrial glue that ad- heres the foam to the tubing stings my nostrils. (Later, the fumes from this same glue, combined with a lack of ventilation, will cause workers erecting other rides to pass out, angering my father with their reduced productivity.) It's so completely and utterly dark inside that jumping in seems like attempting interdimensional travel. I've tested rides for my father's amusement park before, and teenage bra- vado has always trumped common sense, but this thing—he calls it the Cannonball Loop—is giving me second thoughts.

I'm sixteen years old and about to become the Chuck Yeager of this monument to the total perversion of physics.

"Andy!"

I look down at my father. He's tall, about six-two, with a booming voice that adds a few inches. His hair, neatly combed, gives him the im-maculate appearance of a G.I. Joe doll. Bellowing is a standard method of communication for him. It's strange to see him look so small.

"Come on!"

Today he is impatient. There's just a month left before we open for the summer season. The Loop is supposed to be a flagship attraction. It looks like it promises total mayhem, an illusion of risk that is the backbone of any amusement park.

Except that here, in the place my father calls Action Park, risk has never been an illusion. If something looks dangerous, that's because it is.

"Andy! We don't have all day!"

Paranoia enters my thoughts. *There are six of us kids. Maybe six is too many. Maybe he's decided five is better.*

My hands grip the edges of the Loop's entrance. My father never twists my arm. He never has to. If I don't test it, he'll offer an em-ployee a hundred bucks to do it. I know it's my choice, the same one he gives anybody who passes through the turnstiles. Buy the ticket, take the ride. I think Hunter S. Thompson said that, but surely, even if he were on all the drugs in the world, Hunter S. Thompson would not go down the Cannonball Loop.

I blink sweat from my eyes. The words my father recently uttered to a visiting newspaper reporter ring in my head. "I'm going to be the Walt Disney of New Jersey," he said, gesturing at the tangled and dysfunctional aberration he expected would launch him into amuse-ment park history.

Being the son of the Walt Disney of New Jersey sounded pretty good, I had to admit.

I take a deep breath, tuck my arms into my chest, and do what I always do when my father calls me to action.

I jump in.

WHEN DISNEYLAND OPENED ITS GATES FOR THE FIRST TIME ON JULY 17, 1955, seventy million people were watching on television. In less than a year's time, Walt Disney had turned 200 acres of orange groves in Anaheim, California, into a wonderland. Cinderella hugged little girls. Rides spun, and children laughed like they were on helium. A future president, Ronald Reagan, hosted the opening ceremony. Staring into the ABC cameras, Disney beamed. He had willed his $17 million dream into reality.

Watching him, you'd never realize the shit show people were walking into.

Traffic into the park backed up for more than seven miles. When families finally pulled in, kids nursing full bladders popped out of their cars and began urinating in the parking lot. A plumber's strike meant that most of the drinking fountains weren't working, a problem exacerbated by the one-hundred-degree heat. The temperature was melting the freshly poured asphalt and turning the pavement into quicksand. Counterfeiters had forged tickets, so almost 30,000 people, double the expected number, stuffed themselves into the park. Over capacity, the ferryboat ride nearly capsized. It was bedlam.

Despite these calamities, Disney had no choice but to open. He had agreed to the opening-day broadcast months in advance, and there was no rescheduling. Backed into a corner, he did the best he could. When a ride malfunctioned, he diverted the cameras to another part of the park. When he saw a huge pile of dirt left over from construction, he had someone stick a sign at the top: LOOKOUT MOUNTAIN.

Women snapped their shoes in half on the gooey paths. Children searched for water like they were stranded in the desert.

On television, though, there were only smiling faces. Walt knew where to point the camera.

Disney eventually smoothed out the rough edges, scrubbing any trace of imperfection from his fantasy. There was no chipping paint, no loose wiring, no surly Snow White. The reward for the steep admission price was total immersion into a fantasy; you could forget about real life.

Action Park made the same promise, but it never smoothed out its rough edges. Through the twenty summers it was open, every day was opening day.

MY FATHER'S NAME WAS GENE MULVIHILL, AND, BEFORE HE OPENED Action Park, he had no experience of any kind running an amusement operation. In contrast to Disney's carefully conceived fantasy lands, my father pieced together a series of ambitious and often ill-advised attractions on the side of a ski mountain in rural New Jersey that he had come to own virtually by accident.

He started slowly, installing go-karts, small-scale Formula One racers, and unusual contraptions developed in West Germany with no demonstrable history of safe operation. Then came the water slides, speedboats, and Broadway-style shows. The crowds grew from a handful of curious locals to more than a million people annually. We went from selling off-brand soda and taking out local newspaper ads to getting a Pepsi sponsorship and seeing our logo on McDonald's tray liners. My father, who had simply wanted to find a way to make money off a ski resort in the summer, found himself an unlikely pioneer in the amusement industry.

Unlike most theme parks, Action Park did not strap in patrons and let them passively experience the rides. A roller coaster, thrilling as it may be, asks nothing of its occupants, and each ride is the same as the last. My father seized upon the idea that we were all tired of being coddled, of society dictating our behaviors and lecturing us on our vices. He vowed that visitors to Action Park would be the authors of their own adventures, prompting its best-known slogan: "Where you're the center of the action!" Guests riding down an asbestos chute on a plastic cart could choose whether to adopt a leisurely pace or tear down at thirty miles per hour and risk hitting a sharp turn that would eject them into the woods. They decided when to dive off a cliff and whether to aim for open water or their friend's head. They could listen when the attendants told them to stay in the speedboats, or they could tumble into the marsh water and risk getting bit by a snapping turtle.

It was not long before our visitors reworked our advertising to better reflect their experiences: "Action Park: Where you're the center of the accident."

The risk did not keep people away. The risk is what drew them to us.

Their cars emerged from the Lincoln Tunnel, from Newark, New York, and New Haven, a chain of impatient day-trippers blaring their horns as traffic backed up on the tiny, two-lane roadway leading to the property. After screaming at the parking-lot attendants scrambling to keep up with the incoming masses, they burst out of their vehicles and flew past the ticket window, flashing their frequent-visitor discount cards.

In those searing New Jersey summers, they quickly stripped out of their Sasson jeans and down to their bathing suits, young men and women alike, gleefully crowding around rides while Bruce Springsteen and Southside Johnny blared through pole-mounted loudspeakers, the soundtrack for their contusions. They careened down towering water slides that spit them into shallow pools at such velocity that they sometimes overshot and landed in the dirt, laughing or bleeding—often both. They lost their grip on swinging ropes and plunged into freezing mountain water that made their bodies seize up in shock while their friends cheered on their encroaching hypothermia. They emerged from lakes stinking of spilled diesel fuel from overworked boat motors, too delirious with enthusiasm to realize that they were now flammable.

In their haste to get to the next attraction, people would stumble and skin their bare knees or elbows. Undaunted, they would straighten themselves up and continue, too caught up in the excitement of the place to worry about a few bruises. Repeat visitors stuffed their pockets with Band-Aids and sported scabs and scars along their arms and legs. The fourteen-dollar admission bought them an escape from the mundane, from the rules and regulations forced upon them by their bosses, teachers, or parents.

"People like not being restricted," my father told reporters who inevitably asked why his customers were bleeding. "They want to be in control."

His philosophy became the park's identity. My dad didn't have the budget to stand out from an increasingly crowded amusement industry. He set himself apart by promising guests that they were in charge of their own thrills.

That approach made us national news. *The New York Times* called my father's creation "the area's most distinctive expression of the amusement park in our age." They also called it a "human zoo." Both of these things were true.

The park yanked my siblings and me from idle adolescence and tasked us with corralling and protecting the guests who took its promises of risk to heart. Other kids worked at fast-food restaurants. We spent fourteen-hour days wrangling adults and saving lives. We bonded over the outsized responsibilities, the park morphing from a playground for paying customers to our second home. Two of my brothers met their wives there. I spent ten summers walking through a tangible manifestation of our father's psyche, every ride and attraction a tribute to his impulses. I bled into the dirt as it erupted around me. I watched it grow from a small assembly of modest attractions to a sprawling adventure land that even the mighty Disney attempted to emulate. I pulled gasping swimmers from churning water. I patrolled the grounds on a dirt bike, becoming my father's eyes and ears. I found my first love there. I forged lifelong relationships. I saw death. I grew up.

Action Park has become a campfire tale, an urban legend, a can-you-believe-this snapshot of our culture that seemed to predate liability laws and lawyers. The state of New Jersey had never seen anything like it and had little idea how to control it. My father loomed large in the small town of Vernon, keeping hundreds of people employed and using his political savvy—as well as his sometimes-questionable legal means—to make sure his passion project remained afloat. The state would fine other parks or threaten them with shutdowns when a guest stubbed a toe. Action Park remained open for twenty years despite injuries being a near-hourly occurrence.

The price for its success was sometimes paid by visitors, not all of whom came out alive, and sometimes by my father. The state once held a three-day hearing to discuss his outlandish approach to business and how best to deal with him. I'm pretty sure that never happened to Walt.

The park admitted anyone, misfits and clergymen, rich and poor, young and old, and told them it was theirs to do with as they pleased; never again would they have such freedom in their lives. The churn went on all day, people bouncing from the miniature race cars to the Colorado River Ride to the Kamikaze slide. Come closing time, at 10:00 p.m., they'd reluctantly head to their cars, making plans to return while showing off their scrapes and abrasions. Back home, exhausted and exhilarated, they would grab a pair of scissors and cut off the plastic wrist strap that acted as proof of admission.

It looked almost exactly like a hospital bracelet.

FROM THE TOP OF THE LOOP, I CAN SEE A CHURCH STEEPLE, TO which I quickly aim a fervent prayer before diving in. It is like jumping into a cement mixer. The blackness envelops me, the momentum pulling my body down the slide as though it were vacuum-pressured. There is a brief sensation of being upended by the circle, my back sliding along the foam surface before it levels out, and I'm returned to an upright position. There is no sense of up or down, only the g-forces tugging at my limbs the way one would torture a Stretch Armstrong doll. I'm unceremoniously spit out the other end, loose asphalt scraping my exposed skin. The experience is less a ride than a violent encounter with a supernatural force.

I stand up, dizzy. Later, we will tell visitors to lay motionless for a moment after coming out of the Loop, like divers who need to decompress.

My father waves his arms with excitement. I am the proof of concept, and my survival pleases him. It means profits.

"How was it?"

I want to tell him it felt like being flushed out of a toilet bowl, that there is nothing pleasant about it. The creases around his eyes and the smile taking over his face make me swallow my words.

"It's great," I tell him. "It's awesome."

He beams.

After my triumphant test ride, the next person to slide down the Loop without padding or a helmet smashes his face into the wall of the tube when he hits that first terrible corner, losing his two front teeth. The guy after him isn't much luckier. He cuts his arm on the teeth, which are still stuck in the slide.

No one would hear of this for years. Like Walt, my father knew exactly where to point the camera.

The mountain.

The poster commemorating the opening of the Alpine Slide, our first real attraction. Side effects included skin abrasions, anaphylaxis, and loss of consciousness.

Chapter One

FORT NONSENSE

"Anyone waiting for a chance to hit the ski slopes might consider Vernon Valley's new Alpine Slide as an alternative. It has all the excitement and thrills of a bobsled ride except that it takes place on a $500,000 asbestos chute. Fun for ages 6 to 60."

Daily Record (Morris County, NJ), September 7, 1977

lashes of my father's life, before the mountain consumed and upended all of our lives—who he was, what he did—throb like a strobe light. I knew that he once worked on Wall Street and that, when I was around five, our family moved from a modest home in New Providence to a ten-acre lot next to the Great Swamp National Wildlife Refuge in Harding Township, New Jersey. My mother helped design the sprawling house they built there—the result of my father's successful mutual-fund brokerage business, Mayflower Securities. Years later, when *Vanity Fair* profiled him for allegedly swindling the US ambassador to France in a real estate deal that went south, they referred to him as a "rural schemer" and a "minor legend" on Wall Street.

He took offense to both labels. "Rural?" he said. "Minor?"

The house in Harding was large enough to accommodate his desire for a large family. It was also an outlet for my father's appetite for movement and activity, broadcasting his distaste for sedentary loafing. He erected a gymnasium with an indoor basketball court. We had a pool and a tennis court, the latter of which was lit so he could play at night, striking balls with Bruce Lee–like groans—*ki-yahh! Ay-yahh!* There was enough land for impromptu baseball, football, and soccer games, and enough trees to get away with hiding *Playboy* magazines in hollow trunks. The dead-end road let us zip around on go-karts and dirt bikes without fear of being smeared by incoming traffic. A pond held two beautiful ducks that paddled across its surface until my father skipped a large rock across the water and accidentally killed one. It was years before he confessed.

He had met my mother, Gail, while she was out on a date with someone else. Relentless, he pursued her with the same single-minded determination that defined everything in his life. They were married while he was enlisted in the Marine Corps. When my mother was pregnant with their first child, he began selling Kirby vacuum cleaners door-to-door. He would barge into homes, launching into his sales patter and demonstrating how easy it was to assemble the cleaner. (It was not easy at all without practice, as customers soon found out.) Emboldened by his success, he started selling mutual funds on the belief that, if he could sell vacuums, he could sell anything. When he realized he was better at the stock market than his boss, he decided to go into business for himself. His staff ballooned, filling up multiple offices in New York and New Jersey.

The secret to his success, he said, was motivating his salesmen by stoking their egos. There were lavish parties with nine-hundred-pound ice sculptures and car giveaways, trips and flowing booze, competitions and trophies. Once he gave a six-foot award to a salesman less than five feet tall, the gathering erupting in laughter as the man tried to drag it back to his seat.

One of the stockbrokers, Joe Stone, came over for dinner one night. My father took the kids aside, a brood six strong that he often made march with military precision for guests. We had to salute him when we were done.

"You have to call him the Great . . . Joe Stone," he said.

"What?" said my younger brother Jimmy.

"The Great . . . Joe Stone," my father said.

"The Great Joe Stone," I said, happy to help.

"No!" he snapped. "A pause! The Great . . . Joe Stone."

We did as we were told. Joe Stone beamed the entire night.

My father was strict about schoolwork and chores. The Marine Corps instilled in him a love of militant structure. He wore a buzz cut for most of my early childhood, letting his hair grow out only when the culture of the '70s demanded it. But, somehow, a mischievousness co-existed with all of this, one that always seemed at odds with his demand for domestic order. Once, on a family trip to Colorado, he visited a friend who raised organic, grass-fed lamb. We brought home metal suitcases full of frozen raw meat, our clothes shunted off to the side, the meat's juices beginning to drip as it thawed on the drive back home. Our car smelled like a butcher shop for weeks. Another time, he came home late from work and scooped up my two sleeping older brothers, then just small boys, so he could take them to a carnival he had seen while driving. He barreled through things, rarely pausing to consider logistics. One February, he was playing a highly competitive game of tennis with a friend of his named Bob Brennan in New York City. With the score tied after two hours of play, the club closed. My father tried to persuade the staff to leave the lights on, but they refused. It was snowing, and no other indoor club was open.

"What we'll do," my father told Bob, "is we'll go to Puerto Rico."

The two of them drove to Kennedy Airport and flew to San Juan, where they continued playing on a hotel court until it was dark and they were again asked to move along. They found a second hotel with a court. Instead of checking in, they figured out how to turn on the lights by themselves. My father was able to secure the victory before they were chased off by the staff.

There never seemed to be a barrier between his impulses and his actions. The voice in our heads that says *stop* or *wait* or *let's think this over* was silent for him.

Which explains the mountain.

THE MOUNTAIN WAS IN VERNON, A LAKE AND FARMING COMMUNITY in Sussex County, New Jersey, roughly an hour from our house. The town covered sixty-eight square miles, most of it connected by roads that wouldn't allow vehicles to exceed forty miles per hour. No one seemed to mind. The atmosphere was relaxed and unhurried. There was one high school, one bank, and no fast-food restaurants. The residents had only recently started to outnumber the cows. Legend had it that when George Washington's troops passed through hills thirty miles south during the Revolution, they began constructing a barricade at Washington's behest to stave off the boredom that permeated the area. The sign read: FORT NONSENSE. It was a hint of things to come.

Vernon's biggest industry had originally been mining. Then farming. Then an entrepreneur named Jack Kurlander visited and decided its undulating terrain would be perfect for skiing. He opened a resort called Great Gorge in 1965. The other resort, Vernon Valley, was erected a few years later by a small group of investors who believed there was untapped potential in a second slope within driving distance of New York City. Great Gorge appealed to serious skiers who wanted to get their practice in before heading out west. The new investors promised more novice and intermediate trails to accommodate beginners.

Vernon Valley was happy to pander to the casual crowd. They hired cute girls from the high school in nearby Sparta and had them load skiers on the chair lifts while sporting impossibly tight ski pants. Skiers went down the mountain in jeans and leather jackets. It was a quintessentially Jersey slope.

Fearing an exodus, Great Gorge countered by opening a petting zoo. It was a mistake. A worker fended off an attacking ostrich by stuffing a paintbrush in its mouth. It died of lead poisoning. At one point, someone brought in a kangaroo that would box the maintenance workers. The kangaroo went undefeated, a marsupial George Foreman.

Through a mutual friend, the Vernon Valley people approached my father for a loan. He had long held a variety of interests in other businesses, some wildly successful, some not. An attempt to raise giant shrimp in Florida resulted in mass casualties, with the survivors barely reaching two inches in length. He agreed to lend the resort $25,000 for improvements.

While my father looked forward to a return on his investment, he was almost as enthusiastic about getting free admission to the resort. Soon, we were all careening down the mountain, the entire family ebullient that this bastardized version of Vermont was so close to us. He sent us off to grade school with our pockets stuffed full of ski-lift tickets, lubricating our social lives. I'm certain that I avoided a handful of prepubescent beatings because I could produce a pass to a winter paradise.

We kept visiting, even after the resort's operators began missing loan payments.

In the arms race to compete with Great Gorge, the Vernon Valley people overextended themselves. They had spent too much and endured too many warm winters. The banks commenced foreclosure, and my father, smelling blood, bought the resort for pennies on the dollar in 1972. (Though not all of it: A large chunk of land running through the top of the mountain was leased from the state's Department of Environmental Protection, a fact that would later come back to haunt him.) He had never, to anyone's knowledge, exhibited any interest in owning a ski resort. Then again, he had never expressed a passion for giant shrimp, either.

"Guess what?" he told my mother. "We own Vernon Valley." He might as well have said that we now owned a salvage-diving operation or a circus.

"Why?" she asked.

"I decided it might be fun," he said. That was all the explanation she was going to get.

Wall Street had taught him to be bold and brash, to act quickly while others fretted and deliberated. He soon became a snow-caked P. T. Barnum, distancing himself from Great Gorge with an assortment of attractions. He offered night skiing, with trails illuminated by floodlights, and kept the slopes open twenty-four hours for all-night ski parties. He hired Suzy Chaffee, an Olympic alpine ski racer later known for her ChapStick commercials and made-for-TV movies like *Ski Lift to Death*, to perform demonstrations. During a fuel crisis and the resulting gas shortages, he partnered with the local pump station and bought tanks of fuel so no one would be stranded if the stations decided to close on the weekends. He marketed the fact that the snowmaking operation was the largest in the country, its air and water guns working overtime in the middle of the night, and set up a telephone hotline so people could call for the latest weather conditions.

"We're taking the risk out of skiing," he told the press. "Not the risk of personal injury, of course. The risk of the weather not cooperating."

He mastered the weather. People came.

He kept the booze flowing in the Hexagon Lounge, a six-sided bar that allowed the unpolished locals to mingle with families from the Upper West Side. So many people came up and down the entrance stairs in heavy ski boots that the foot traffic rounded off the edges of the steps. If there was ice on the surface, Jimmy and I could surf over them in our shoes, toes pointed down.

Amid the increasing flow of customers, it was easy to get in the lift line without a ticket. During one busy Saturday, someone cut in line wearing an old pair of wooden skis. An employee asked where his lift pass was. When he didn't produce it, the employee ran to a utility room and burst out wielding an ax, like Jack Nicholson in *The Shining*.

"Thief!" he yelled, hacking the skis off at the tips.

Guests screamed and fled the scene as best they could, their feet bolted to giant sticks. My father had put two of the maintenance workers up to it, both for his own amusement and as a cautionary tale for line cutters. The story spread. People paid.

The resort did well enough that my father eventually acquired Great Gorge from Kurlander, cementing his conquest of the region's ski business. He had moved on from Mayflower, eager to get out from under the thumb of regulatory hassles. By the mid-1970s, more people were learning to ski at Vernon Valley than anywhere else in the country.

Despite the success of the resort, my father could never come to terms with the idea that he owned something he could monetize only a few months out of the year. Even at its zenith—with the ski parties and the corporate retreat specials—the best he could hope for was one hundred days of business, and even that was only by openly defying the laws of nature with snowmaking. A terrible winter could still ruin him, as it had countless other resorts. It gnawed at him.

And then he had an idea.

"LOOK AT THIS," HE HAD SAID, WAVING A COPY OF *TIME* **IN OUR FACES** during dinner, the pages slick with salad dressing. We all ate whenever he came home from work. Sometimes that was six o'clock. Sometimes it was nine.

He read from the article: "'Americans will spend $960 million going to theme parks this year, more than they spend to attend all the major sporting events combined.' Nine hundred and sixty million!"

"So that's what we're doing?" my older sister, Julie, said, a touch of wariness in her voice. "A theme park?"

He had raised us as skiers and campers, not roller-coaster devotees. Though we had made the requisite American pilgrimage to the Disney parks, the Ferris wheels of the Jersey Shore held little appeal. Theme parks outside of Walt's dominion had not yet become grand spectacles. Some were ambitious. Others looked ramshackle, their creaky contraptions seemingly on the verge of causing cotton-candy-tinged tragedy.

"Not just a theme park, Rosebud," he said, using his nickname for her. "A theme park where you control the action."

"Like driving?" Topher said. Christopher, or Topher, was the youngest of the six kids. He was a cheerful optimist. The park would soon test that.

"Right." He cited *Time* again. "'People are tired of passive experiences. They want to be active participants in rides.' How many times have I said that?"

He had said it many times. My father was a participant in life, a reveler who hosted family gatherings and employee bashes. He assumed everyone felt the same.

Time went on. The bicentennial was upon us. Vietnam was over. We weren't in the throes of any political scandal. Americans, it said, had been bracing for disaster for too long. Now, they wanted to take the wheel.

In its infinite periodical wisdom, *Time* had encapsulated my father's ambitions perfectly. Tired of relying on winter, he would bring the resort into the warmer months.

What *Time* didn't—and couldn't—anticipate was his methodology. He wouldn't build his salute to autonomy in Anaheim, California, where Disneyland had sprung up two decades prior, nor over a flat parcel of land in Florida chosen for its convenient location and malleable landscape. He intended to build a theme park on the side of a mountain in the middle of New Jersey.

As a kid, he had made his way through Palisades Amusement Park, a cliffside destination in Bergen County across the Hudson River. Palisades loomed large for people, especially children, in the 1950s and '60s, advertising in comic books and even leaving a small gap in the fence open for kids who couldn't afford the admission. Its signature attraction was the Cyclone, a dizzying wooden roller coaster that originated in Coney Island and was popular enough to duplicate in several other territories. Cynical and distasteful journalists described it as "a cure for unwanted pregnancies." Nurses were on hand to administer smelling salts to disoriented passengers.

I'm sure he saw the faces of the people who dared get on the Cyclone—expressions that mixed fear with excitement. It felt like a risk, a wager of thrills against your lunch or your consciousness. Seen at a formative age, those faces stay with you. I would know.

The Cyclone had one mark against it. Like virtually all amusement rides, the experience was predestined. My father's rides, whatever they might be, had to put the rider in complete control.

He began a scouting mission. He visited the beachside parks at the Jersey Shore, like Seaside Heights. He went to Coney Island, which had fallen into disrepair and looked almost dystopian. In these places, he saw the familiar. Another collection of spinning, mechanical rides was not in his plans. (Not to imply he had plans. That would take long-term financing and patience, neither of which he possessed.)

He took fleeting, disinterested glances at Great Adventure, a park that had recently opened just two hours south of New York City in the Pine Barrens of Jackson, New Jersey. It had a safari, a mining ride, hot air balloons, and a log flume, which sent guests down a water-filled chute in a passenger sled. No one would mistake it for Disneyland, but it did a brisk business.

Where Great Adventure went awry, my father thought, was investing tens of millions of dollars in rides that didn't provide half the excitement of attractions he could erect for a fraction of the price. He was convinced that increasing the thrill factor was the only way someone on a shoestring budget could compete with the giants of the amusement industry.

He decided to expand the search. A ski-trade publication made mention of a daring new contraption that sounded intriguing. Curious, he traveled all the way to West Germany, where superior foreign engineering had triumphed in creating new ways to accelerate the human body. There, he found a majestic fiberglass slide that undulated and curved down an incline. Riders mounted a small, sled-like plastic cart mounted on two wheels and plastic runners with brakes they could control with a joystick positioned flush against their crotch. Once seated, they plummeted down a half-mile-long chute made of durable, all-purpose asbestos. It took skill to know when to slow down around curves and when to plow forward. It was a "dry" ride that could monetize the property in the summer months, similar to a bobsled run without the snow. The manufacturer, DEMAG, called this monument to mesothelioma the Alpine Slide.

DEMAG referred my father to their North American dealer, a resort owner named Stig Albertsson. Albertsson operated the Bromley resort in Vermont and swore to my father that the Alpine, which he was in the process of installing at his own property, would transform both of their businesses. No longer would he be a slave to the seasons. No longer would the property sit, unused and unexploited, for most of the year. This would be the spark that lit the fuse. If the Alpine worked, my father told us, an amusement park would erupt all around it. There were only sketches in his head—motor rides, perhaps one of the water slides gaining in popularity around the country, maybe live shows. The specifics were vague, but the response he wanted to elicit was not. He wanted thrills and adventure. He wanted more of the faces he had seen at Palisades Park.

He was in the ideal place. Vernon was a sleepy town and presented few regulatory obstacles to building self-propelled attractions. It was as if someone had handed my father a blank canvas. He decided to call it the Vernon Valley Fun Farm, a mixed bit of alliteration that sounded to me like a place where people would come to pet goats.

How do you react when your father proclaims he wants to open a theme park? I imagined myself growing fat on free concession food and tumbling from one ride to the next, cutting in line and laughing all the way down. I would be Augustus Gloop, risking a combination overdose of sugar and fun. Jimmy and Topher were equally enraptured. Pete and Splinter, my two oldest brothers, spoke of a possible empire.

Julie remained cynical. "We're going to become carnies," she said. I rolled my eyes. There couldn't possibly be any downside.

"Dad," I said to him one day. "Are Jimmy and I going to work at the park?"

My father was silent. He did this often, staring off into the middle distance, sifting through any of the dozen thoughts going through his head at any given time. Questions went ignored until they came up in his neurological queue.

"Of course," he said, looking slightly amused, as though the idea that we wouldn't was strange. "You all will."

I was thirteen, Jimmy twelve. "Won't we need working papers?" I said.

My father just laughed. Later, I'd understand why. I brought up a rule as though it were an obstacle, something to be concerned with and not merely a nuisance to cast aside. This was amusing to him, the idea of being restrained, of acknowledging an authority other than his own. He was building an amusement park on the side of a mountain. What rules was he supposed to be following?

THAT SPRING, I COUNTED THE DAYS UNTIL SCHOOL WAS OVER. SEV-enth grade had become a cursory responsibility, something that was getting in the way of helping out on the mountain, where construction crews had already broken ground. The ski-lift passes were old news. Soon, I would be doling out golden tickets to world-class rides. When I mentioned this to friends, I expected envy. Instead, I received puzzled looks.

"Here?" they would ask. "On the mountain?" Explaining what my father was up to and meeting confusion, if not outrage, would become a recurring element in my life.

At the kitchen table, as my mother helped me with my homework, I peppered her with questions. Would she work there? (No. She had six children to raise.) Does my father know how to build a theme park? (No, but that had never stopped him before.) Would there be goats? (Ask your father.)

When I was finally free for the summer, Jimmy and I hovered near him for instructions. "Wear old clothes," he said. Then he paused. "Have you had your tetanus shots?"

The next day, we were covered, head to toe, in filth, shovels loosely gripped in our blistering adolescent hands. We threw clumps of dirt and mountain rock for hours, making a trench for the Alpine Slide. When our backs began to stiffen, we switched to raking and laying down rolls of sod layered with bright green grass and ink-black dirt, coughing and wheezing like authentic Vernon coal miners. Grown men with heaving muscles and missing teeth dug beside us, grunting their disapproval at our comparative inefficiency.

I looked up and saw Charlie O'Brien, the construction foreman and a former marine gunnery sergeant, coming toward us. Charlie had worked as head snowmaker at Great Gorge for years. My father had inherited him with the resort, along with the lift chairs and the Hexagon Lounge. He was an ornery man who wore his Irish heritage like a costume: red hair dotting his thick wrists and fingers, belly overlapping his belt. His glass eye sometimes caught the sun's reflection.

Charlie never talked about what happened to his eye. Rumor had it he lost it in some kind of explosion on the mountain. He refused to sue, endearing him to both Jack Kurlander and my dad. Charlie was one of three people in my father's employ who did not have two working eyeballs. Now that I was also working for him, this gave me pause.

Charlie examined our carefully arranged sod. "Get some water on that before it burns up and Gene has my ass," he said. My father considered dry, brown grass an unpardonable sin. It would have to be nurtured around the clock so it wouldn't wilt and perish in the summer heat.

I unfurled a garden hose and let the water wash over the sod, waiting for Charlie to turn his back so I could take a sip. "That's some good work, college boy," he said. Charlie called me "college boy" because he once saw me reading a book.

Charlie turned his attention to the men nearby, and the clouds of dirt erupted faster and faster. If Charlie caught you slacking, he would fire you, but experienced workers knew it rarely mattered. He kept a bottle of Dewar's Scotch in his desk drawer and was often inebriated enough to forget what he had said by the following morning. The rumor was that he had totaled his car more than once. But Charlie was also a former soldier, stout and formidable, and commanded respect. He would work sixteen-hour shifts for days on end. A few pulls on a bottle to keep warm during the frigid snowmaking sessions was, my father thought, a small indiscretion to forgive.

I don't know how the workers stood up to the grueling effort. One morning, I woke up sick to my stomach and walked downstairs, where my father was alone, drinking coffee. I told him I didn't feel well and that Mom usually made me toast. He nodded and grabbed two pieces of bread. He turned on the electric stovetop and held the slices on the red-hot coils.

"Faster than a toaster," he said.

The slices blackened. He doused them in sugar. I ate them. It made me feel better. I went to work.

AT SIX O'CLOCK EACH MORNING, WE PILED INTO A STATION WAGON with Pete and Splinter, the car pausing every twenty feet or so to pick up more of the neighborhood kids my father had recruited for duty. Pete corralled them into the car, impatient. No one wore a seat belt.

Over time, Pete's nickname became the Needle, because he enjoyed doing what older brothers are supposed to do: torment the smaller and weaker siblings. Jimmy and I bore the brunt of his wrath. Even as we grew bigger, he found new ways to maintain his dominance. Once, sleeping in my bed, I awoke to a massive stranger picking me up by my shirt and pinning me against the wall. I screamed out in terror.

"Ja!" he roared. "Ve are goink to kill you!"

In the darkness, I could hear Pete cackling. He turned on the lights and watched as I tried to regain my bearings. Nearby, one of his friends from college—a massive Norwegian from the Dartmouth ski jumping team whose head almost scraped the ceiling—laughed deeply from his belly.

"Pete, you dumb asshole," I said as he headed for Jimmy's room, muscle in tow.

Splinter, whose real name was Eugene Mulvihill III, considered such juvenile activity beneath him. Because some people knew our father as Chip, as in "chip off the old block," people took to calling my brother Splinter, an increasingly complicated wood-based nomenclature. Splinter was slightly aloof and spoke in measured tones, as though he needed to pause and consider someone's intelligence before responding. I noticed he spoke to Jimmy very slowly.

In their late teens, Pete and Splinter did not lay sod. They would drop us off, then drive on. Splinter worked with the adult laborers assembling the Alpine lanes. Pete headed for a separate section of the property, across Route 94, the main two-lane road threading through town.

"What are you doing over there, Pete?" I would ask.

"It's top secret," he said. "You can't be trusted. You'd blow the whole operation. You and the little feral child there."

He nodded at John Thornton, a neighborhood kid about my age

who sometimes refused to wear shoes and spent the day working in his bare feet. "I'm protesting," is all John would say by way of explanation. A contrarian, he argued with Charlie over the best way to rake rocks.

Jimmy rode in uncharacteristic silence, knowing that, if he didn't piss Pete off, he could suck the backwash out of his used beer cans on the way home. "You want some?" Pete would sneer, tossing the near-empties at Jimmy's head. "Here, you little punk."

Meanwhile, I picked at my blisters but got no sympathy from Splinter. At my age, he toiled in the bowels of the resort, trying to organize the rented ski boots back into matching pairs while rats leapt out of the piles and scurried up his arms. Nearby, an old resort hand smeared cleaning solvent on the skis while a cigarette dangled from his lips, threatening to send the whole place up in flames. Because I was under no direct threat of immolation, my brother dismissed my complaints.

Arriving each day, we saw things taking shape, my father patrolling the grounds on his dirt bike, his mere presence enough to incite frenzied activity. Despite his motivational speeches, the work stretched well past the planned opening on the Fourth of July and into August, which drove my father from rah-rah addresses to regular paroxysms of screaming. Charlie protested that there was no precedent for what Gene wanted, comparing it to paving a roadway down a mountain. If you saw them arguing for the first time, you would expect it to end in violence. This was simply how they communicated, two boisterous marines lobbing orders and complaints at each other. It would stop just as suddenly as it started, their voices returning to normal volume.

"I need more fucking men here!" Charlie would say. Then, "How's Gail?"

"She's great," my father would say. "How's Rose?"

"Fantastic."

My father had inherited an entire crew of snowmakers from the previous owners of Great Gorge. Charlie O'Brien was their leader, and his fleet consisted of men with names like Big Al, Indian, Bunk, and Wacky Joe, the lift mechanic. Wacky Joe once climbed from one chair lift to another on the cable that dangled dozens of feet in the air, scrambling down the line like a capuchin monkey. Big Al was a member of the Laziers, a family made up of roughly twenty people that lived near the resort in a cluster of blue-collar houses known as Lazierville. Big Al, their patriarch, could pull wooden fence posts from the ground with his bare hands. Some of the workers called him Sasquatch, a man so legendary he had earned two nicknames.

The men often piled into old army trucks the resort kept on hand, faces dirty and tools stacked up in the back, dispatched from one operational emergency to the next. In the years to come, they would be the hands that helped shape the park, like the workers who dynamite-blasted Mount Rushmore. No task was beyond their reach, from welding to painting to plumbing.

At times, they frightened me, these men with missing teeth who lived in ramshackle buildings dotting the margins of the resort. It took a special breed of human to be able to scale a mountain in the middle of the night, clothes soaked through with water in sub-zero temperatures, to shoot a blend of water and freezing air to overrule Mother Nature. My father grew to see them as a unit he could deploy no matter the season. Earning their loyalty was not easy, but my father trained them to fall into step. They wanted to please him, to get his approval, just as the men at Mayflower had. He treated these laborers no differently than he would affluent business partners or neighbors. He threw elaborate parties for them. He handed out Thanksgiving turkeys to their families. Once, he gave Charlie a car (which Charlie promptly wrecked, but that was beside the point). My father seemed to sense when his workers needed reinforcement and when they needed material goods. Managing and inspiring people was his specialty.

"I'm tired of digging," I told him on several occasions.

"You're part of the expansion," he said, instantly elevating my mood and status. It was as good as a turkey.

As he argued with Charlie one afternoon, I gazed up at the mountain, this massive natural formation onto which he was projecting his imagination. It was ill-defined then, but we chipped and carved and dug, and soon an image began to form, one of a steep, twisting track that somehow managed to look both wildly out of place and completely appropriate. The sheer scope of the work was so impressive, the way he directed his workforce to create something out of nothing. Soon, he would be famous, and I would have to feign humility when people asked if my father was *the* Gene Mulvihill.

I looked back at my father. He was peeing into a ditch.

We kept digging.

IN THE DAYS LEADING INTO THE OPENING OF THE RIDE, JUST BE-fore Labor Day weekend of 1976, my father must have had some inkling of what poor Walt had endured more than twenty years earlier. Sensing his concerns, we kept our distance from him. He was never visibly nervous, but word traveled through the household that the Alpine Slide was a risky undertaking. It cost half a million dollars, money that was cobbled together from investors and resort capital. He had leveraged and balanced his assets as precariously as Vernon Valley's previous owners had, a path that led them to financial ruin. The park's protracted construction had consumed most of the summer. There was little time left to reap profits, if any were forthcoming. We would not be homeless if it failed, but the financial loss would be a blow. More important, it would dash my seemingly attainable dreams of a permanent adolescence.

The morning of the opening, we all watched as a stream of cars pulled off Route 94 and branched off to the resort entrance. Julie madly pressed a clicker for a head count.

"How many?" I asked her.

"Hundreds," she said.

Heading for a ski resort in warm weather was a foreign concept for people, so my father took out newspaper ads that trumpeted live music, beer, and events like tobacco-spitting competitions to stir up the town's rural demographic. In those early days, he hosted bluegrass festivals with hippies and hillbillies, a mountainside bash fueled by beer, weed, and skinny-dipping in the snowmaking ponds. People who owned homes nearby woke up to partygoers sleeping in their yards and, if their doors were unlocked, passed out on their couches.

The real attraction, though, would be the slide, which my father hyped up as not just a ride but a revolution in outdoor recreation. People had never seen anything like it. It was an amusement attraction you could control. His agreement with Stig Albertsson required that the Vernon Valley Fun Farm have the only one within a two-hundred-mile radius. Road-tripping teenagers and families from the tristate area looking for one last summer thrill veered toward us, intrigued by the promise of a new kind of adrenaline rush.

"I have investigated this sport thoroughly," he told reporters, sounding like an Olympic committee member. They leaned forward, curious. No one had to "investigate" the Dumbo ride at Disneyland. They had come expecting a cheap carnival ride like the kind temporarily erected by transients at county fairs. The permanent tracks winding up the foot of the mountain promised something else. Later, he would tell us he thought he saw some spies from Great Adventure there, looking to see what the crazy mountain man was up to.

The guests stood in line for two hours to fork over two dollars and fifty cents (a dollar fifty for kids) and jump on the ski lift to be transported twenty-seven hundred feet up the mountain to the launch station. At the top, attendants, including Splinter, nudged them into motion. Seated on the carts, the riders rolled along the surface and banked into the curves, gaining confidence—and speed—with each subsequent trip down, their rear ends cradled by the carts' molded plastic. Pushing the joystick forward raised the brakes and lowered the wheels, making them go faster. Pulling it back activated the brakes and retracted the wheels, slowing them down.

My father had settled on two lanes for visitors. One was designated the slow lane for overly cautious beginners with an iron grip on the brake ("scaredy cats," he sniffed). The second was for the adventurous. A parent might be riding down with a ten-month-old on their lap on one track. Next to them, a teenager would be speeding like he was on the Autobahn and laughing maniacally. There was no seat belt, helmet, or pads.

"They don't want helmets," my father said, parrying questions from inquisitive reporters who noticed a lack of safety features. "They want the wind in their hair!"

As far as he was concerned, once they paid, people could do whatever they wanted. This was a basic tenet of his philosophy on life, which mandated minimal intervention from any kind of non-familial authority. "Let them have fun," he said. "Let them do what they want to do."

The transformative effect of the freedom was startling. People who stood listlessly in the hot sun waiting their turn grew excited as soon as they sat on the seat. They snatched up discount ticket books for repeat trips and wore digital watches so they could time their runs and brag to friends about their personal records. They stood at the foot of the ride watching others make the descent in a blur of denim and plastic, shouting instructions like cornermen in boxing.

As more riders piled on, the price of freedom began to reveal itself. The control granted by the Alpine was accompanied by a measure of risk, much of it self-imposed. Attendants would tell guests to go slow and mind the brake until they got used to it. The guests would nod, completely oblivious to the safety instructions, then proceed to make every mistake they were warned to avoid. If you stuck your arm or leg out to balance yourself, it was like holding your body against a sander. The surface of the track scraped off your flesh, leaving an oozing, blistering wound. For superficial injuries, we sprayed a pink iodine liquid that bubbled up like acid and made the tender skin flare with pain. The teenage boys took it stoically. Younger kids hissed through their teeth. On busy days, the area around the slide could look like a leper colony. We eventually put up photos of these ghastly wounds at the top of the ride, a visual reminder of the potential for carnage.

There were dangers beyond the track peeling people like potatoes. If you went down too slowly, someone behind you would smash into your cart, creating a brain-jarring collision of bone, plastic, and fiberglass. Dads, not realizing the consequences of their greater mass, playfully rammed into their kids, sending them tumbling into the air like rag dolls. We tried to space riders at least fifty yards apart, but attendants at the top had blind spots where the track dipped out of sight. Mischievous guests would wait until they were farther down and then stop, hoping their buddy would blindly ram into them. Others took note of slow patrons in the fast lane and punished their hesitation by spearing them from behind. The sound was like two enormous NFL players colliding with a crunch of equipment, the displaced bodies giggling or moaning depending on the force of impact.

If you were thrown clear, you'd skid on the grass with so much momentum that pollen would be injected into your skin. It never happened at the park, but a few people ejected from the Alpine at other places went into anaphylactic shock. Someone wrote a paper for a medical journal about it.

If you wiped out, the cart—which weighed twenty pounds— could come crashing back down on you like an anvil in a cartoon. Because of the slide's proximity to the woods, people flying off the track could smash into a tree or find themselves falling into a pile of rocks. We quickly put in hay bales to cushion the falls, only to realize they created even more of a hazard. People flicked their used cigarette butts everywhere. We had two fires before we realized we had created a tinderbox.

The potential for a raging blaze aside, *Time* was right. People did want to be in control. Only a few stopped to consider what was actually happening—that unprotected bodies were traveling at thirty miles per hour and occasionally getting shot into the sky like they had been ejected from a fighter-plane cockpit. Those who did backed away, holding their children behind them in a protective posture. A few reporters showed up to file a participatory story, took one look, and refused to get on the slide. My father tried to assuage concerns over its potential for destruction. "My seventy-one-year-old mother loves it," he told reporters. While this was technically true, he didn't tell them my grandmother went down when the slide was closed, a few inches at a time.

He was giddy over the success of the Alpine, keeping it open through November. The only thing that would interfere with business was precipitation. If the track was wet, the carts would hydroplane when the brakes were applied, and the guests would skid across the water. A gathering storm meant we had to shut it down. My father could manipulate snow, but he could not control the rain. At the sight of crowds dispersing, he shook his fist at the skies.

I was good on the Alpine, but Jimmy was king. He learned all the finer points—where to brake, when to take off, how to balance your weight so you didn't lean too far to the side. My father ushered Jimmy up to a newspaper reporter covering the ride, boasting of his son's fifty-five-second record. (It normally took an average of three minutes to go down.) Charlie O'Brien's son, Kelly, was in second place. My father tried to get them to race to settle it.

"I can't believe Jimmy has the record," he told Kelly. "You can beat that kid."

Then he'd heckle Jimmy. "That Kelly kid has got some moves," he said. "He's coming after your record." Instigating conflict gave him tremendous pleasure. He chuckled as the two sat in the chair lift, staring daggers into each other.

Kelly shot down the slide, his long, wavy brown hair flying behind him, but Jimmy was too slick. He remained champion.

Soon, I noticed Jimmy was taking fewer trips on the ride. Like a great athlete with a peerless record, I thought he wanted to leave on top. When I asked him, he looked at me with big, mournful eyes. "You didn't hear?" he said.

An employee chasing Jimmy's record streaked down the slide at such velocity that, when he was thrown clear, the momentum had caused the track to gouge the back of his legs and butt so badly that he needed two hundred stitches. Riding the asbestos lightning had scraped his ass almost completely off his body.

"Was he naked or something?" I asked.

"It was one of those pickle-smuggling bathing suits the Europeans wear," Jimmy said, and we both frowned. If you went hard on the Alpine, you needed jeans at minimum. Motorcycle leathers were better. Light clothing would essentially disintegrate from the friction and had to be peeled off weeping flesh like a used bandage.

The boy's detached rear end became legend, and the Alpine ended the season with something of a reputation. Nevertheless, it was a resounding success. My father spent that fall repeatedly handing Wacky Joe bags stuffed with thousands of dollars in cash. The money room at the ski resort was unstaffed in the summer, and he had nowhere to stash his profits. "In the trunk, Wacky Joe!" he whispered. Worried about being robbed, my father would lock the weekend's profits in his car until there was no more room for them. He sold adrenaline, and people were buying.

TIRED OF BLOWING MY NOSE AND SEEING BLACK SNOT COME OUT, I pleaded for a promotion from the ditch digging. I was climbing out of bed with the posture of a horseshoe, my back screaming for relief. I worried that I was on my way to becoming a snowmaker, perpetually inebriated and missing an eye, yelling at children for reading books.

"All right," my father said. "You can unload the carts."

When the chair lift stopped at the top of the mountain, the carts dangling from the back of the lift had to be pulled off and handed to the riders. It was less responsibility than I wanted but more than I had. I left a disgruntled Jimmy to toil in the shadow of Charlie O'Brien's large belly.

Within the first half hour of unloading and retrieving carts, my back hurt worse than ever. Instead of digging rocks, I was moving plastic boulders. Riders discarded the equipment all over the slope, leaving them at the scene of a crash. Jimmy made periodic visits to heckle me. So did John Thornton. The first time John got on the

Alpine, he tried to slow down using his bare feet, Fred Flintstone-style. He wept.

At lunch, Jimmy and I would jump in the carts and race down to the bottom of the hill, where any pain in my muscles disappeared. *I cannot believe this is my job,* I thought. The chill in the fall air made goosebumps rise on my arms and caused my eyes to tear. The sleeves of my T-shirt would billow as I picked up speed, a wide grin forming on my face. Hay bales and trees passed in a blur. Jimmy showed me how to tug on the strap that was mounted on the front of the carts and used to hang them on the lift, which put more weight on the wheels. It allowed us to go even faster, satisfying an inexplicable need to push our limits. The increased speed and the accompanying risk of injury was intoxicating. We went again and again, sometimes racing down the dual lanes, racing until dark, racing until our father waved us in because it was time to go home.

From across Route 94, I began to hear the din of motors, a hint of Pete's mystery project. He was testing dune buggies, then putting them back into storage for next summer. Even Julie began to come around, talking about an outdoor roller-skating rink that she would supervise. My father was reinvesting the profits from the Alpine. The park, which would soon grow dormant to make room for the skiers, would explode once the ground thawed. Though he loved to ski, my father couldn't reinvent slopes. The park was a place where he could shape everything to his exacting specifications.

One day, late into the season, I looked up and saw someone urinating from the chair lift, the stream arcing over the grass and across the surface of the slide. A woman going down on a cart screamed, swerving to avoid the pee. She tumbled off the track and swore at the man above her, who was laughing hysterically.

"You think that happens in Vermont?" Jimmy said.

"No," I said.

Watching the man empty his bladder from seventy-five feet in the air, I started to feel a little disconcerted. The Vernon Valley Fun Farm was promising autonomy for all. I wondered if my father had considered that even though people craved control, not everyone could necessarily handle the responsibility.

Fort Nonsense, I thought, and watched as the stream slowed to a trickle.

Two patrons failing to observe a safe distance from each other on the Alpine Slide.

The Lolas. Sobriety optional.

Chapter Two

FUEL

"If you're in control, you're not going fast enough."

Parnelli Jones, professional automobile racer

The summer of 1977 was a proof-of-concept season, with my father wanting to make sure the Alpine was no passing fad. He offered just one new attraction: grass skiing, a warm-weather activity where people wore boots fitted with what looked like tank treads and rolled down the slope on dirt, sometimes tumbling from an errant rock or pebble. Grass skiing did not prove popular, but the Alpine continued to draw crowds, and so he decided it was time to move forward. One ride was not enough. Expansion and growth were necessary.

He believed the best way of going about this was to legalize drunk driving.

He called it Motor World. It was in the same lower plot of land across the main roadway where Pete had busied himself getting the dune buggies ready. Because the Alpine's opening had been delayed, those vehicles had largely sat dormant. At first, Pete explained, our father had merely wanted to allow guests to traverse a wooded area on the buggies, dodging trees as they hit the gas. Over the cold months, when he incubated ideas, he plotted something far more ambitious.

Now, in the late spring of 1978, there stood a prefabricated aluminum garage that housed a small fleet of three-quarter-scale Formula One racers, the first of their kind on the East Coast. Also called Lola cars after the British car company that made them, these were slightly shrunken versions of the arrow-shaped vehicles that tore through Monaco every year. They were not toys. The engine of the Lola T506 vibrated through your stomach and made your testicles rattle.

"Eight grand each," Pete said. "They top out at fifty miles per hour, but that's only because we put governors under the gas pedal. These things can go ninety." Considering some of the questionable judgment already exhibited on the Alpine, I had a suspicion guests would approach these vehicles with a mixture of excitement and gross negligence. It didn't matter. While my friends played with Hot Wheels, plastic lanes snaking around their bedrooms, I watched as an entire automotive world was laid out before me. Big Al and Charlie supervised the paving of a huge track that wound through the field like a miniature Le Mans. In the middle were the ride attendants and a digital clock that displayed lap times. It was accurate to one hundredth of a second.

"Now we can time how long you'd last with a girl," Jimmy said, snorting. At fourteen, Jimmy was beginning to approach the opposite sex with a little bit of a swagger. That didn't quite match his experience, which, like mine, was precisely zero. I had already caught him bragging of his Alpine prowess to the occasional female visitor. Now,

I suspected, he would likely drop whatever records he secured in Motor World into conversation with other objects of his affection.

Jimmy and I both snuck in laps, but we were too young to work at Motor World and technically shouldn't have been allowed on the track at all. You had to be seventeen years old and present a valid driver's license to operate a Lola car. (Kids with a learner's permit could get on with a parent's consent.) At the time, New Jersey printed licenses on paper with no picture. Kids successfully forged them all the time by punching out the birthday numbers with a hole puncher and switching them to buy alcohol. Attendants would eye one of these dubious licenses, then look at the prospective driver, who would often tug their hat brim down to cover acne or braces.

They encountered little resistance. Taking a cue from the obedient employees at the Disney parks, my father told us that we should never utter the word *no* to guests. Snow White, he said, would never reject anyone. He seemed oblivious to the fact that Snow White wasn't charged with making sure people didn't run each other over with gas-powered racing vehicles.

That mandate made attendants in Motor World largely powerless to stop both juvenile drivers and people who had been drinking. There was also the fact that the attendants were teenagers themselves and often cowed to the adults waiting in line, forgetting that the balance of power had shifted in their favor inside the park.

"Sir," one would say. "I think you've been drinking. Have you been drinking?"

"Move, kid," the guest would say, ignoring the question. Then they'd climb into the Lola and go swerving along the half-mile track, narrowly avoiding mowing down the crowd standing near the edge of the asphalt. We quickly developed a rule. If two wheels ran over on the grass, the driver would get a warning. Four wheels and they'd be kicked off the Lolas for the day. It was our improvised version of a sobriety test.

We were not as vigilant with the dune buggies. These were off-road vehicles made by Honda that guests could take on the rougher, wooded area adjacent to the track. Riders would follow a guide deep into the woods, where they could career around freely. To offset the inevitable wipeouts, the buggies had a roll bar built behind the open driver's seat, like you see in auto racing. Another set of bars was in front. While these were intended for safety, riders took them as license to drive like lunatics without fear of being trapped under the crumpled body of the vehicle. They whipped around the lot, taking off on small hills that briefly allowed all four wheels to leave the ground.

Balancing a dune buggy while taking sharp turns was difficult, and overzealous drivers sometimes found themselves losing control of the vehicles. The first weekend they were available, all ten dune buggies met cruel ends, their riders pulling themselves from the wreckage, a handful sobbing as they crawled away. Fortunately, my father had mandated helmets. It was one of the few times he decided safety equipment would be necessary. This measure likely saved many attendees from becoming vegetables.

The dune buggy apocalypse drove the mechanic insane. My father had recruited a guy named Mike Kramer because of Kramer's reputation as a first-class engine jockey for a track in North Carolina. Kramer was short, bearded, and raced Volvo station wagons as a hobby. He was meticulous in maintaining the vehicles, treating them like collectors' classics. It did not occur to him that they would be abused by people who considered auto accidents a recreational activity.

"The fuck. . . . the fuck is this?" he said, surveying the mangled dune buggies in his shop the following Monday. The garage had turned into a junkyard. "I just got all of these ready."

Pete shrugged.

"SON OF A BITCH!" Kramer screamed, banging a mechanic's wrench into a tray, glasses askew. Kramer developed a hostile working relationship with the ride attendants, insisting they didn't do enough to protect the fleet. It was residual vitriol from my father, who hated seeing his investments mangled and yelled at Kramer to pull it together.

Kramer would often stay late, tinkering with a peculiar machine that looked like one of the evil Dalek robots from *Doctor Who*. Every time someone asked about it, he'd throw a tarp over it and shake his head, waving off further inquiry. Jimmy and I considered the possibility that he was building a bulletproof vehicle he would eventually take on a rampage.

Kramer was also responsible for maintaining the Super Go-Karts, twenty vehicles that each had an open-chassis seat, positioned low to the ground, and hummed with a high-decibel engine that made the area sound like an actual speedway. Because of their size, people underestimated their ability to take off in a matter of seconds, like a spooked horse. The drivers' necks snapped backward upon acceleration and then forward upon braking. On some of the karts, a design flaw caused the gas cap to come off as people drove along the track. The fuel would splash out behind them, hitting drivers a few lengths behind.

"My eyes!" one guest cried, veering off course and smashing into the giant truck tires lining the track. Later, we replaced the tires with metal rails, because the go-karts could sail directly over the rubber barrier if the angle was right, crinkling the nose of the vehicle as it speared itself into the dirt.

With each collision or spinout, Kramer would become a forensic auto detective, trying to figure out what had gone wrong. It was almost always the fault of the driver, and Kramer would mutter his diagnostic finding: "These people are fucking nuts."

In fairness to patrons, it was unusual for them to get this level of control over such powerful machines in an amusement park. If a similar attraction existed somewhere else, as was the case with the Lolas and go-karts, my father would make sure his went a step further—faster, more daring, bigger, better. If the Lolas went forty miles per hour in California, his would go fifty. If someone had go-karts that ambled along a serene path, he would allow our guests to race them wheel-to-wheel.

It was a much-needed break from reality. The year prior, in New York City, David Berkowitz, the Son of Sam, had been on a murder spree, later claiming he was under the control of a talking dog. That same summer, a blackout had sent the entire city into chaos. Stressed-out residents came to Vernon in groups, flooring the gas and forgetting their troubles. The Lolas became addictive, with people constantly repeating the track to try to beat their own best times, which were handed to them on a small ticket at the end. One man spent one hundred dollars in a single afternoon trying to outdo himself. My father even organized a Lola Grand Prix later in the year, inviting fifty people with the best times to race. The winner got a portable color television. To avoid disaster, Kramer only allowed them on the track one at a time.

Amid the revving engines and drunken swerves of patrons, a romance flourished between Pete and one of the ride attendants, a tough, no-nonsense girl named Ellen. A black belt in karate, Ellen had the interpersonal skills to deal with braying guests. Her comparatively soft-spoken sister, Erin, also worked at Motor World. Part of Erin's job was to let people know when they had reached the final lap of the four allowed on the Lola track. To signal the drivers, she waved a checkered flag. Often, people completely ignored it.

"Sir," Erin would say. "Please return the car to the starting line."

"Fuuuuuuuuuuck . . ." the drivers would say before disappearing around a curve and out of sight, then zooming back into view to add, "yoooooooooooou!"

The honor system was clearly not working.

Erin was patient and a valued employee, but Ellen's other referral was not. A neighborhood kid she enlisted broke into the park in the middle of the night, made off with a Lola, and took it for a joyride down Route 94. He figured out how to deactivate the governor that limited the car's speed and tore off like a Daytona 500 finalist. Police followed in pursuit for miles before they apprehended him.

Maybe it was then that I began to wonder whether the park was broadcasting on a frequency only a special kind of lunatic could hear.

AS THE PARK GREW IN THE COMING YEARS, IT ALWAYS REFLECTED my father's interests. The Alpine was his homage to skiing, a rapid descent down a mountain path that rewarded skill. With its high-throttle races, Motor World told a story about his passion for speed and competition. The faster he could get from one point to another, the better. Being forced to stand idle was probably the only thing he truly feared.

His friends later told me that, in his early Wall Street days, Gene would take the ferry into New York amid a morass of commuters. When the ferry docked, he would suddenly burst forth, cutting through the congestion of bodies, jabbing them with his elbows and shoulders like a running back so he could be the first off the boat. Waiting for other people to make room for him was unthinkable.

Later on, he began driving to the train station to get into the city. One morning, worried he might miss the train, he sped through a school zone. A police cruiser saw him barrel through and gave chase, but had to stop for the crossing children. When the cops finally caught up, my father had left his car and was already on the train.

Unable to prove he was the one driving, the police could do nothing more than issue a parking ticket.

This story made the newspaper. It would be the first of many unflattering press clippings.

He was caught parking illegally so often that a vengeful meter maid once plastered his car with tickets, obscuring the windows. He scraped off just enough of them to see through the windshield to drive home. Another time, with my mother in the car, he was going one hundred miles per hour.

"Slow down," she said, her fingernails sinking into the seat. "Slow down."

Seeing the lights of a police cruiser behind them, she was delighted that he would finally have his comeuppance. When the officer walked up to the car, he noticed that Gene's insurance card was issued by USAA, which serviced veterans. Gene and the cop got into an exchange about the Marine Corps, at which point the officer learned my father was a captain.

"*Semper fi*, Mr. Mulvihill," the cop said, saluting him. "On your way, sir."

My mother stewed the entire way home. If my father believed he could get anyway with anything, it was because he got away with everything.

Speed was only part of it. From the days he sold vacuums and the salesmen's results were tracked in chalk on a leaderboard at the Kirby offices, my father considered everything a contest. That all of us grew up to be competitive came as little surprise. Over dinner, he would charge us with taking up positions in political or business discussions and then encourage us to defend our assigned beliefs. (Splinter often boasted he was on the "wrong" side of a debate but had the skills to win the argument anyway.) We were rarely given quarter for being young. He relished our exasperation, if only to teach us that life could prove frustrating, and we had better become used to it.

Sometimes this led to a sense of gross injustice. Once, when he was involved in a houseboat business, he reserved one of the vessels for a Caribbean family vacation with four of us: me, Julie, Pete, and Jimmy. For reasons we could never quite grasp, my father brought only a minimal amount of food along for the trip. He rationed out sandwiches like he expected to get lost at sea, leading to frequent complaints of hunger from all of us.

"Okay, okay," he said, capitulating to our protests. He produced a small stash of individually wrapped chocolate coins, which immediately made all of us begin to salivate. As we reached for them, he brushed us away. "We're going to play cards for them," he said.

While Pete and Julie could put up a semblance of a fight in poker, Jimmy and I were easy marks, and none of us were a match for our father. Using the chocolate coins as chips, he proceeded to wipe us all out, offering no allowance for the fact that most of his rivals could barely hold five cards at once in their tiny hands. His lanky arm swept the delicious currency away as we looked on with a sense of hopelessness. At least when you lose in Vegas, the casinos will comp you some food. This trip was due to last for days. Starvation seemed like a real possibility. Satisfied we had learned the perils of gambling, he eventually handed over the chocolates.

When he was not stirring dissent among the children, he was transforming even mundane episodes into matters of winning and losing. One oft-repeated story involved my father boarding an airplane for a long flight. The plane hit turbulence, and soon the passengers and attendants were vomiting. Only my father and a single flight attendant had not. He decided this was some kind of competition. Grabbing the provided air-sickness bag, he poured a can of tomato juice into it. When the stewardess came around, he began gulping from it. She ran to the bathroom, spewing. My father had "won."

Time and again, rides would go up in the park with lanes, speed, and the ability to set records and conquer. To my father, fun had winners and losers.

AS MUCH AS HE LOVED COMPETITION, HE TOOK AS MUCH DELIGHT, perhaps more, in watching other people release themselves from speed limits both literal and metaphorical.

His face lit up as Pete told us a story over dinner one night. He was getting something to eat when he heard a crackle over his radio. "There is a situation at the Super Go-Karts," an attendant said.

Because there was always some kind of "situation," Pete took his time returning to Motor World. When he got there, he saw a woman behind the wheel of a go-kart with what looked like a scarf wrapped around her face. She clearly had no control of the vehicle, smashed through a chain-link fence, and was careening toward pedestrians, who screamed and jumped out of the way. Unable to slow down, she headed directly for Pete.

To avoid being run over, Pete stepped to the side—"like a mata-dor," he said—and jumped on top of the go-kart. The woman drove through another section of fencing, smashing Pete's head on the metal bar in the process. She then drove the go-kart into a tree, wheels spinning. Pete, likely woozy from the head trauma, still had the presence of mind to hit the kill switch. When he looked back toward the track, he saw eight other women driving in the same frenzied manner. Pete, who hadn't been exposed to much religious diversity in New Jersey, speculated that they were part of a spiritual sect that disallowed driving.

"That's fantastic!" my father said, pouring a tablespoon's worth of salt on his salad. He doused everything he ate in salt. He put salt on pancakes. "You see the opportunities we're bringing to people?"

"What if someone gets hurt?" Julie said.

Pete, not without reason, pointed out that he had smashed his head into a steel pipe and had been having memory problems.

"A guest, I mean," Julie said.

"Ski laws," Gene said.

Historically, if you skied into a tree, it was your fault. However, when a novice skier named James Sunday lost control and hit a boulder next to a slope in Vermont in 1974 and became a quadriplegic, he sued and won $1.5 million from the resort. Ever since, insurance rates had been rising, and the ski industry was lobbying to go back to the status quo. New Jersey was helpful in this regard, having recently endorsed a law that said that the liability fell on the individual, not the operator. Skiers had to assess their own experience and choose slopes wisely. It fit my father's philosophy. He believed every person was the architect of their own fate. Specifically, he believed a court would agree every person was responsible for themselves. It was not a recklessness that seized my father so much as a sense of imperviousness. He did not often stop to mull over consequences, believing they would either never materialize or that they would not be of sufficient seriousness to prevent him from doing what he wanted to do. He assumed others felt the same.

Attending a football game while enrolled at Lehigh University, he had a bit too much to drink and tumbled out of the stands, landing on the ground ten or so feet below. A man named Billy Porter, who would become a close friend of his, met up with him in the bathroom right after. Porter's memory of meeting my father is watching him urinate blood, profoundly and utterly unconcerned with any possible damage done to his internal organs. Asking my father about people totaling Lola cars seemed quaint in comparison.

"So, what if someone gets hurt?" Julie pressed.

"The important thing is to drag them off to the side so no one trips on them," he said, chuckling.

"Dad!" Julie said.

"I'm joking, Rosebud," he said.

My mother sighed. No matter how busy my father was, Sunday dinners were sacrosanct. They were a time for the entire brood to get together and leave business behind. Now, the family was part of the business. As a result, the dinner conversation was veering away from school and other topics and toward his ambitions for the park. He discussed strategy and our respective roles. As laborers, Jimmy and I were now inexplicably digging swimming-pool-sized holes in the ground. I also took the occasional shift fetching the Alpine carts. Pete covered Motor World. Splinter, the Alpine. Julie, the roller rink. Each of us pulled our own weight, fueled by the work ethic he handed down to us. Once, we spent multiple weekends in a row putting up a ten-foot-tall metal fence around our ten-acre property, a complicated task that involved navigating trees and other obstacles. He could have hired someone to do it, but he had a fleet of perfectly good laborers in the house already. He always expected us to help. Plus, we needed the spending money. There was no allowance, no stipend for the effort of simply existing. Family vacations were on our parents' dime, but records, and junk food, and everything else that fueled adolescence, were not.

After finishing the excavation of the holes, Jimmy and I were tasked with manning them. They turned out to be skateboard bowls, making the park one of the first in the country to have a dedicated skate area in 1978. My father hired Bobby Piercy, a professional skateboarder from California, to oversee its design. Bobby was more interested in the waitressing bunnies at the neighboring Playboy Club Hotel, however, and rarely strayed from their company. Bobby actually missed several of his scheduled flights to New Jersey, prompting my father to have a friend physically drag him onto the plane. I was pretty sure that was technically kidnapping.

As Bobby radiated California cool, Jimmy, Kelly O'Brien, and I rented out skateboards and helmets to people curious to try the burgeoning sport. Because few had the ability to make any real use of the ten-foot-deep bowls, our job consisted mainly of handing out Band-Aids. My father buried the bowls in dirt the next summer, erasing evidence of their existence. He was unfazed. "Try ten things, eight fail, doesn't matter," he said. "The two that score will make up for it."

While Jimmy and I continued to moan about swinging pickaxes and offering first aid to clumsy skateboarders, we agreed it was better than Topher's role. He wore the dog suit.

No one was sure where the dog suit had come from, but it was a clear attempt to mimic the costumed Disney characters. The dog costume helped foster a kind of alternative reality for parkgoers, one in which they could fancy themselves Formula One drivers while interacting with a non-copyrighted dog.

Topher hated it. It was stifling hot, and my mother refused to let him launder it in the washing machine, insisting it might harbor actual fleas. It was dark brown and hung listlessly from his eleven-year-old frame, which was tall but thin. He looked like the world's saddest McGruff.

"I'm just some no-name dog," Topher sulked. Families arranged for their kids to pose for pictures, not realizing the kid inside the suit was probably younger than they were. Unlike the Disney mascots, our dog was also chatty. Hearing Topher converse with guests, I wondered if David Berkowitz had ever visited the park.

The costume was so saggy, and Topher so unimposing, that he became a target. Once, I came upon him wriggling against a light pole. A group of drunks had taken the arms of the costume and tied them around the fixture, trapping him in the afternoon heat. Guests walked right past him, oblivious to his struggles and muffled pleas for help.

"Assholes," Topher said, taking in great gulps of air as I freed him. His dog head was heavy with sweat. He vowed never to wear it again.

"You can wear the dog suit," my father said, "or you can wear the pig suit."

Topher stuck with the dog suit.

EMBOLDENED BY THE SUCCESS OF THE LOLAS, MY FATHER BECAME preoccupied with growing out the entire motorized area. If it needed fuel, it belonged here. He collected things that went fast and faster still, scooping up anything that could accelerate and filling up virtually every corner of the dedicated property with vehicles that guests could race or wreck. In this hazy tract, Motor World's atmosphere was different from the one surrounding the Alpine Slide or even the skate park. From across Route 94, my ears partially obscured by a skate helmet, I could hear the chants: "Wreck the boats! Wreck the boats!"

On a break, I walked across the road and stood out in the rain next to Pete. We watched as people zipped around in speedboats that were roughly two-thirds the size of a full-scale version. Powerful engines that seemed way out of proportion for their flimsy plastic frames weighed them down. They populated a mucky-looking lake in Motor World with a small island in the middle.

"Why are they upset?" I asked.

"When it rains, we close down all the motorized rides except for the boats," Pete said. "The lines get long. They get pissed and start to revolt." Once someone got in a boat, he said, it was almost impossible to get them out until they ran out of gas.

The boats made a zipping sound as they looped around the island, noses pointed up in the air as if driven by junior cartel smugglers on the run from the Coast Guard. Two teenagers sped directly at each other, hair blowing back, bearing down on the throttle.

"Don't do that!" Pete yelled. "Don't you do that!"

The hulls collided with a *thonk* noise. Both speedboats began to capsize, spilling the occupants into the water.

"Serves them right," Pete said.

One of them managed to get back into the boat and began cycling around the island again as Erin, the area's traffic cop, tried to wave him in. The other climbed back on the dock, dripping with water and reeking of gasoline.

"There's fuel all over my shorts!" he shouted. "My dick is burning, man!"

"Go to the office," Pete said. "They have soap."

Fuel and engine oil leaked from the motors, giving the entire lake a greasy sheen, like the top of a pizza.

Kramer looked at the water, taking a drag of his cigarette. "These people are maniacs," he said. "Delinquents." He had adopted the steely gaze of a war veteran, immune to the sights of vehicular gore.

People who had been tossed into the water often started screaming. "Something brushed against my leg!" they would wail as they waded toward land, looking back as though a shark might emerge from the four-foot depths.

"Snakes," Pete said. "Some of them are copperheads. We have snapping turtles, too. They can take a toe." Doing laps in the boats first thing in the morning, Pete said, usually scared them off.

The relative sophistication of the motor-powered rides didn't prevent us from installing low-cost attractions as well. Adjacent to the speedboat lake was a giant pile of hay bales that stretched more than ten feet in the air. They formed a winding labyrinth that resembled an obstacle course constructed for a rat in a laboratory. A sign next to it read: HUMAN MAZE.

A buddy of mine from school, Artie Williams, worked as the maze attendant. He was a good tennis player and read *The New York Times* every day without fail. These would normally be insufferable qualities for a teenager, but Artie managed to remain likable. He said he often heard muffled pleas for help from inside the maze. "People don't understand it's actually complicated and hard to get out of," he said. "They think it's like one of those things you draw a line through in a puzzle book. I wouldn't go in without a rope tied around my waist."

Snakes occasionally made their way into the bales, he said, popping out and causing people to sprint away in a mad panic, getting themselves even more lost than before. In the middle of summer, the bales trapped heat, effectively turning the maze into a suffocating furnace. People emerged from the exit soaked in sweat and gasping. "Water, water," they whispered, dry lips cracking. One of these disappearances actually made the local newspaper.

After a week, I saw a sign go up near the entrance:

DANGER
People Have Been Lost in This Maze for Up to Nine Hours

"It's good to warn them up front," Artie said, a *New York Times* tucked under his armpit.

As Motor World swelled, so did the rest of the park. New attractions seemed to erupt from the ground weekly, and other areas found new purpose. My father put in batting cages and basketball courts. The ski lift became the Sky Ride, a "scenic forty-minute tour through the mountain landscape." Trails of pot smoke surrounded the lifts.

Then there was the water slide, which would change everything.

Water slides were a relatively new phenomenon in the country. In 1971, a California campground owner named Dick Croul laid out the first one, a concrete trough covered in resin. People liked it, and soon slides were popping up on the West Coast, where the weather generally cooperated. George Millay, the guy behind SeaWorld, had opened Wet 'n Wild Orlando in 1977. No one thought much of doing anything similar on the East Coast except for my father, who again saw an opportunity to cede control to the guests. Unlike other parks, we didn't need to build expensive and ugly towers over flat land. We built our slides into the hill.

Our first, which was later known as the Green Water Slide, was made from fiberglass and had two lanes that curved to a pool at the bottom. Julie spent days filling the pool with water she siphoned from one of the lakes and carted over to the job site using an old fire truck my father had bought from the Vernon Township Fire Department to move water for the snowmaking machines. Julie drove it in halting spurts across the park, throwing herself violently about the cabin. When she stopped, she would unwind the massive fire hose and aim it in the general direction of the pool, every muscle in her body working to keep it under control.

"You're doing great, Rosebud!" my father shouted.

Compared to the demolition derbies in Motor World, the potential for misadventure on the slide was minimal, though it still harbored hidden dangers. The snowmakers had not done the best or most complete job of connecting the joints of the sections, causing some to jut out. If you went down the four hundred feet of track without riding one of the required foam mats, you could scrape your exposed skin over the joints. The defect would result in anything from a bruise to a gash. The slides also angered anyone who rode down with the paper driver's license needed for Motor World: The paper would get soaked. We charged two dollars for twenty minutes of this.

While popular, the slide couldn't hold a candle to Kramer's secret project. Encouraged by Gene to come up with an idea unique to the park, Kramer devised what he called Battle Action Tanks. These were small, engine-powered four-wheelers with a protective chassis built over the driver's seat. A cage crafted from chicken wire allowed people to see out of the camouflage-colored body. Inside, a joystick triggered a series of tennis balls, which shot out of a custom-made cannon at an absolutely ridiculous one hundred miles per hour, allowing the drivers to fire upon one another. Along the perimeter of the area, mounted tennis-ball guns allowed spectators and people waiting in line to attack the tanks. Kramer rigged them to go into a tailspin when someone scored a direct hit, the balls making a satisfying and foreboding *donk* against their armored panels. It was Wimbledon meets Vietnam.

The problem was that we had no efficient system for retrieving the ejected tennis balls. A Roomba-like machine that was supposed to canvass the area and vacuum them up was often broken. Employees would wait for lulls in combat, then sprint into the battlefield to retrieve them. The drivers would immediately turn and fire at the unprotected victims, the balls drilling their heads and torsos.

"Stop, stop!" the attendant would plead. You could hear muffled laughter from inside the units as they emptied their clips: *Thwock-thwock-thwock*.

"Unbelievable," my father said, laughing as the attendant sprinted away from the crossfire. He was ecstatic at the gladiatorial aspect of it all as crowds cheered the roving machines.

As my father soaked in the atmosphere, an attendant absorbed a shot directly to his groin. The worker groaned, folding into himself and falling over, the tennis balls continuing to bounce off him.

"Wonderful," my father said, taking in the landscape of warfare, largely oblivious to the wounded. I soon learned that supervisors assigned Motor World employees who were chronically late to the tanks as a punitive measure.

Kramer was pleased with his handiwork. Rather than idly suffer the destruction of his equipment, he had designed something engineered for abuse. He seemed resigned to the hunger for risk that permeated the park. Attendants at the Alpine would take the carts to his shop, where mechanics fixed the broken ones and modified others to fly down the chute faster by giving them four wheels instead of two. These carts were for employees with advanced expertise only and kept tucked away from the general population. They were liable, Kramer said, to kill somebody.

As Kramer's tanks began to draw long lines, my father grew convinced that the best rides, the rides that would be talked about, not only had to be unique to us but packed with thrills. The concept of the Vernon Valley Fun Farm was already too quaint. The park was evolving, reflecting the increasingly rabid tastes of its patrons. The diesel-drenched success of Motor World and the failure of the comparatively serene skate park proved that people wanted speed and danger, competition and risk. Each tennis ball that threatened to crush a testicle was an exclamation mark on this demand for more.

They did not want a fun farm. They wanted an action park.

A prototype of the Bailey Ball. Insert one human. Roll down mountain.

Chapter Three

A CRASH COURSE

"We try to generate excitement, what the parks call 'safe danger.' The rides provide the danger, but the environment provides the fantasy, an escape from everyday problems. People go to parks to escape."

Grady Larkins, amusement park designer, August 1979

We all stared at the ball.

The ball was a giant plastic sphere at least ten feet in diameter. It resembled the kind of thing you stuck a hamster in, except this ball was scaled for a human. A human who would, by virtue of being willing to climb inside, presumably possess an intellect comparable to that very same hamster.

I don't know how the ball had been transported here. It had been absent one day and here the next. No one thought it unusual. Workers walked by it without comment. In my father's orbit, the sudden appearance of a medieval-looking contraption was simply not remarkable.

"Go on and get in the ball, Frank," my father said.

I turned to look at Frank, a thirty-something who gave off the chill-dude vibe of someone who ate cereal for dinner. Frank was apparently an employee of the resort's wintertime operations. I had never seen him before. Depending on what my father had planned, I might never see him again.

"Mr. Mulvihill," he said. "Mr. Mulvihill, I don't think . . ."

"Come on," my father said. "You'll be fine."

Frank touched the surface as though it were an alien spacecraft made of a strange alloy. He nudged it as though physical contact might reveal its mysteries. The ball wobbled a bit before growing still. He slid a hand behind the railing surrounding the exterior. It got stuck, prompting a brief panic. With a sheepish grin, Frank plucked it out.

This would soon be the least of Frank's problems.

Inside this ball was another ball, one equipped with a seat and a shoulder harness, like the kind found in race cars (just not our race cars). Ball bearings separated the inner ball from the larger exterior ball, which allowed the inner ball to swivel independently and orient itself so that the seat always remained upright. Behind Frank, stretching in a zigzag pattern down the foot of the mountain, was a long track made from PVC piping like the kind used in plumbing, five or six inches in diameter. On the outer surface of the ball were casters and wheels like the kind found on office chairs. With these context clues, I began to understand Frank's apprehension.

"Once you're in the ball, Frank," Gene said. "You're going to roll along that track . . ."

"I don't think—"

"Don't worry," my father said, acting as though climbing into a giant ball was routine. "You'll roll along the track and come to a gentle stop. You get in there and try it out, and we'll take it for a spin when the ride inspectors come."

Before Frank could protest further, my father handed him a one-hundred-dollar bill. Frank stared at the cash, temporarily placated. He opened a hatch on the ball and Charlie and Big Al helped him in. Once Frank was strapped to the seat, the two began rolling him around the grass like they were bored children playing with a toy, shoving him from one side to another. Inside, a stoic Frank remained upright. Mostly. The seat sometimes drooped to the side, leaving Frank to rotate into the fetal position, knees bunched up to his torso like the world's most bizarre ultrasound. Though he was one hundred dollars richer, Frank still seemed very concerned.

"You're not gonna find this at Disney," my father said, beaming.

Rarely did he stop to consider that there might be a very good reason for that.

BY 1979, THE VERNON VALLEY FUN FARM WAS UNDERGOING A META-morphosis. For one thing, it was no longer the Vernon Valley Fun Farm, a name few people had used and which had never even appeared on an entrance sign. He trusted that people would find their way to our mountain theme park and not mistake it for one of the other mountain theme parks, of which there were precisely zero. Dismissing the Fun Farm label as too rural, he declared we would undergo a "massive rebranding." On our shoestring ad budget, that amounted to printing up new brochures and correcting newspaper copy. He was now referring to his summer escape as Action Park and had become obsessed with locating attractions that would live up to the promise of that name. Motor World and the Alpine Slide were drawing crowds, but visitors would stay for just a few hours, at most. He wanted them there all day, migrating from one ride to the next, stopping only for food and beer or to marvel at the towering contraptions in front of them. He wanted people so drunk on fun that they would have to be ushered out at closing time, dismayed at having to return to a life of rules and regulations.

More important, he wanted rides that defined his park, just as It's a Small World defined Disney. The tennis ball tanks were one-of-a-kind. They may have come at the cost of Kramer's sanity, but my father wanted more.

In scouting for these thrills, he became part of a national movement that had started more than twenty years earlier. The success of Disneyland, in the mid-fifties, kicked off an amusement park gold rush. Investors clamored to erect the Disneyland of the northeast or the Disneyland of the Rockies, all with singular ride experiences. Magic Mountain opened in Golden, Colorado, in 1957 with themed areas including an Old West mock-up and Storybook Lane, a fairy tale destination. Guests could ride a boat ride similar to Disney's Jungle Cruise with a tree rigged to fall and narrowly "miss" the vessel.

Pleasure Island opened two years later near Boston. Boasting a space rocket ride and a mechanical Moby Dick, it was hampered by Boston's short summers and closed in 1969. So did Magic Mountain, which suffered from cost overruns and reopened as Heritage Square under different management in 1971. Both were designed in part by Cornelius Vanderbilt Wood, who had helped Disney with his parks but decided to strike out on his own.

Wood also designed Freedomland USA, which opened in the Bronx in 1960 and carved out sections to pay homage to American history. The park set controlled fires to recall Chicago's famous blazes, giving visitors the opportunity to experience a tragic historical event for their own amusement. Kids could face the flames and pump water to try to extinguish the gas-powered inferno. (Inevitably, some uncontrolled fires started before the opening. The resulting ash was dumped near the caved-in buildings for authenticity's sake.)

There was an earthquake simulator meant to make visitors feel like they were in San Francisco as the ground opened beneath them. Admission was cheap—fifty cents at first—and people stayed all day, but it was a lost cause. Construction and development expenses kept the park from turning a profit. It closed after four seasons.

The lesson, if one could learn it, was that amusement parks were among the most volatile of businesses, prone to shifts in consumer tastes, cost overruns, hazards, weather, and even cultural context: Freedomland's attendance was said to have plummeted following John F. Kennedy's assassination in 1963. In trying to avoid the unpredictability of the ski seasons, my father had simply traded one kind of uncertainty for another. It was easy for a theme park to misstep, to bankroll the wrong kinds of rides. None of these other parks found a sustainable model or an enduring theme, even with the help of a Disney-anointed genius like Wood. Yet here was Gene Mulvihill, an independent operator without the massive financial support of the big conglomerates like Warner Brothers, which owned Six Flags, or Marriott, Mattel, and Anheuser-Busch, which backed other parks. When industry people came by and saw Motor World or the Alpine, they would ask which third-party operator he had hired to oversee them, which massive corporation was giving him his funding.

There was no one. It was just Gene and his kids.

Though he looked for attractions year-round, his opportunity for making additions was the lull between the end of the ski season and Memorial Day. My father's clock started when the snow began to melt. In that window, he had to erect rides, test them, make adjustments, and then open them. All this activity was compressed like a film played back at double speed and scored by a symphony of expletives from overworked snowmakers.

In his search for the unique, he was willing to entertain ideas from anyone. He met inventors at industry conventions he attended in Florida and answered letters he received in the mail. He had a stack of brochures that leaned precariously from a perch on his desk, all of them full of breathless copy about "rip-roaring excitement" and rides that were "the new standard in fun." They had names like Avalanche, Slide-a-Ride, and the Wave Pool. I stumbled across a pamphlet for Robinson's Racing Pigs, with photos of determined little hogs tearing across a dirt track like fat, pink stallions.

At night, he sifted through piles of concepts, asking himself questions about whether an attraction would be a worthwhile addition. Was it fun? Was there anything else like it? Most important, did it leave the person in control?

He worried about capacity—the number of guests who could pass through a ride in an hour. The higher the number, the greater the admission take. Someone could go down the Green Water Slide in fifteen seconds, which worked out to 240 people an hour. This was excellent churn, reducing the amount of time they had to spend in line and increasing the overall capacity of the park. Lower-capacity rides needed a bigger wow factor. As in, "Wow, that looks amazing," or, "Wow, that looks dangerous."

If a ride had a brochure, that meant it was being peddled everywhere. There could never be a guarantee it would not rise in another park, diminishing its stature at ours.

He needed innovators. He needed men like Ken Bailey.

Ken Bailey was the man who came up with the idea for the ball. He called it the Man in the Ball in the Ball. When everyone got tired of saying that, which happened immediately, we just called it the Bailey Ball.

Bailey was a very excitable man who had a childlike enthusiasm for rides. He peddled the ball, his most sensational idea, at the amusement conventions my father frequented. Ken said he got the idea while working as a custodian in a Kmart and accidentally spilling a bunch of Wiffle balls on the floor. As they rolled around, Bailey imagined a person inside of each one.

The amusement people listened to this and wrote off Ken as insane. Rather than raise alarms, their abundance of caution pleased my father. It meant he would be the first to have a Bailey Ball.

"This," he announced, "is what ambition looks like."

To me, it was what a janitor moonlighting as a ride engineer looked like, but that did not appear to dissuade him. He loved the idea of an eccentric in his midst. He adored Ken's enthusiasm and thought he could be the next big thing in amusements. He envisioned Ken as one of his Imagineers, the famed theme-park developers who brainstormed ideas for the Disney parks. My father flew him to New Jersey and told him he could start laying his track on the side of the mountain.

"When?" Ken asked.

"Today," my father said.

I think the decisiveness surprised Ken. There was no protracted deliberation or projection sheet prepared. Some of my father's friends would later describe this business approach as Ready, Fire, Aim.

That day, I watched as Ken immediately got to work. I asked if he had built a trial ball back in Canada, maybe a smaller prototype, something to demonstrate that it was practical.

"Nuh uh," he said, tongue jutting from his mouth as he glued the PVC together. "First one."

AS KEN MADE MAJOR AND POTENTIALLY DESTRUCTIVE ALTERA-tions to the face of the mountain, no one acknowledged that my father didn't have permits or approvals for any of this. He had absolutely no patience for things like site inspections, zoning restrictions, or feasibility studies. There was really no infrastructure in place for the state to cope with any of it, either. New Jersey's Department of Labor was responsible for granting permits for amusement rides, but my father argued that he wasn't installing "rides" in any conventional sense. They were "sporting attractions," and thus the state had no actual jurisdiction. The state never wanted to test that theory and thus was reticent to hand out fines or make demands for changes, lest a court of law find my father's argument valid. Getting the state's permission was mostly academic, anyway. It just wanted proof of insurance and evidence that the ride was not currently on fire. My father boasted of coverage from London and World Assurance, Limited, a company bold enough to cover his liability-prone participation park. He would proudly hand over proof of insurance to skeptical state regulators. No one bothered to question London and World's endless confidence in him. That would come later.

By the 1970s, amusement park safety was becoming a hot button topic not only in New Jersey but around the country. In 1975, the state had passed the Carnival and Amusement Ride Safety Act, which mandated annual inspections, maintenance records, and liability coverage, among other things. New Jersey was one of the few states that bothered with such legislation. In two-thirds of the country, there was nothing at all regulating rides. That always became controversial when an accident occurred. The US Consumer Product Safety Commission estimated that between six thousand and eight thousand people were injured in theme parks every year, bruised or clobbered in their pursuit of escapism. At Six Flags Magic Mountain in Valencia, California, a woman fell to her death from the formidable Colossus coaster, which reached speeds of sixty miles per hour. At Disneyland, a teenage worker was caught in a revolving wall and crushed to death in the America Sings attraction, prompting her parents to sue, and the park to offer a settlement.

Following one of these well-publicized mishaps, editorials in newspapers pondered whether there should be some kind of federal regulation of amusement parks. Parents of victims ruefully pointed out that Pennsylvania regulated hair stylists and charm schools but not amusement rides. Park owners wanted to remain self-governed and often blamed guests for their own injuries. When the CPSC wanted information from Disney about the Skyway tramway rides following three deaths on a similar gondola ride at an Illinois park, Disney management revolted, getting a court injunction that barred officials from investigating it. The industry knew it was in an arms race, building bigger and faster and more audacious roller coasters and attractions, and did not need the plodding oversight of government to slow them down. Today, it would be the gondola. Tomorrow, they would come for Goofy's Playhouse.

This suited my father just fine. Regulation was a nuisance. He had no patience for bureaucracy of any kind and was happy to wade into the Wild West of ride design. Permits and approvals were red lights that slowed progress and made him restless. Most of what he was installing was new to the East Coast, if not the entire industry. Early on, it was difficult for inspectors to gauge potential dangers because they had no idea what they were looking at. As a result, they were just as inept as my father believed most government agencies to be.

We would watch as officials from the state eyeballed the Alpine, looking at the track for any obvious cracks. They stood on the carts to make sure they would bear their weight. Then they'd stack sandbags on them and send them down the chute. When the carts didn't fly off the track, they appeared satisfied. The whole exercise was pointless, since no two rides on the Alpine were ever the same. Give those sandbags two beers and control of the joystick, and things would be much different.

If my father thought there might be even a slight amount of push-back, he enlisted an orthopedist named Dr. Sugar to stand by while the inspectors made their rounds. Dr. Sugar was in his fifties with snow-capped hair and a perfectly groomed beard that gave him the air of an authority figure—a theme-park surgeon general. He blithely endorsed whatever it was my father wanted to do. Like Frank, Dr. Sugar had seemingly materialized out of nowhere.

"It is my professional medical opinion," he would say, "that the Man in the Ball in the Ball is safe."

"Why is a medical doctor here?" Pete asked Splinter.

Splinter shrugged.

If inspectors found a problem that couldn't be soothed by Dr. Sugar, like the abrasive joints on the Green Water Slide, my father took their recommendations for repairs as suggestions. "Thanks, guys," he would say. "We'll address that immediately."

When they left, I asked, "Should I ask Charlie to look at that?"

Sometimes, he would say yes. Sometimes, he dismissed the recommendations as minor gripes. It could be difficult to persuade him to refine or perfect rides that were in operation. Once something was up, it was considered done. He was not irrational or negligent. If there was an immediate issue, like a nail sticking out of a railing, he would have it fixed. But maintaining attractions was not as interesting to him as building new ones. Part of it was his desire to have a sprawling park. Part of it was that he had waited all winter to begin playing with his toys. And part of it was the thought of people walking by a ride bearing a Closed sign and coming away disappointed. Like brown sod, this was unthinkable.

"Is it safe?" someone might ask of a new and winding attraction that could have used another week of fine-tuning.

"Safe enough," he would say.

Perhaps the best illustration of my father's approach to risk assessment is the day we realized he was not interested in performing any. During a family vacation to some ranch land he had bought near

Aspen, Colorado, we piled into a Jeep to make a short drive along a steep dirt road. As more of us piled in, clown-car style, it became obvious that we would not all fit. My father ordered Julie and Pete to climb on top of the roof and cling to the luggage rack. As the Jeep lumbered along the bumpy road, we could hear the two of them swearing and protesting, asking him to slow down. An Adidas sneaker sometimes popped in and out of view as they lost their footing on the slick surface.

"Hey, you two!" he said, barking out the open window. "Stop fooling around up there!"

Armed with a complete disregard for risk, he found it fun to conceive of things that would excite and delight people and drew crude sketches of rides that were almost purely conceptual, lacking principles of engineering, human anatomy, or physics.

"What are you doing, Dad?" I once asked him as he hunched over a piece of notebook paper with a red marker.

He held it up. A stick figure appeared to be plummeting from a building. An inscription appeared next to it:

DEATH DIVE

"How does that work?" I asked, not entirely certain I wanted to know given that I might be compelled to testify about it at some point.

"Guy climbs up to a platform," he said. "Guy jumps off. Real high. Real scary."

"Where does he land?"

He looked at the paper. "He slides, really. First, he's perpendicular. Then the path slowly starts to curve. In time, he's traveling horizontally and comes to a stop. The slope slows everything down." For my father, the thrill came first. He worked backward from there.

When he was ready to begin building, he looked for investors.

Some capital came from park profits. Some came from his other businesses, which were wildly eclectic and ranged from real estate investment to smelting silver on a hunch it would rapidly increase in value. Others were more pragmatic, like magnetic imaging used in medicine and, later, a wise bet on the future of a personal cell phone network, which he correctly believed would revolutionize the world. (After securing a gigantic early portable phone, he would call us at home and implore us to guess which street he was calling from.)

At times, it seemed as though my father pursued other ventures just so he would have money to sink into the park. Yet, even when his wells were tapped dry, he could count on a reliable stream of cash from Bob Brennan, the tennis partner who traveled with him to Puerto Rico and a hugely successful businessman in his own right.

My father first met Bob when Bob was just a teenager. Bob's father sold my father insurance, and Gene would sometimes go over to the Brennan house to pay the bill. Just a kid, Bob was awed by this energetic, enthusiastic man ten years his senior who seemed to be working on a dozen things at once.

"Stay away from that man," Bob's father told him. "He's a crazy man. He's from the moon."

Bob didn't listen and found major success under Gene's tutelage at Mayflower Securities. He stayed on at Mayflower after Gene got out, converting it into First Jersey Securities and making a fortune. Bob was fond of affirmations and acronyms, which he found useful for motivating himself. BAYCOB was Be All You're Capable of Becoming. SCHRIDE was Self-confidence, Courage, Honesty, Responsibility, Impatience with yourself not others, Determination, and Enthusiasm (that one was rather unwieldy). This shorthand was adopted by his fleet of aggressive salesmen, who later pushed shares of Great American Recreation, Incorporated, or GAR, the Action Park parent company, as the next Disney. GAR had an eclectic board of directors, including a man named Amos Phillips, who was well connected in Vernon and very wealthy from his steelmaking business but incredibly frugal. Missing an eye like Charlie O'Brien, Phillips opted to cover the empty socket with a Band-Aid, which would flutter as he inhaled. It was quite horrific, but you got used to it.

Gene, Bob, and Amos would walk the park grounds, Gene selling Bob on blobs of mud where towering rides with delighted patrons would one day rise. When Bob found a lead on some financing, he would sometimes co-sign the loan for Gene, lending significant heft to the transaction. In addition to being wildly successful, Bob feted Jimmy Carter at his residence. He appeared in Super Bowl commercials, stepping off a helicopter and inviting people to invest with First Jersey. His name meant a lot, and he deferred to Gene, whom he considered his mentor. He demanded no profit forecast, no complex web of accounting. There were other investors, but Bob was the most loyal. Gene was equally devoted to his friend, even when Bob later went to prison for bankruptcy fraud.

So the assembly line was in place. Anything my father dreamed, anything he found, he could fund and build. No inspectors would oppose it. His army of mountain men would build it in record time, and it would open before the industrial glue could cure. No obstacles prevented him from taking his impulses and rendering them in steel or fiberglass.

One day, not long after Bob came for a visit, there was a flurry of activity in one of the empty parking lots. Charlie and some out-of-work welders began assembling an enclosed slide with a loop at the bottom. It was one of my father's ideas. He had sketched it out on a napkin. He called it the Cannonball Loop.

"That's fucked up," Jimmy said, staring at it.

My father offered some of the employees one hundred dollars to try it out. No one would.

GIVEN THE CHOICE, I WOULD HAVE SPENT THE ENTIRE YEAR HELP-
ing build my father's park, nodding sagely over blueprints and sug-
gesting strategically placed soft-pretzel stands. In reality, trips to the
park in the spring were discouraged, and working there after school
was out of the question because of the hour-long commute each way.
Instead, my parents expected me to be a studious tenth grader. My
brother Pete was at Dartmouth. Splinter was studying engineering
at Lehigh. My father took education seriously, as though one generation of wayward Mulvihills would turn the whole family tree into
the shanty Irish. We all spent hours on homework each night and on
weekends. My mother bounced from one kid's absurdly difficult
math question to another, leaving my father undisturbed in his office
to make phone calls and sketch unfathomably precarious rides.

I attended Newark Academy, once an all-boys institution that
taught grades six through twelve. The school had an air of informal-
ity to it, with long stretches of time between class periods. Nomadic
students could crawl out through a window to a reservoir that was
just behind the building and get some sun or burn off excess energy.
The school was also across the street from the Livingston Mall,
where we strolled around giant water fountains, messed up record
store displays, and gawked at older girls. The latter often proved difficult because the mall was dimly lit, like an Italian restaurant.

I had a core group of friends and rarely strayed from their circle.
There was Artie Williams, who manned the Human Maze in Motor
World; Mac Harris, whom I had known since grade school; and Chaz,
a wrestler who was constantly starving himself and running around
in plastic in an effort to make weight, the cuffs of his garbage bag
pants engorged with collected sweat. I also hung out with kids a year
ahead of me. There was Benji Bressler, who never had money but

carried a wallet anyway; and Fast Eddie, whose older brother bounced at the hottest bar in New Jersey, the Final Exam, and regaled us with tales of drunken indiscretion.

Any of them could have landed a job at the park in a flash. Artie was one of the few who accepted. I managed to get Fast Eddie hired for one summer, but he kept people slightly on edge. He carried a water jug filled with juice to work but wouldn't let anyone drink from it. The working theory was that he didn't want what he considered the unhygienic trash of Sussex County giving him some kind of disease. A rumor grew that he had mixed vodka in with the juice, and that was why he refused to share. The truth was probably a little of both.

Mac caddied at the golf course and argued that my father, who played there, was already paying him pretty well in tips. Gene liked Mac quite a bit. Once, when over at the house, Mac emerged from our pool and grabbed a towel with the Heineken logo on it, wrapping it around his shoulders. Seeing this, my father pointed at him.

"Look," he yelled. "It's Captain Heineken!"

Mac seemed astounded that my father had put us all to work in the service of his park. "You're like the von Trapps," Mac said.

"Well," I said, "I think he sees potential in the recreation business." I said this as though my father had ever consulted a projection or had any kind of long-term plan other than getting people inside the park and letting them run amok.

When Mac was not caddying, he preferred to spend his time in pursuit of alcohol with a level of dedication usually associated with graduate studies. He drank like a fish and would stop at nothing to acquire beer. I seldom drank before the state's legal drinking age of eighteen, but Mac's enthusiasm for underage imbibing sometimes became infectious. Finally, I agreed to go on what amounted to my first beer run.

"We'll take a friend's brother's ID," Mac said, announcing his latest methodology. That weekend, the two of us biked into Madison, a neighboring town where we were less likely to be outed as the sixteen-year-old children we were. We pulled two empty wagons behind us and found a liquor store. I stared at the sign on the counter: MUST BE 18 OR OVER TO PURCHASE ALCOHOL.

"Give me two cases of Michelob," Mac said, handing over the license. We thought it was best for Mac to do the talking because he was sprouting a little fuzz over his lip.

"Why Michelob?" I asked him when we were back outside. No one remarked upon two kids heaving beer into their little red wagons.

"You don't want to ask for Budweiser," he said. "Michelob sounds more sophisticated."

We rode the bikes uphill, our thighs burning from the effort. We headed for my house with the beers because my parents were both away for the day, my father off to see some structurally suspect ride, and my mother tagging along. The beer drowning out coherent thought, I decided it would be a good idea to place a golf ball on top of an empty bottle and try to smack the ball without breaking the glass.

We broke all the bottles from both cases, sprinkling shards of glass around my father's golf tee, which he hovered over regularly. Seeing the mess was sobering. I could not believe I had been so brazen. Even this minor rebellion gnawed at my stomach. My mother was prone to corporal punishment with a wooden spoon, from which Jimmy often ran, but which I accepted with resignation. "A wooden spoon to tune you to the moon," she'd say, taking unusual delight in the word play while lashing her children with kitchenware.

I was older now, but a tuning to the moon, or beyond, was assured. I took a wet/dry vacuum to the yard, quickly sucking up the glass and periodically turning off the machine so I could listen for my father's car pulling into the driveway. By the time he arrived, we had erased all evidence of our misbehavior. We repressed our beer burps and waved to him as he walked inside.

"Captain Heineken!" he yelled, pointing at Mac.

NORMALLY, MAC AND I DIDN'T BEHAVE LIKE SUCH DEGENERATES. I considered myself an athlete and looked up to Pete, who had captained his soccer team to a state championship. My father was very fit, staying active via tennis, basketball, and early-morning jogs, though his unusual gait—more of a limping hobble, as though he were an escapee from a chain gang—drew attention.

"I saw your father out jogging," a neighbor once said. "If you can call that jogging."

He encouraged us to play sports. I enjoyed soccer, even making it to the state finals one year, but soccer was not my father's game. Long and lean, he preferred basketball, and the Mulvihill siblings spent many evenings squaring off in physical games on our home court. These were not playful skirmishes but serious competitions, which sometimes resulted in Julie crying, storming off the court, and then returning with a vengeance.

Soccer and sibling basketball did not fully satisfy my need for cutthroat competition. For this, I turned to the violence of hockey. The Newark Academy Minutemen were a scrappy team but effective. We played teams that appeared to have a surplus of resources, including their own home rinks and sparkling equipment. We were like beer leaguers playing the Soviet Red Army. If I got smacked, I would bide my time until the perfect opportunity arose for a crushing retaliatory hit. I did not realize it then, but this tempered reaction to violence would later serve me well at the park.

My mother attended many of the games. My father rarely came.

He was not aloof, but six active kids meant he had to choose his spots wisely. He also didn't relate to hockey the way he related to basketball.

"Not sure I get it," he said, doodling on a napkin.

When we won the Northern New Jersey Interscholastic League's Division B State Championship, I had the game-winning assist, passing the puck to co-captain Andy "Fat Man" Rothschild. I don't recall my dad attending, or even knowing that I was the other co-captain. I snipped out some newspaper notices, just in case he wanted to get the highlights later.

One day he looked over at my bag full of equipment, stink lines practically emanating from the sweaty foam padding. The season was long over, which meant I hadn't aired it out in months. As he stared at the gear, I thought he might ask about the big game.

"I've got an idea," he said.

TWO HOURS LATER, THE CANNONBALL LOOP WAS EJECTING ME LIKE a spitball through a straw out onto the mats that had been laid down at the exit. (It's too bad he didn't ask after I guzzled the Michelobs. The beers might have helped numb the limb-trembling terror.) At the bottom of the Loop, I was elated to be alive but also very disoriented.

I was the first human to make it through, a badge of honor that helped quell the grilled cheese fighting its way back up my esophagus. The descent through darkness, my body contorted by centrifugal force, was unpleasant in the extreme. Space and time ceased to have meaning. The enjoyment came not from the experience but from the bragging doled out thereafter. My father had created the first amusement ride to be endured, not enjoyed. He thought it would become our trademark and returned to his doodling, this time for a slogan. *Can you survive . . . the Cannonball Loop?*

The Loop would require another trial without the benefit of armor, as we could never mandate that guests wear padding to descend a water slide. Like someone who had already broken the sound barrier, I watched from the sidelines as a new maverick ascended the hill. His name was Glen Smocovich. I had seen him around, working construction and later as a ride attendant on the Green Water Slide. He was from Queens and about my age. His parents kept a lake house in Vernon. He was not wearing any equipment. Instead, he was shirtless and applying copious amounts of suntan lotion. He was sinewy, like an Olympic diver, with gobs of lotion clumped all over his torso. I realized he was using it as a lubricant, greasing himself up like a gloved finger going in for a prostate exam.

In a flash, Glen disappeared into the tube. There was a loud thud from inside, like the sound a shoe makes bouncing against the drum of a dryer. He shot out the other end and skidded fifteen feet, slamming into the hay bales someone had dragged out. He held his nose as blood poured from between his fingers.

My father handed him a hundred dollars.

The ride didn't open.

Not that summer, anyway.

UPON LEARNING OF MY MAIDEN VOYAGE DOWN THE LOOP AND Glen's shattered nose, my mother forbid me from going into the Bailey Ball. That's when Frank materialized.

We gathered at the foot of the mountain—me, my father, Charlie O'Brien, Dr. Sugar, and Ken Bailey. Also present was an inspector from the Department of Labor, who seemed to recoil at the sight of the mountain track. That he was there at all was something of a formality, but the Bailey Ball would nonetheless need to demonstrate some basic regard for human life in order to be rubber-stamped.

My father had wanted to see the ball in action first thing in the morning, hoping to get it open the following day, but the inspector was running late. It was growing hot, the first searing day we had experienced that summer. Because of the delay, Frank had been in the ball, cooking, for more than half an hour. He was already at the mouth of the track, six hundred feet up the mountain.

When everyone was in place, Ken gave a thumbs-up. Big Al pushed the ball from its starting position down the graded slope. Things went well for the first fifteen seconds or so, with Frank remaining upright in the center of the ball. But on the first turn to go back across the mountain, the ball didn't stay in the groove. It broke free and began rolling straight downhill.

Ken's face fell. He had been working up until the last minute gluing the PVC pipes together, not realizing they were warping under the heat. I could already see gaps in the tubing. Damaged by the hot sun, the plastic was expanding, severing the rail that was supposed to give the ball direction. Now it was free, unburdened by the track. The ball had achieved autonomy.

It gained momentum, tumbling uncontrollably down the face of the slope and picking up tremendous speed. Inside, Frank spun helplessly, unable to stop. He could not abandon the craft, as the door opened only from the outside. At this speed, the seat was unable to keep him secure. One second he would be upright. The next, his feet would be pointing toward the sky. His mouth was open in what I could only presume was a scream, but the ball sealed off any sounds.

When the contraption made it to the bottom without any visible damage, and Frank still appeared conscious, I exhaled. But it didn't stop. It began rolling at high speed toward us like the boulder in *Raiders of the Lost Ark*. We scattered, my dad and I scurrying to the left, and Ken and Charlie to the right. Dr. Sugar and the inspector were frozen, each of their faces a rictus of terror.

We gave chase as Frank and the ball rolled through the parking lot, narrowly missing the inspector's car. It spun past construction workers, who looked up from their shovels and heavy machinery to see a man bouncing around inside what appeared to be a diving bell. It cleared a small hill, briefly going airborne, then zipped right across Route 94, the two-lane road splitting the park. Cars honked and slammed on their brakes. If there had been opposing traffic, Frank would have become part of a real-life game of *Pong*, volleying from one bumper to another.

Still in pursuit, we followed the ball toward a small lake in Motor World that had been earmarked for a fleet of tiny bumper boats for children. The area wasn't open yet, but the empty boats were being tested and floated on the surface. The ball soared over the grass and smashed into several of them, scattering the others with rippling waves from the impact, which launched some of the boats several feet in the air.

Charlie and Ken waded into the water looking for the hatch. After some difficulty, they got it open. Charlie pulled Frank out by grabbing him under his armpits like a baby. Frank crawled up the bank, coughing and sputtering. There was blood on his shirt, but it was hard to know where it was coming from. He splayed across the grass as we all stared at the ball, which bobbed in the water like it was attached to a fishing lure.

We did not ask for the inspector's report, nor did we ever hear of it being filed. Ken Bailey returned to Canada. The snowmakers cleared away the PVC. Told to dispose of the Bailey Ball, they rolled it into the woods, where it remained for many years.

My father was unbowed. He kept drawing and doodling, telling us about things that were not yet there but soon would be. "Just wait," he said. "Just wait."

A promotional image of the speedboats. Actual guests were seldom this well behaved.

Chapter Four

THE PEOPLE MOVERS

"As the park's name implies, participation is the name of its game, but you will find spectators oohing and aahing at the base of the high-speed Kamikaze Slide. Bathing suits are a must, and it's advisable to wear shorts over them because the ride can have . . . an abrasive action."

Daily Record, September 5, 1980

O f the many inspirations my father took from the Disney parks, he held a special affection for their monorail. Debuting in Walt Disney World in 1971, the electric-rail passenger vehicle shuttled guests from the entrance to the hotels and on toward the park at an efficient fifty-five miles per hour. Another transit method, the PeopleMover, transported people above Tomorrowland in what amounted to a sightseeing tour.

As Action Park began to grow and expand, the problem of what to do with locomoting guests became more and more pressing. To get from Motor World to the aquatic area dubbed Water World, you had to hike up a big hill and then cross Route 94 on foot, dodging traffic and hoping a distracted driver in an AMC Gremlin wouldn't turn you into paste. On the other side was another hill leading toward the rest of the rides. It became a test of physical endurance for young and old alike, a gauntlet guests had to navigate before they could earn the right to have fun.

My father's solution was the Transmobile, a three-thousand-foot-long electric artery running from Motor World across the road to the ski lodge and on to the entrance to Water World. It would, he said, revolutionize how people maneuvered around the park. Instead of intoxicated and stumbling, they could be intoxicated and stationary. While Disney's monorail resembled an elevated subway train, the Transmobile featured small, open-air carts that held four passengers over a raised track and moved at four to seven miles per hour. Given its considerable height of ten to twenty feet, it was one of the few rides in the park that came with a safety belt.

My father bought it from DEMAG, the same West German outfit that had sold him the Alpine Slide. (Undoubtedly, he negotiated a package discount.) It was cutting-edge, which he loved, and expensive, which he didn't. Bob Brennan took care of the latter, raising money for what Gene considered a necessary weapon in his arsenal. The Transmobile was not only the present but the future. Eventually, it would connect the park sections, the park to the resort, and the resort to the nearby Playboy Club. (The Club was a hotel once earmarked for the legalized gambling that had failed to spread across the state. Now, it lurked in the margins of the area like a blacked-out adult bookstore.) My father hoped the Transmobile would someday run through the entire valley, enabling his planned domination of the area. Some of the snowmakers called it the People Mover, after the Disney transit system.

The People Mover had one issue. In order to fulfill its practical function, it needed to cross Route 94 via a bridge. While only a narrow two-lane path, Route 94 was nonetheless subject to the jurisdiction of the New Jersey Department of Transportation, as well as Vernon's own supervisors. These were entities whose gears turned slowly or not at all. Clearing the red tape to build a bridge could take years.

My father did not think in years. He had started constructing the Transmobile before asking anyone for permission, trusting he would solve that problem later. His men worked on it seven days a week. He had become the cartoon coyote who laid railroad track right off the cliff before bothering to look down. He could not cross the road, but he could not stop, either. It appeared to be an untenable situation, one that set the stage for what would become a years-long struggle between the quaint township high on its own bucolic nature and my father, whom the townspeople perceived as a threat to their tranquillity.

To him, it was as if Anaheim didn't want Disneyland. To realize his dream, he would have to smother the opposition, be it local, state, or federal.

"What do you think he'll do?" I asked Julie as we stared at the ever-growing People Mover track.

"Probably something he shouldn't," she said.

VERNON'S POPULATION HAD BLOSSOMED IN THE 1970S, WITH MORE and more people from the tristate area considering it a slice of Vermont within driving distance. They bought up homes and filled its single high school with their children. From some of the windows of those homes, they could not see any cars or roads. Vernon had all the charm of a rustic scene in an oil painting. When my father talked of building a sprawling amusement park that would bring millions of dollars to the local economy, some of the residents were wary of what else it might bring.

They were known as NIMBYs, as in Not In My Backyard. Sometimes my father used his own term, "the Crazies." The NIMBYs and Crazies spoke up at town meetings, peppering him with questions on how big he expected the park to get, what kind of patrons he anticipated attracting, and how bad traffic would become. Vernon was a bedroom community, and it wanted to remain that way. People didn't usually open or operate major businesses in town. Most commuted to the city for employment. My father was introducing a new industry—recreation—that threatened the serenity of their quaint little utopia.

"Don't they realize," he said, working up a head of steam, "that big business means their property taxes will go *down*?"

There was another problem, one that largely went unspoken but seemed to metastasize over time. In building a resort within driving distance of New York City, my father was inviting a multi-ethnic brand of tourism. For decades, Vernon had been predominantly white. There was no mass transit to or from the area, cutting it off from the multiculturalism of the city. That led to a shielded perspective, one that feared an influx of people who did not look like the average Vernon resident. A local could wake up, drive their truck over to the gas station, and thanks to the park, encounter the first black person they'd seen in years. A contingent of citizens didn't like these visitors and didn't want them—"the element," some called them—in their town. While those objectors were not many, they were vocal.

My father, who didn't care about color, religion, or class, tried to assuage their concerns, dancing delicately around institutional racism. He tried to tie in what he was doing with taxes that would cover the cost of their children's educations. Vernon had no other industry, he said. His was free of factory pollution. (We would wind up accidentally gassing several people with ozone, but that came later.) It employed all the teenagers in town. He argued methodically, pointedly, reasonably. They would nod. Then he'd leave the meetings and the townspeople would begin to buzz with unease about his growth strategy and ethnic mixing.

He knew of their whispered concerns because he had sources embedded in the community. One of them was Father Boland, an Irish-Catholic priest who bonded with Gene over their shared Irish roots. The two had met when Father Boland came into Vernon for the first time and visited the mountain on Charlie O'Brien's invitation. As Father Boland explained it, Charlie had brought him around to the Hexagon Lounge, when my father appeared, face red with rage, and began a torrent of verbal abuse directed at Charlie about litter.

"Why would anyone come here?" he screamed. "Look at these papers everywhere!"

There was one piece of paper on the ground, Father Boland remembered.

After letting Gene spew profanities, Charlie introduced Father Boland as the new priest in town. My father's demeanor changed immediately. He tried to make friends with priests, he once said to me, because he found their company comforting.

With his thick shock of dark hair and kind face, Father Boland became a regular sight at the park. He seemed charmed by my father's imagination and concrete convictions. His ability to will things into existence excited the reverend.

"What will be going here?" Father Boland would ask, staring at a mess of tubing and shovels. My father would paint him a picture of something grand. Sometimes Father Boland would be awed. Sometimes he would shake his head. My father once described plans to mount a rope across the water so people could swing on it.

"Gene, that's just an old swimming hole," he said. "You can't charge admission for that!"

"Can and will," my father said.

Thanks to chatty parishioners, Father Boland had all the town gossip and sometimes relayed which way the wind was blowing. Gene could then try to curry favor in targeted spots. The town might need a parking lot repaved or a soccer field seeded. He would dispatch the snowmakers like a band of merry drunken men and have them toil until the land was transformed, earning my father points for civic and charitable duty. He wanted to be Vernon's favorite adopted son.

It wasn't so much bribery as a microcosm of politics in the real world. When one of his proposals came up for a vote and there was little resistance from township officials due to his philanthropy, he smiled, knowing he had scored one over the NIMBYs and Crazies. If it failed, he would go in search of another blight or project to tackle, another town fundraiser to host.

Father Boland sometimes found himself in the position of defending Gene, stirring into the local conversation that Gene had installed a pool free of charge for local migrant workers who worked with a group of nuns. Such information kept people on their toes. Yes, Gene Mulvihill was taking over Vernon, but he had also *helped the nuns*, so how bad could he be? Father Boland had an impeccable reputation and was able to deliver a perspective on my father that was not immediately obvious to people dealing with his development demands.

It was not until later that I discovered the bond between my father and Father Boland ran much deeper. A month after meeting Gene, Father Boland visited a man who was sick and dying. It was raining, and the man's roof was leaking. Drops of water collected in cups and saucers the man had set down on the floor. Despondent, Father

Boland mentioned it to Gene, who was busy directing contractors on a project near the resort. Gene huddled with his men, then sent them away.

By the end of the day, the dying man's roof was no longer leaking. No one brought it up at meetings, and my father asked Father Boland not to use it as currency for his plans. Like many of his better deeds, it would remain a well-kept secret for years. Sometimes, he wanted the camera pointed away from him.

FATHER BOLAND WAS NOT GENE'S ONLY CONDUIT TO VERNON. Often, my father would let a man named John Steinbach run interference. The two had been friends since grade school. My father was extremely loyal to John, just as he was with all of his close friends, but the bonds forged in youth were strongest. When he bought the resort, he hired John as a bartender at the Hexagon Lounge. Soon, word spread among the town gossips that John's stepfather was famous. This was true. He was once the biggest mobster in the state of New Jersey.

Abner "Longie" Zwillman was six feet two inches tall and got his start selling produce from a rented horse and cart in Newark. When people paid for their fruit, he also offered to sell them a penny or nickel ticket to an illegal lotto. It was a numbers racket, and it introduced Zwillman to the pleasures of trafficking in vice. A teenager during Prohibition, he imported alcohol from Canada and carried himself like a veteran bootlegger. When the Lindbergh baby was kidnapped and held for ransom in 1932, Zwillman offered a fat reward for information. The police roadblocks were cramping his business.

Eventually, Zwillman stepped up for a piece of the syndicate crime dynasty when it looked like a fellow member, Dutch Schultz, was headed for prison. When that didn't happen, and Schultz returned to claim his territory, Schultz was gunned down in a diner. While Zwillman wasn't implicated in the crime, it was a convenient bit of homicide.

He later married John's mother, Mary, and seemed to ease up on the criminal mayhem a little bit, hunkering down in a twenty-room mansion with his bride and stepson in West Orange, New Jersey.

Gene once took my mother over to John's before heading out for New Year's Eve. Soon, it began to snow, and the roads steadily got worse.

"No one's going anywhere," Zwillman said. "You're going to have your party here."

My parents spent the evening under the care of a mobster serving them lobster and champagne. Later, when my mother's Protestant parents objected to her marrying Gene, they claimed it was due to his Catholicism. I imagined evenings spent in the company of Longie might have also played a part.

I don't think my father considered Zwillman much of a big deal. His own father, Dockie, was a union organizer and ex-boxer. He had no connection to organized crime but was not to be trifled with. (Dockie was always lovely to me, taking me out for ice cream and to Woolworths, lazy afternoons he called "bumming.") To add to my father's protective umbrella, his cousin Donna was married to a West Orange police officer. Between the three of them, you'd be hard-pressed to mess with Gene or John and not have someone to answer to. I don't know if it taught him to ignore authority, but my father often acted as though there would be no repercussions for his actions—as if Zwillman, Dockie, or a relative with a badge would forever be there to make a phone call and allow him to slide.

Longie's lawless ways ended when he died under some controversy. He was found hanging in his basement, and bruises on his body indicated it might have been an "assisted" suicide, an act possibly perpetuated by those concerned he might talk to law enforcement to avoid a tax problem. When John's mother passed and John received his inheritance, he stopped bartending and started investing money in whatever my father was cooking up. The money wasn't his only useful trait, though; he was also devilishly handsome. John looked like Paul Newman and was always well dressed. Women liked him. So did men. He befriended local officials. The mythology of the mob appeared to captivate people. John, for his part, would do pretty much anything Gene asked, always mindful that his old friend had never considered him a pariah because of his infamous stepfather. Rather, Gene took a mischievous delight in the loose association, embarrassing John whenever the two were in the company of new business partners.

"Do you know who his father was?" Gene would ask. "My God!" Then he'd mime holding a machine gun. Some people felt this was a very subversive method of intimidation, as though Gene was implying he was connected and not one to be crossed. In truth, my father's relationship with the mafia following Zwillman's passing extended to having seen the *Godfather* movies. But if people believed it, he wasn't in a hurry to correct them. It was a tool to be put in the box and deployed when necessary.

When religion and implied organized-crime affiliations failed him, my father turned to the other weapons in his arsenal. His children.

At the park one day, he pointed to a kid about my age. He was working on the Alpine Slide. "You see that guy?" he asked.

I did.

"You'd better make friends with that kid," he said.

I asked him why.

"You just be friends with him," he said, and walked away.

As ordered, I struck up a conversation with the kid, a lanky teenager with dirty blond hair and a farmer's tan from wearing a muscle shirt at the top of the Alpine. Hefting carts off the lift had pumped up his shoulders. His name was Chuck Kilby.

"My dad is on the township committee," he said.

"Right," I said.

When my father realized Chuck and I had no interest in exchanging intelligence, he turned to Pete's girlfriend, Ellen, whose father happened to be a state trooper who lived next door to the Kilbys. Slowly, the trooper tried to ingratiate Gene into the Kilby household, occasionally bringing his name up the same way vaccines introduce low doses of a virus. But nothing could persuade Kilby to turn away from the idea that Gene had come to swallow Vernon whole.

WHILE MY FATHER NAVIGATED THE WATERS OF SMALL-TOWN DIPLO-macy, I had political concerns of my own. My chance at being named school president was in danger due to a nemesis named Harold Grodberg.

I had been elected class president in ninth, tenth, and eleventh grades, and elected vice-president of the school that last year. It amounted to a popularity contest with a tiny voting base, but I didn't care. I saw my father able to organize people and shift their thinking, and I wanted to see if I could do that, too. Candidates ran on joke platforms seeking more variety in school lunches and getting homework credit for watching the *ABC Afterschool Special*. I took it seriously. I was friends with the departing incumbent, who provided a valuable endorsement. My appointment seemed all but assured.

Then Grodberg showed up. He had a slight potbelly and wore sweater-vests, sometimes the same one two days in a row. I scoffed at his candidacy and glided through my campaign without a care in the world. I was like JFK to his stodgy Nixon. I could speak to anyone, from the burnouts to the football players. In this, I mirrored my father, who refused to pay attention to class distinctions and treated everyone equally.

I thought I had positioned myself well, but I underestimated Grodberg's tenacity. Knowing older kids were indifferent to school politics, he went after the six, seventh, and eighth graders, whose minds he could easily manipulate. He was a hungry upstart, rallying students with rousing speeches and outlandish guarantees.

"If I'm elected, I promise you this," he said, pounding a makeshift podium that housed the AV equipment. "I will sit on the school's board of directors!"

"That is such bullshit!" I said. No student had ever sat on the board. I turned to Mac, who was staring out the window at nothing. "They're not gonna let him do that."

"Raise an objection," Mac said.

"It's not court," I said.

"I vow to you," Grodberg said, "that our mac and cheese will be warm again!"

This platform of lies and deceit swayed people I had counted on to be loyal. Grodberg won the election, albeit by a slim margin.

"You didn't do anything wrong," Mac said, sipping a beer. "People just want a fresh face." Despite the damage he was doing to his brain cells, Captain Heineken was sometimes capable of sage insight.

Still, I didn't handle the loss well. I spent time ruminating over which wheels I should have greased and whose soccer field I had proverbially failed to seed. To his credit, Grodberg made good on his promise to join the board of directors. When I edited the school yearbook, I had him hold a picture frame over his face and stand next to the wall with the rest of the board members' photos. I suppose it was my way of conceding the victory.

While wallowing in my defeat, I discovered my father was friends with someone who knew Morton Blackwell, a conservative activist involved with Ronald Reagan's 1980 presidential campaign.

"Do you think you could get me a job with the campaign?" I asked him.

I wanted to do something after losing office. Maybe I could win vicariously through Reagan, whose values I admired. We shared a love for freedom and a distaste for socialism, and helping out with his candidacy was appealing. The problem was that my father was anticipating an explosion of visitors at the park. Workers swarmed the property, racing to get new attractions open in time for the start of the season. Ride attendants in bathing suits pulled double duty, picking up shovels. The place was vibrating with a mania and energy, my father bouncing from one half-finished ride to another on his dirt bike. There was always a rush, but this was unprecedented.

"Tourism is going through the roof," he said. "Great Adventure is turning away cars!"

Because it had tolls, the Atlantic City Expressway was a good barometer of how many people were visiting the state. According to reports, more than eleven million people went through the Expressway during the first half of the year, up from roughly eight million the year prior. There was a recession, and gas prices had gone up, so people were seeking out day trips closer to home. Atlantic City, and its legalized gambling, beckoned them. So did national parks. The state blanketed the population with tens of thousands of brochures touting tourist destinations, including Action Park. The cover read: *Jersey's Got It!*

My father saw this as an opportunity to wow a stream of visitors with attractions they couldn't find anywhere else. He added two new lanes to the Alpine, for a total of four. (We'd eventually have six, three of which were serviced by a second chair lift.) Miniature speed-boats were up and running. He told a reporter he was preparing a hot-air-balloon landing port, though that never materialized. The tourism board had even corralled German journalists to visit attrac-tions in the state in the hopes they could get Europeans to plan over-seas visits. The Germans sat in the dining hall of the ski lodge and watched as one of the publicity people showed them projection slides of the rides.

"This is the Alpine Slide," she said, clicking over to a photo of a man in a tight graphic T-shirt and two-toned sunglasses spiriting down the track. The journalists murmured and nodded at each other, smiling.

"And this is the Cannonball Loop," she said, showing them a picture of a giant death straw. They looked astonished. We later learned many of the journalists were actually editors of prestigious publications, and some had PhDs. Our flippant attitude toward gravity alarmed them.

While international visitors were unlikely, people from inside the state were a different story. My father sensed an influx of attendees coming, and he wanted to dazzle them. It was no wonder that he was trying to charm and squash his political opposition by any means necessary.

For these reasons, I expected him to say no, to require me to re-main at the park as it was on the verge of a major expansion. Part of me wanted him to insist I stay and continue to help. But he was also an admirer of Reagan and seemed impressed I was taking an inter-est in the future of the country. "If it won't be for long," he said, "I'll make a call."

Within the week, I was told to report to Reagan's national cam-paign headquarters in Arlington, Virginia. I borrowed the family station wagon and drove there. Walking into the offices, banks of phones buzzing and purposeful young adults weaving between metal desks, I felt reinvigorated. I was convinced that, with Reagan at the helm, the nation would escape its fiscal crisis. Under the oppressive leadership of the incumbent Jimmy Carter, we could only slide further into debt. I was prepared to give it my all under the tutelage of these hungry and impassioned volunteers. Let Harold Grodberg worry about the school lunch menu. In my own small way, I might have some effect on the future of the country.

Some days, I stuffed envelopes at the campaign office. Mostly, though, I made copies and ran errands. I also went on road trips with volunteers to different cities, where I assisted in training college students to conduct mock elections so they could identify Reagan supporters among students who were largely apathetic about politics. With Reagan winning the school elections, and the results getting coverage in the local press, the impression would be that the youth of America was behind him. It was an intriguing sleight-of-hand that clued me in to the importance of appearances, of controlling the narrative in a way my father had perfected.

In July, we traveled to Detroit for the Republican National Convention, where it was all but assured that Reagan would officially be named the Republican nominee. The day we arrived, a virus turned me into a bedridden mess. I felt so sick that I wasn't sure I was going to live to see Reagan's triumph in November. I held my campaign button like a healing crystal and dialed my parents from the Michigan State dorm where the campaign had put me up.

My grandmother answered. (My grandfather called her Turkey. No one was really sure why.)

"Is Mom there?" I said, rasping.

"Your parents are in Europe," she said. "I think your father is looking at some of those amusements."

My mother would never hear my dying words because my father wanted some German-made deathmobile.

"Okay," I said, and hung up.

After a few days convalescing, I made my way to the convention floor, my brain feeling like it was stuffed with gauze. Reagan was giving his acceptance speech, and I wasn't going to miss it.

As he spoke, I headed over to the phone banks and called Mac. "You hear that?" I said, lifting the receiver above the din. "That's Ronald Reagan!"

"Holy shit," Mac said. We discussed my contributions that helped lead to this historic moment. Then he asked me, "Did anyone tell you about the Larsson kid?"

I had trouble hearing Mac through the roar of the convention. "Who's the Larsson kid?"

"He wiped out on the Alpine, man. It's not good." The crowd smothered his words.

"The Alpine? How bad?"

"He's in a coma."

We tried speaking more, but the noise was too much. I hung up on Mac and listened as Reagan chided the current administration for weakening the economy and failing to combat the energy crisis. He said the system had grown fat and needed a diet. Tax cuts were necessary. We could no longer allow the Soviets to stockpile arms unchecked. Most important, he said, the government would do the work of the people without intruding on their lives.

It sounded familiar. My father didn't have professional speechwriters, but the sentiment was the same. I began to see what he had been driving at and how it matched the country's mood. The park was a metaphor for individuality. People didn't need to be legislated into submission, relegated to narrow corridors of living. Action Park was America. Six Flags and its pre-set coaster paths was communist

China. I did not understand how anyone could support any authority forcibly dictating how others should live. It was too George Orwell, too suffocating.

Thousands of balloons were released, bouncing around the arena. Reagan stood for rapturous applause, waving to the throngs of people who held up signs and roared their approval.

Freedom was a good thing. Individualism was a good thing.

What was that about the Larsson kid?

"YOU'RE PALE AS SHIT," JULIE SAID. WHILE I WAS INDOORS STUFF-ing envelopes, Julie had been operating the Green Water Slide and its new neighbor, the Blue Water Slide, for weeks. She looked like a Coppertone ad.

The shame I felt over my albino complexion worsened when I caught sight of a new water slide employee. After extensive prodding, Julie told me her name was Ginette Molina. Ginette was a stunning beauty with a fetching overbite in a tight blue bathing suit. She and her sister, Nicole, had started as ride attendants while I had been away serving my country. I contemplated going up to her, but Julie pointed out my new Young Republican outfit: a button-down shirt, shorts, black socks, and loafers. I thought I looked sharp.

"You look like an idiot," Julie said.

I took a final, longing look at Ginette as Julie pulled me away. The park was erupting, just as my father had vowed, construction debris shunted off and piled into isolated mounds. Before, I had been there on a near-daily basis and had grown accustomed to its steady evolution. Seeing it after some time away was startling. It had morphed into a mini-metropolis, with new attractions thrilling the deluge of guests my father had anticipated. Despite an increasingly vocal chorus of dissent, his political jockeying was working.

Julie and I continued walking uphill, past adults in flip-flops and children dripping wet from the slides. Speakers mounted on poles blared "Stayin' Alive" with a persistent crackle. Bulky Sony Walkman tape players, just introduced, tugged on the flimsy waistbands of bathing suits. It seemed busier and more vibrant than ever before, throngs of people racing around us, our lagging bodies an impediment to the next attraction.

"There," Julie said, and pointed to the left.

Sunken into the hill below was a grotto, a coagulation of people milling around on a platform next to the water. Over the pool was a rope that dangled from a high steel bar that traversed the surface. Separate from the group was Glen Smocovich, the kid from the Cannonball Loop. He held a giant metal hook on a pole, which he used to pull the rope back toward the group. I couldn't hear him, but I could see he was demonstrating how to grab the line, squatting down until his knees were in his chest. This was the swimming hole my father had told Father Boland about.

"Dad is calling it the Tarzan Swing," Julie said. That was smart, as Tarzan was not copyrighted and therefore not subject to licensing fees. "Watch."

Glen passed the rope to the next person in line, who broke away from his giggling friends to grab it like he was about to climb it for gym class. His body was rod-straight, knees locked in place, completely the opposite of what Glen had just demonstrated. He swung across the water in a wide arc, legs outstretched. Suddenly, he lost his grip. As he came down, his frame took on the limbs-askew pose of the figure on those folding signs that warn of slippery floors. He belly flopped into the water, then paddled back to the deck while the entire crowd heckled him.

Glen corralled the rope a second time, again bending his knees to illustrate the correct posture. The next guest also ignored him completely. The kid swung, but his thin arms didn't have the strength to hold on. He fell straight down. A girl let go almost as soon as she clenched the rope, falling into the water with the grace of a cinder block. I winced. The crowd roared. Glen used the pole to drag people back to shore. Emerging, they seemed to be shivering violently.

"The water is from the mountaintop lake," Julie said. "It's fifty degrees."

"I don't get it," I said, watching more of them land with a splash. "Does anyone make it?"

"You're just supposed to make it to the middle of the pool," Julie said. No one had yet managed that. "But the crowd has fun either way."

I saw money changing hands.

"Are they *betting*?" I asked Julie.

Longie Zwillman would have thrived here.

We continued to walk, surrounded by the sounds of screaming, roaring, and splashing. "Look up there," Julie said. "That's the Kamikaze."

There, at a forty-five-degree angle, stood a massive slide surrounded by the biggest crowd I had ever seen at the park. From the top, I could see tiny figures shooting down its surface and creating a break in the water tension like a car tire zipping through a puddle. I had never seen human bodies move at that speed outside of a vehicle. They came down the slide screaming before the surface turned level, slowing their momentum and allowing them to skim across a long, narrow pool. When they reached bottom, the crowd threw their arms up in a wild and raucous applause.

"Why is everyone just standing around at the bottom?" I said.

"You'll see," Julie said.

A woman sailed down the slide and into the pool, bouncing over the water like the surface was made of rubber: *plip-plip-plip*. She stood up, slightly discombobulated, and waved to the cheering crowd.

They seemed overly enthusiastic about her success. Through a part in the mob, I suddenly understood. Everyone could see her bare breasts. The water had blasted her bathing suit top completely off. Numb and disoriented from the ride, she was oblivious.

"Oh, my God," I said. "Oh, my *God*. Does Dad know about this?" Julie nodded. It was obscene, obviously, but not premeditated. The ride wasn't designed to disrobe. I could imagine Dad's reaction. *It's not a big deal,* he'd say. *No one is complaining.* I wondered how Ronald Reagan would feel about this.

Julie stationed me at the top of the Kamikaze. For the rest of the summer, I watched as growing lines of people funneled themselves down the slide. Some women told their boyfriends to tighten the knot of their suit before they went down. Men lost their loose-fitting bathing trunks, exposing their genitals to crowds as they scrambled to find them. Tops floated in the pool like water lilies. Kids passing by were fascinated by the display. From the top of the ride, I could see the whites of their eyeballs soaking in the anatomy lesson.

When Julie asked Kamikaze attendants to rotate to other areas, they protested. Some threatened to quit. "You can see more tits here than a strip club," one whispered to me, a spotter who stood midway down the slide. He looked to be about fourteen.

Julie seemed exasperated by the display. She thought it was lurid and argued that families might be reluctant to drag their children along if there was a possibility of seeing nipples.

My father shrugged. "It happens by accident," he said. "Should I shut the ride down?" That, we knew, was rhetorical.

THE TARZAN AND KAMIKAZE RIDES WERE HUGE HITS THAT SUMMER. Near the Alpine, though, the mood felt overcast. The lines wound down the mountain, but near the top, attendees hefted carts without their usual gusto. The Larsson story had spread among the employees like a campfire tale, and I slowly gathered the details.

George Larsson was a nineteen-year-old from the neighboring town of Sparta. He had worked at the resort as a ski-lift operator for part of the winter and had come back to socialize. I had never met him but knew someone who had. He told me Larsson was a good wrestler and had gone undefeated the previous season. In the summer, he worked for his dad's roofing firm. He spent an entire day riding down the Alpine's fast lane. He had become adept at careening down at a near-record clip, just as Jimmy had, and decided to ramp up the difficulty level by using one of the carts that had been customized by the Motor World mechanics to go faster. Worse, he had insisted on continuing even after it had started to rain. The ride always closed in bad weather because the brakes stopped working.

At roughly six in the evening, the ride was shuttered to the public. Larsson, still riding, turned to look at a friend on a parallel track while banking into a ninety-degree turn. He lost control, flew off the track, and rolled down the embankment, coming to a stop only after he struck his head on a rock. The area was inaccessible to ambulances, so employees carried him down the slope. He wound up in the intensive-care unit with severe brain trauma. He spent a week in a coma before he died.

The ski resort's general manager, a man named Wesley Smith, was doubling as our spokesperson. He decided to play offense with the press. "The ride didn't injure Larsson," he said. "It was a rock twenty-five feet away that hurt him." He found it necessary, I supposed, to deflect the notion that the park was negligent. Wesley Smith was controlling the narrative. Still, it bothered me a lot. Smith also noted that Larsson was on the ride without authorization and after normal operating hours. He referred to a sign posted near the slide: RIDE AT YOUR OWN RISK.

Employees seemed divided. Some believed Larsson pushed things too far, discounting common sense for a thrill. He had overdosed on adrenaline. Others believed the ride attendants had been too permissive in letting him put himself at risk. A sign wasn't enough, they said. Someone should have told him not to do it.

My father shut the ride down for two days. An inspector came out, put a sack of potatoes on the cart, and watched it go down the mountain without falling off. They deemed this successful and said Larsson had gone down at an "excessive speed," though no one really knew what constituted excessive speed on the ride. There was no rule book. My father had a paved access road put in so EMTs could get to injured guests. The park received citations for the lack of ambulance access and failure to report the accident in a timely fashion, but no fines. Rumors swirled that Larsson's parents would sue.

Whatever my father may have thought about rider responsibility—and Larsson clearly tempted fate—he was shaken up by what had happened. He peppered employees with questions about what Larsson had done wrong. He took Jimmy and me aside. "You treat this with respect," he said. He meant both the accident and the Alpine Slide. All three of us felt the same shivering dread. It could have been one of us.

After Larsson's death, the Department of Labor got a stack of overdue accident reports from the park. Ninety-five people had been treated for injuries ranging from bruises to fractures, scrapes to burns, bumps to concussions. Over forty percent of the injuries came from the Alpine. I didn't know who had withheld the reports, but I knew my father's philosophy when it came to cooperating with agencies that could slow him down. One had to minimize interference. Missing paperwork was another strategy for maintaining course.

The accident sparked another wave of conversation about the safety of amusement parks. A water slide in Wildwood, New Jersey, had recently come apart, causing six people to fall thirty feet. Luckily, their injuries were moderate because they landed on sand instead of the boardwalk. For a time, it felt like theme parks had become the next big evil in the eyes of the media, replacing video games and rock music. Dorney Park in Pennsylvania told the newspapers they used on-site inspectors. We could only remind people what our park was and what it was not.

"The ride is in the control of the individual," Smith told a reporter. "This is an action park where people are doing physical things to themselves. Their situation is not totally in our control."

It would become a mantra.

THE ONLY THING THAT DREW ANYONE'S ATTENTION AWAY FROM THE accident that summer was the Transmobile. In August, it became fully operational, and my father held a dedication ceremony for it. "This is the transportation system of the future," he told the press. New Jersey state senator Wayne Dumont attended, lending the whole thing an air of importance. Despite the pageantry, the system seemed kind of rickety, the carts trembling as they carried people from one area to the next. When a state inspector named Harry Crane gave it a cursory once-over, the cart he was riding in slid backward and careened down a slope in the track, smashing into another cart and sending him to the hospital with bruises. Harry was affable enough, and usually seemed more interested in the show at the Kamikaze than anything else. No fine was issued.

I was less impressed with the mechanics of the system than the fact it existed at all. A bridge had materialized overnight across Route 94. I couldn't believe my father had somehow persuaded state bureaucrats to cooperate.

I asked Julie and Jimmy what had happened. I asked my father, who shrugged and credited "an efficient workaround." I asked Charlie O'Brien. No one had the entire story, but each had details. In the middle of the night, someone—Charlie would not say who—operated a crane that lifted the flat section of bridge over the road. Workers scrambled to secure it in place. The next morning, a town official drove under it as the work was being finished. He pulled into the park and demanded to know who from the state was responsible for approving it. A Department of Transportation employee emerged, shook his hand, and explained all the necessary permits were in place. Satisfied, the man went on his way.

I asked who the transportation worker was. No one knew, but people kept saying he was well dressed and quite handsome, like Paul Newman. They said he looked a lot like John Steinbach.

The Wave Pool, my father's attempt to replicate the Jersey Shore.

Chapter Five

THE WAVE

"For ten minutes each half hour, the pool seems innocent enough. Then the eight 75-horsepower engines surge into action, producing rolling whitecaps three to four feet in height. Swimming amid the 'debris' of rented and brought rafts in the eight-and-a-half-foot deep end of the pool was like experiencing the aftermath of a shipwreck."

Sunday News (Lancaster, Pennsylvania), August 9, 1981

The first time I mentioned to my father that I spent my rare days off from the park at the Jersey Shore with my friends, he looked at me uncomprehendingly. Though it was the most normal thing in the world for a seventeen-year-old in New Jersey, he acted as though I had said I enjoyed the occasional trip to the moon.

"Why?" he said. "Why would you bother?"

To him, the park was a permanent vacation, one that provided all the escapism anyone could require. In his eyes, I was making the ninety-minute drive to the shore for nothing. But that was the point—the nothing. The shore wasn't expecting anything of me. I had no responsibilities. I hung out with my friends, aping my father's penchant for associating with characters. There were kids like Chuckie Baby—who resembled Chuck Barris of *The Gong Show* fame and once responded to a bunch of seniors crashing one of his house parties by chasing them out with a 12-gauge shotgun—and Rich Szuch, whose family owned a house on the shore and whose bed I once puked on to such a degree that his mother had to disassemble the frame in order to clean it up. (This made me realize that I might have been a character recruited into Rich's life, my first existential crisis.) I chased flocks of seagulls. I surfed—or tried, anyway—and went water skiing. I was free to enjoy the sun and the saltwater or just stretch out on an empty bulkhead. I watched as people in the water let the tide wash over them, monitored by lifeguards who never once had to move from their perches.

I thought it was perfect.

I did not realize my father believed he could improve upon it.

For months, he had been hovering near a massive concrete-lined hole in the ground that grew deeper and wider every time I walked by. It soon sprouted an enclosed operating room that housed enormous fans and pumps that throbbed with so much power they sucked the insulation right off the walls. Workers, led by Charlie O'Brien, funneled lake water from the snowmaking pipes on the mountain into the hole. It was cumbersome work and wore Charlie down. He became surly, growling at employees. Gene often pulled Charlie aside, their voices quickly growing loud enough to turn the head of anyone within twenty feet.

"I can't do six months of work in four!" Charlie roared.

"I want my hole!" Gene bellowed. "Fourth of July!" This was the cut-off date for maximizing revenue. If a ride missed the big holiday weekend because it was still under construction, my father considered it a catastrophe. The sting of the Alpine opening in September had never left him. He continued throwing manpower at the problem, expecting seven-day work weeks. Day by day, the snowmakers' habit of drinking during their shifts seemed more and more reasonable.

As my father and the workers sparred, a murky liquid surface began rising in the pool, growing over a period of days to nearly seven hundred thousand gallons. It was as though their expletive-laden exchanges were incantations that had conjured a strange and secret brew. When the fans kicked on, the water rose like a sheet-covered ghost, a forty-inch wave chopping away at your legs, chest, or face with enough force to push you backward. It was a facsimile of the ocean, a not-quite-right replica of nature. Apparently, something like it had been built in Berlin in the 1960s to test the integrity of German ship hulls, researchers watching to see how much force it took to capsize small-scale models attempting to resist the churning water.

Somehow, a recreations manufacturer got hold of the technology and co-opted it for amusement purposes. They called it the Wave Pool. There was one at an indoor aquatic complex in Decatur, Alabama. Others were scattered in public parks around the country. None of them had our demographic, which could charitably be described as increasingly manic. I wasn't sure we needed military-grade technology sloshing them around in water ten feet deep. Some could barely be trusted to remain upright on land.

"People won't need to go to the shore," my father said, looking directly at me. "We're bringing it to them! It's gonna be big, big, big. Phenomenal!" He gave a thumbs-up to the laborers, who were wiring the pole-mounted speakers that would soon be pumping top-forty radio into the water-clogged ears of the pool's occupants. Its dimensions nearly two-thirds the size of a football field, the cost of the pool's construction was heading well into the six figures, a price tag I heard from one sibling and passed along to another until it got back to Julie.

"Low sevens," she whispered to me.

I stared into the churning muck, the bleachy smell of chlorine working hard to eradicate whatever parasites were lurking in the siphoned lake sludge. The rusty snowmaking pipes had discolored the mountain water. It looked like a vat of iced tea. I pitied whoever would be in charge of policing this scene.

"You're head lifeguard," my father said.

WHILE THE WAVE POOL WAS MY FATHER'S BIGGEST INVESTMENT TO date, he really had no other choice. By 1981, the amusement industry was changing fast. There was an increasing consumer desire for more of everything, an appetite for thrills that bordered on gluttony. It was not enough to have six or seven major attractions. There needed to be dozens, all of them unique. Kennywood, one of the northeast's largest parks, now offered six roller coasters. Disney World was putting the finishing touches on Epcot, a massive new world that would offer a glimpse of the future in a giant, orb-shaped building that resembled a golf ball. Great Adventure had introduced a Roaring Rapids ride modeled after the Congo River in Africa. Guests were strapped into boats that went through a series of minor obstacles before launching off a waterfall. They barely got wet, my father scoffed, and the big thrill—a thirty-foot slide that went through the waterfall—was tame. It reportedly cost six million dollars, which my father considered a complete waste of capital. He still measured the worth of a ride by the amount of adrenaline pumping through bodies, not how much it put the operator into debt.

Despite his lack of awe for the new rides, a few things had become clear to him. For one, he said, we needed a flagship attraction in the "wet" category of water-based experiences that could surpass the wow factor of the Roaring Rapids. At a trade show, footage of the Wave Pool's formidable machinery manipulating the water bowled him over. It appealed to his snowmaking sensibilities. It was another way of subverting nature.

Second, we needed a ride that could "eat" people. This was amusement-industry slang for something so massive and with such capacity that it could entertain hundreds of guests for a prolonged period, freeing up other attractions in the park. The Wave Pool was perfect.

Finally, we needed to increase our advertising efforts. Great Adventure was pushing the Rapids all over television, a ceaseless barrage of propaganda stuffed between Saturday-morning cartoons. We needed to break away from the primitive newspaper ad and its rote recitation of attractions. People needed to see what we offered in action.

In order to stretch his modest ad budget, my father tasked Julie, who had expressed interest in marketing, with producing a commercial. It would emphasize the unparalleled freedom he allowed each guest—thirty seconds of cascading bodies sliding, racing, and climbing. He told her he wanted to capture the relentless pace of the people in the park, who practically sprinted from one ride to the next. The details—who would shoot this, edit it, air it, act in it—were all left up to her. Just as he trusted himself to figure things out, he believed all of us could, too. That Julie could not program the family VCR was irrelevant.

Julie sought out the assistance of an ad agency, but they didn't understand what made the park special. She wound up writing the commercial herself, which highlighted everything we offered, from the Lolas to the Kamikaze. She even came up with the tagline: *"There's nothing in the world like Action Park, where you control the action."* She scored a camera crew and got a discounted rate on some editing time at a New York television station by agreeing to visit late at night, gamely walking the streets to and from her car in the hope she wouldn't wind up on a milk carton.

Once she had it done, my father watched the spot over and over again. "It's perfect, Rosebud," he told Julie. "Just perfect." Only his family, it seemed, could fully understand his vision.

A little later, I saw the ad on television when the station cut to a commercial block. I immediately recognized Glen Smocovich, who had bravely tested the Cannonball Loop and, against all odds, still had use of his legs. Now going by the nickname Smoke, he was roughly my age—seventeen—and well built, with a shock of surfer-dude hair he regularly bleached with lemon juice. Ever my father's daughter, Julie had enlisted park employees to act in the spot because she wouldn't have to pay them extra.

It was a fast, kinetic half minute that made a visit to Action Park look as exciting as a trip on a space shuttle. It occurred to me that the park was no longer a secret handshake of sorts, a whispered commodity between teenagers. Now, everyone within an afternoon's driving distance could see it. Television gave it the one thing my father could not, and the same thing it had given Disney all those years ago: the blessing of the cathode-ray tube, which surely only broadcast things worth someone's time and money.

"Action Park," Smoke said. "Like, whoa!"

The commercial would change everything.

WHILE JULIE WAS BUSY PROMOTING US, I WAS COPING WITH MY NEW role as head lifeguard, which gave me the responsibility of putting together a team. His mediocre acting aside, Smoke was an easy choice as my first recruit. He had his lifeguard certification and was a good swimmer. Telling him he could sit and tan all day while watching a bunch of well-endowed attendees splash around in a pool didn't require an additional sales pitch. He would undoubtedly use the opportunity to make his appearance in our low-budget commercial sound like he was in the entertainment industry. Already, he had been telling girls he was an extra in *The Empire Strikes Back*.

"I thought you lived in Queens," one said.

"They shot a lot of it there," he said.

After Smoke signed up, I roped in Tommy Smith, also known as Smitty, a Vernon local who grew up around a lake and could chop through water like a fish; Vinnie Mancuso, an aspiring bodybuilder who brought his lunch (skinless chicken, unseasoned broccoli) in plastic containers and sank to the bottom of the pool because he had no body fat; Denise DeSimon, one-third of a sister trio in Water World with Buffy and Lauren DeSimon; and Kip Merritt, who started as a ski instructor and moved over to construction. Later, I recruited Doug Rounds, a senior in high school who may have been the best swimmer in the county. Long and lean, Doug glided in water but cautioned that he would use his skill judiciously—routine flailing would not move him from his chair, only dramatic matters of life and death. Chuck Kilby eventually joined as well, a promotion that my father hoped would further endear us to Jim Kilby. Still others would join: Lynette, blond and pneumatic, who could swim just as well as any of them; and Nancy Hallam, humorless and immune to Smoke's advances.

As head of lifeguard operations at the Wave Pool, I established a dress code to distinguish this new, elevated park clique from mere ride attendants. I settled on red Adidas surf shorts and a white tank top for the guys, and a red, one-piece Lycra suit for the girls. The ladies' swimsuits were so cheap they became semi-transparent when they got wet. This prompted their aghast mothers to sew lining into the fabric to preserve their daughters' reputations. Only Denise DeSimon refused the extra layer, preferring to strut around unencumbered by modesty. Later, a teenager named Bob Krahulik took notice of the male uniform and began walking into the park dressed in identical attire with a whistle around his neck. Assuming he was an employee, the ticket attendant let him walk right in. By conservative estimate, he did this a total of twelve times before someone finally caught on. It turned out that he was a certified lifeguard and swam on a local school swim team, so we eventually wound up offering him the job he was pretending to do.

"Well, I'm here anyway," he said.

Not having any real idea about how to whip a squad of lifeguards into shape, I invented a regimen. It included taking turns rescuing a janitor's jumpsuit that had been stuffed with sand bags, the head still missing from its trial run through the Cannonball Loop. They all did well dragging it up from the depths, but the dummy only weighed about one hundred and twenty pounds. Park attendees could easily be double that, as well as inebriated, and were likely to resist rescue out of panic or ignorance. This inanimate, decapitated bag of pounded rock was, I suspected, smarter than some of our guests.

The night before the Wave Pool opened, I felt a surge of pride. I was finally stepping into a more demanding role, one I had coveted since moving dirt with toothless snowmakers. I decided to hold my first-ever staff meeting near the gasoline-polluted pond housing the speedboats. I explained what this attraction meant to my father, who was pinning his hopes and a significant line of credit on it bringing in more business—business that would, in turn, keep them all employed for that season and beyond. I cautioned them that parkgoers could be abrasive, petulant, and prone to disobeying instructions. I brought them to Motor World because I wanted them to see how people could behave. I motioned to a man in a speedboat who, having long since exceeded his allotted number of laps, was laughing as a worker waved her arms and insisted he come back in. He gave her the middle finger, then tried ramming the dock.

"This is what I mean," I told them.

All of them nodded, but I wasn't sure they were listening. Only Vinnie, who once worked on the Alpine and had been friends with George Larsson, had the park experience to take the warning seriously.

LIKE SOLDIERS TAKING THE BEACHES OF NORMANDY, HUNDREDS OF people poured into the Wave Pool when it opened on Memorial Day weekend 1981. The manufacturer, WaveTek, had a recommended capacity, but no one knew the number. It was listed somewhere in the phone-book-sized operator's manual my father had thrown into the corner of his office, uninterested in its annoying limitations.

Whatever the tally was, we were clearly in violation of it. The Jersey Shore had an unlimited expanse, offering each visitor their own private oasis away from everyone else. The Wave Pool packed attendees in with such congestion that people were practically elbow-to-elbow. Previously, Water World's only bodies of water were small pools that held just one or two people coming off a slide. Here, there were hundreds. You could've walked on their heads like a frog hopping on lily pads and never have to touch the water. The pool was so enormous that you couldn't have a conversation with anyone on the other side of it.

Unlike our other rides, there was no queue. People dove in from anywhere, splashing into the shallow end or sinking like stones into the deep end. Most tended to come in on the right side, since that was closer to the pool-area entrance. They jumped into water that was just deep enough to cover their head or neck, unprepared for the waves battering their faces. This area was immediately designated the Death Zone by Smoke, who nonetheless took up sentry duty and paid close attention to signs of trouble. He did this even as Lynette and Denise filled his peripheral vision, their clingy red suits tight enough to look like a second skin.

The waves were on a timer—twenty minutes on, ten minutes off—to give swimmers a break from their pummeling aggression. We had a digital countdown display, similar to a scoreboard, that let people know when the waves were coming. If they got in during a lull, they happily paddled about with a false sense of security, some sitting on the tiny rafts, mats, and inner tubes rented out at a stand nearby.

When the waves hit, their force caught our guests unprepared. Powered by the insulation-sucking fans, the waves struck with the same violent menace originally meant to create a series of mini-shipwrecks. Most people on the flotation rentals capsized. Devoid of their occupants, the tubes looked like soggy Cheerios floating in milk. The canvas rafts, made to hold one person, were often overstuffed with three or four. They were also prone to trapping people under-water, plugging the limited space between swimmers and preventing anyone from surfacing. If one occupant went under, the others would try to help. Pretty soon, the small party would all be in peril.

"I can't see shit," Smoke said, angling for a better view through the sea of people and the still-murky water. "Fuck. Look at that guy."

Smoke pointed to a broad-shouldered teenager waving his arms and bobbing in and out of the water. I got Lynette's attention, and she jumped in to help, only for the guy to suddenly break into a grin, flip his middle fingers, and cut underneath the surface like a dolphin. He was in no trouble.

"Asshole," Smoke seethed.

By noon, the congestion began spilling out onto the margins of the pool. The wraparound deck was full of people tugging their dripping swim trunks over their exposed cracks. Others dove in without bothering to remove their sweatpants or jeans. Children ran laps, the wet concrete threatening to send them sliding into a leg cast. Teenagers with gold chains around their necks scanned the pool, looking for friends. When they found them, they would dive in with the express goal of landing on someone's head. Their target would resurface, distributing headlocks in retribution.

The waves produced an anticipatory nervous energy. Pushed by the fans via massive air vents—it was like a network of leaf blowers—the water rose more than three feet above the surface, looming over its victims and appearing to pause before collapsing on top of them. Instinctually, people put their arms over their heads or turned away. It made no difference. Few could remain standing if they were in the waist-deep areas. Without a firm footing, they'd be carried away. The waves abruptly cut off conversations.

"I'm thinking of taking the boys to—*OMPHLEGGHM*," one woman said, unable to finish her thought before being claimed by the pool. It was like watching the Rapture.

We were all armed with buoys, ring-shaped chunks of high-density foam that we could toss to people having trouble with the tide. By the end of the day, we had used them all repeatedly, not realizing that they had absorbed water and developed the density of a brick. When one hairy-chested occupant struggled to swim against the current, Vinnie tossed him a waterlogged buoy. His powerful arms made it sail like a Frisbee. It landed just as the swimmer was surfacing, smacking his face and shattering his nose.

"Gahhhh!" he cried.

Consumed with their own struggles, no one in the pool paid him any mind. I waded in and escorted him out and to the infirmary, tiny red droplets leaking from his face and dotting the pathway.

Smoke made our first dive-in save, dragging out a swimmer who had been tossed out of his raft by the waves and left to flail in the water. Smoke got him to dry land immediately. I exhaled in relief. *This is manageable*, I thought. *Everything will be okay. Action Park is "like, whoa," but that's all.*

Then came another. Lynette jumped in. Then two people began going under at once. Smoke pulled a man out as another began panic-paddling right next to him. Dragged beneath the surface by the hysterical guest, Smoke began punching him in the head to make him loosen his grip. The mood had become manic. From that point on, none of us was ever out of the pool long enough to dry off. Vinnie Mancuso didn't bother sitting down the rest of his shift. I saw fear in some of the guards' eyes. They were exhausted and scared, the full weight of the responsibility beginning to slump their shoulders. A summer job had turned into a struggle to keep people alive.

There was no B squad. We all worked from 10:00 a.m. to sunset that day, eating lunch on our feet, our arms scratched from people clawing at us as we wrangled them to the deck. I started interrogating the rescues, searching for evidence of some kind of misunderstanding or defect. Something we could fix.

"Why did you go under?" I asked one man. A soggy Van Halen shirt clung to his protruding stomach. "Are you okay in the water?"

"Yeah," he said. "I've been in the Central Park fountain."

A boy came up to me. "Mister," he said. "How deep is the water?"

"Over your head," I said. "Don't go in."

I turned around. When I turned back, he was upside down in a tube, legs pumping in the air like he was riding an invisible bicycle. I pulled him out. "What happened?"

"You're supposed to pull me out before I drown," he said.

"You need to be more careful," I said, a paternal hand on his shoulder.

"Eat a dick," he said and dived back in.

A horrible realization came over me. The Wave Pool's occupants had taken on a collective, stupid consciousness, one that paid no mind to the threat of drowning. The commercial had sterilized the park. Nothing on television could be hazardous. Nothing could happen to them.

With the water cloudy from body oils, suntan lotion, and other excretions, it was impossible to peer over the edge of the pool and see the bottom. After we finally ushered everyone out, I dove in and made two passes, convinced I was going to find dead bodies that had been obscured by the filth. Satisfied I did not have to summon the coroner, I went directly to my father, who was reviewing attendance numbers.

"Eleven thousand people," he announced. "That's twice our best day!" I had witnessed it firsthand but had not been able to process the math. A blast of furnace-hot weather, Wave Pool hype, and the commercial had colluded to create a surplus of humanity.

I collapsed into his leather office chair, exhausted from the heat and exertion. "We got a problem," I said, waiting for him to look up. He didn't. I explained that, if we couldn't see the bottom of the pool, that meant we couldn't see any people at the bottom of the pool.

"Andy," he said, shaking his head. "You can't see the bottom of the ocean, either."

"So?"

"So, that doesn't mean you stop people from swimming in it if they want."

This was Gene Logic, which used nature to explain why things weren't really as dangerous as I feared they might be. *Sure, you could fall off the Alpine and crack your head open,* he'd say. *But you can also get into a car accident on the way to the park! Don't go outside, you might die of a bee sting! Come on! People want to have fun!*

I wanted to point out that the concept of acceptable risk includes understanding the risk, which was not necessarily the case with the pool and its unique method of assaulting people with water. In my weary and sun-stroked state, I just mumbled something about limiting the number of swimmers going in at once and having a designated point of entry. These seemed like small but manageable victories.

"We're not making people wait in line," he said. My father hated lines. They reminded him of the DMV.

"Then let me turn the fans down," I said. "At least let me do that."

"I would make them stronger if I could," he said. "I'm gonna ask the design people about that." He looked around his office. "Where's the operator's manual?"

The next day, we upped the chlorination in the Wave Pool to cut through the oily sheen on the surface. We became amateur chemists, mixing calcium chloride with baking soda without any real idea of how to filter such a massive body of water. On days we got it wrong, kids would emerge from the pool wincing, their eyes red with irritation. For ten hours, we performed a ballet of rescue and retrieval, dragging out and admonishing people who came out sputtering after nearly being killed by their own lackadaisical attitude. Because the countdown display had gone unnoticed, I tried using a bullhorn to announce when the waves were coming. It merged into the tinny sound of the speakers blaring "Celebration" by Kool & the Gang on an endless loop and was ignored by all.

At the end of the long weekend, Julie and I held a meeting of the lifeguards. We sat around a cafeteria table in silence. Vinnie Mancuso kept his head down, staring at the skinless chicken he hadn't had time to eat.

"You guys did great," I said. Lynette was sobbing.

"We need to shut this fucking thing down," Smoke said, black circles around his eyes.

"I know what the problem is," Julie said, her face adopting the emotionless gaze of middle management. It startled me. "We had a lot of church groups that got bused in from the Bronx this weekend."

"We get buses every weekend!" Smoke shot back. "The bottom line is, New Yorkers cannot fucking swim! These are land people!"

We talked about all the things my father was not going to do, like force people to wait in line. We discussed the drunk who had scalped himself diving into six inches of water, briefly clearing one end of the pool as he bled into it like a shark-attack victim. Julie refused to entertain the idea of a raise from three dollars and ten cents an hour to accommodate the psychological toll exacted by the job. We agreed that no more than two people should share a raft, and that we probably needed a sign cautioning people about the waves. Doug Rounds recommended everyone get hepatitis shots.

"The commercial is going to keep running," Julie said. "So, I mean . . ." She looked at me. "It's probably going to get a lot busier."

At the end of the meeting, two people threatened to quit. I begged them to stay. The next day, Tommy Smith took to scrawling the letters CFS on the admission bracelets of people who had been dragged from the pool.

"What does that mean?" I asked, watching one such guest bounce to another area of the park.

"Can't Fucking Swim," he said.

MIDWAY THROUGH THE SUMMER, SMOKE AND HIS COUSIN DANNY went to a lifeguard recertification class at the Red Cross. The instructor was demonstrating CPR on a doll that resembled a toddler. A young woman shifted in her seat, uncomfortable. "I don't want to do that," she said.

The instructor asked where she worked. It was a local public pool. She told her not to worry. "The odds of you needing to perform CPR are a million to one. It's unlikely you'll pull out even one person this summer."

Smoke and Danny looked at each other. The guards at the Wave Pool had collectively pulled out one hundred people the weekend prior.

Like surgeons, we grew to adopt the necessary arrogance of people charged with saving lives. Pleased with the increased attendance, my father agreed to spring for varsity-style jackets for the team with "Wave Patrol" and "1981" embroidered over the chest. We wore them to and from the pool, in the employee break room, and while we circulated after our shifts. Wave duty was serious business, reserved for the elite. I turned away candidates at tryouts like a coach dismissing NFL Combine stragglers. We did laps at the beginning of each day, guests applauding as we emerged.

Making the cut cultivated a sense of pride. Ride attendants walked the grounds. We strutted. One member of the Wave Patrol got a vanity license plate on his car using the eight characters allowed: LIFEGARD. When Smoke saw it, he got one, too. His read LIFGUARD, though I wasn't sure he knew about the character limit.

As head lifeguard, I was at the peak of my confidence, my fitness, and my tan. And I had not forgotten Ginette Molina, the seemingly unobtainable beauty who had caught my eye the previous summer. She was back again, migrating from ride to ride as a manager in Water World. I would not be dissuaded by Julie, who declared Ginette out of my league.

"She's two years older," Julie said. In teen years, that was like two decades, but I forged on.

I casually walked over to the Kamikaze, where Ginette was supervising an attendant sending down guests at fifteen-second intervals. We usually waited until the person at the bottom had cleared the pool, but sometimes attendants would get distracted and not notice a person going down too early. If this happened, the unofficial protocol was to scream, "Look the fuck out!" at the oblivious person below. Sometimes this worked. If not, their speeding bodies could collide while the first guest was still looking for their stripped bathing suit at the end of the slide.

Guests were being spaced apart, and I was impressed that Ginette actually took her job seriously. We hit it off and began seeing one another. Ginette's beauty was renowned around the park. I felt like I was dating our version of a prom queen.

While the Wave Patrol helped our social lives, we made enemies, too.

Smoke made a positive identification of the fake victim. He was a lifeguard at Dorney Park, a corporate oasis situated two hours southwest of Vernon in Allentown, Pennsylvania. A creepy clown named Alfundo—for Allentown, Fun, and Dorney—loomed over the entrance. Decked out in our jackets, we crashed his turf in retaliation several times, heckling guards at Dorney's large but otherwise unremarkable swimming pool. We splashed in the water, boorishly channeling our own feral patrons. Then we put on our jackets and sauntered off, secretly envious of the fact that the water there was as clear as glass, unsullied by the sweat of the teeming hordes or residual fuel splashes from Motor World.

When I saw two of the Dorney guys back at our park, I braced for reprisal. Instead, they looked at me with sympathy.

"This is like the end times here, man," one said, looking at the cascade of bodies bouncing, floating, and sinking.

We started to keep a running tally of saves. Near-drownings became abstract black dots on notebook paper. I worked seven days some weeks, sometimes for fourteen days in a row. Weeks of uninterrupted sun exposure seared the tip of my nose and turned it into a bright-red bulb. I stopped going out and instead retreated to the resort condo I was staying in for the summer to avoid the hour-long commute home. There I would lie motionless until the alarm rang. The condo was the model home for the resort units my father was developing, which would eventually swell to more than 1,300 spread across the property. I'm sure some prospective buyers thought I was a squatter.

We continued to have problems with water visibility. A pitched hill that rose up on one side of the Wave Pool was no more than twenty feet high, but it was made up of loose and untended soil covered by brown grass. After several days of rain, the precipitation and the dirt combined to create a thick and viscous sludge. Overnight, it had slobbered down the hill, encroaching past the concrete and into the water. We scooped out the larger globs, leaving an unsightly muck behind.

"It looks like the Jolly Green Giant took a shit in here," Chuck Kilby said.

"We're not closing it," my father said, coming around and anticipating my request. The Wave Pool had become his most sensational attraction. He continued to pepper newspapers in the tristate area with a giant ad that featured a cartoon person surfing a giant tidal wave.

"Let the waves gently rock you to sleep," it read. I don't know who in the fuck wrote that ad.

"It's disgusting," I said, trying to sway him. "Look at this." I stirred some of the water with my toe, disturbing a brown sheen of filth.

"To empty this out," he said, "would take a week, minimum. Then we'd have to fill it back up, which would take another week, minimum." He started to tell me what two weeks of disappointed patrons would do when they came to see his attraction only to be turned away. They'd tell friends, and they'd tell their friends, and pretty soon no one would be here.

He waved me into the pump room. We tweaked the controls to the chlorine pumps and filters, which began to cycle through the water at a rapid rate. A strong chemical odor began to mix with the mud to create a kind of sterile-smelling swampland.

"You let that run today and part of tomorrow and that should clear it," he said. "No more than that."

The pump room was messy, full of discarded potato chip bags, and had unexpected amenities like a cot, a lamp, a dresser, and a stereo—things you might find in a serial killer's van. My father was, thankfully, oblivious, but I knew the reason why. Park gossip had gotten back to me that Smoke had constructed a makeshift bachelor pad inside. He had nailed foam mats to the walls to help dampen the noise generated by his hormones. Walking in to check the fans the next day, the noise they made overwhelmed me. It sounded like a 747 taking off. Smoke was making up the cot.

"How can you stand to be in here?" I shouted.

"You gotta do it quick," he said. "Ten minutes when the fans are off. Then out."

I should have evicted him, but good lifeguards capable of standing up to the demands of the Wave Pool were few and far between. In lieu of a raise my father would never give, letting him have a poorly lit den of inequity on park grounds seemed like a proper compromise at the time.

By way of non-monetary compensation, I also began what became an annual tradition of taking the Wave Patrol on an overnight camping trip on top of the mountain. The bashes were for guards only and were intended to take their minds off the precarious nature of human life. Unfortunately, we nearly killed ourselves in the process.

After toting beer and other necessary supplies up the mountain in Charlie O'Brien's Jeep and Bob Krahulik's Dodge Dart, we settled in around the fire. As it crackled and sparked, I told the Patrol how happy my father was about the Wave Pool's success and how important their work was to the growth of the park. It was supposed to bolster their morale and keep them from quitting, but I meant every word. Their courage in the face of lunacy was inspiring.

Less than sober, we swam across the mountaintop lake that helped feed the snowmaking machines. Swimming under the influence is one way people drown, but we were in our teens and twenties and felt invincible. Plus, we rationalized, if someone was in real trouble, there were a dozen lifeguards around. We made our way across, laughing and talking as we went. The water was refreshingly clean compared to the Wave Pool's mix of sweat and lotion.

Once it got dark, a lifeguard named Dan Giachin suggested shining the headlights of the Jeep in our direction. Dan started the engine, then began backing up to turn the vehicle toward the fire. He must not have known how close to the edge he was, because the rear wheels lost their traction and the Jeep fell straight back on the hill, disappearing from sight.

We ran over to the edge, expecting to see Dan falling backward into darkness, envisioning indifferent snowmakers discovering his mangled form the next morning. Miraculously, the Jeep was sitting on the incline. Tommy Smith forced wooden boards under its rear tires to give it traction to return to level ground, and Dan and the Jeep were saved. When it came to averting disaster, we had become professionals. Later that night, the head parking-lot attendant and only civilian we had invited, Steve Moran, passed out in the lake after getting up to pee in it. I heard the splash and retrieved him. He passed out peacefully on the ground.

The next morning, we all awoke to pounding heads. Chuck Kilby couldn't be roused at all, so the rest of us piled into the cars and left. Chuck would later wake up and discover someone had stolen his shoes. Groggy, he staggered down the mountain on foot wearing moccasins he fashioned out of leaves. He was determined to lay into all of us for abandoning him, but it was not to be. He had walked down the wrong side, ending up in the nearby town of Stockholm.

When Chuck knocked on a stranger's door to ask for a phone, a very alarmed woman greeted him in the doorframe. Just then, a police car happened by. Evaluating Chuck and his moccasins, the officer asked what he was doing.

"I'm from the mountain," Chuck said, as if that would explain everything.

ON A PARTICULARLY CONGESTED WEEKEND BEFORE LABOR DAY, MY father strolled up to the Wave Pool with oversized sunglasses obscuring his face from his forehead to his cheeks. He would periodically emerge from his office to take in the splashing and screaming of patrons, carrying himself like a chef wandering the dining room. "Having fun?" he asked kids, bending over and peering into their faces to better absorb their cheer. He bought ice cream for crowds of people ten deep. The throngs, now reaching fifteen thousand on some days, were causing food shortages. We rationed nachos until our supplier could catch up.

At the pool, he checked the fans to make sure they were cranked high, worried I might give occupants a fighting chance. I marveled at how he always seemed to arrive during a lull, then leave just moments before someone began gurgling for their life, reinforcing his untarnished perspective of the park.

After my father wandered off, Smoke nudged me, pointing to two heavyset women climbing into the pool with a raft. They balanced on it at opposite ends, splashing and shrieking like they were on a teeter-totter. By now, it was obvious to me who was capable of fending for themselves in the pool and who would immediately put themselves in some kind of danger. You learned to recognize the body language of a swimmer, who entered slowly and eased into the depths, and the spastic, who jumped in feet-first, sometimes while still in their jeans.

Smoke stood up and slid off his Ray-Bans, ready to jump in and preempt disaster. We had been at this for months. The beating sun was now peeling off my top layer of skin. My elbow throbbed from knocking it against the edges of the pool. My voice was dry and weak from screaming at people to grab the buoy. Cold fall air chilled my bare legs.

Reflexively, I put my arm out like a turnstile, stopping Smoke from bringing the whistle up to his lips. "No," I said. "Give it a minute."

The two women had come in between wave cycles. Barely keeping upright, they laughed and stuck their arms out for balance.

"They're going under in two seconds," he said.

"Just wait."

The fans came on with a *throoooom*. The women held on with the first cascade, but the second capsized their tiny vessel. They started paddling with frenetic energy, trying to hold on to the side of the raft for support. It floated away from them with the next wave, and they quickly disappeared.

Vinnie tossed in a buoy. One of the women managed to get a grip, but the other ignored it. Smoke flew past me and dove in, grabbing the second woman. Slick with suntan lotion, she kept slipping out from his grasp. Panicking, she put him in a bear hug, dragging them both under. When they resurfaced, he pawed at her bathing suit top, searching for purchase. The fastener came undone, causing the top to slide down. Soon, Smoke was holding her up by her bare breast, embarrassed but desperate to keep her afloat. Lynette jumped in, and together they eventually got her to the side. Exhausted, Smoke began coughing up water. Beside him, the woman turned green and threw up all over Smoke's arm. I couldn't help but laugh, a sinister, reedy cackle that was startling to hear.

I tossed Smoke a towel as he came stomping back over, bits of half-digested hot dog staining his shorts. "What the fuck was that, Andy? Why didn't you let me warn them?"

I looked out at the replica of the Jersey Shore my father had erected, everyone floating freely and soothed by their expectations of rescue, beckoned by a commercial that had sanitized the danger. I told him I didn't know, but I did. Their obliviousness and freedom from consequences had worn on me. For one brief moment, I wanted them to feel as accountable for their own lives as we were.

I told him I was taking a break. On the way out, I passed the countdown timer for the waves. When guests stopped paying attention to it, the lifeguards modified it into a counter for the number of saves in a given day. The display's number read twenty-seven. I reached over and hit a button. It now read twenty-nine.

Getting hang time on Surf Hill.

Chapter Six

AN EDUCATION

"It was bad enough the [Action Park] pavilion concession stand was out of hamburgers, making hot dogs the alternative, but a surcharge for onions? Outrageous."

Courier-Post (South Jersey), July 26, 1981

A s the first Wave Pool season wound to a close, I headed back to the Jersey Shore to stay at my friend Rich Szuch's house. The gentle waves that lapped over the sand provided a stark contrast to the screaming and mania of my father's simulation. I felt stress hiss out of my body like someone had found a pressure nozzle.

I had just graduated from high school, but Rich, Benji Bressler, and the others were a year ahead of me and were already coming off a year of college. I heard stories of women and parties, freewheeling dorms and fraternities that were like something out of *Caligula*. My own looming college experience couldn't get here fast enough. When I told them I had enrolled at Stanford, Rich sighed.

"Unbelievable women," he said. "California quality."

"Actually," Chuckie Baby said, "nine out of ten women in California are hot. The tenth goes to Stanford."

We spent many days and nights like this, inflating my expectations of college, bullshitting, and becoming wandering vagrants around the shore. I braced myself for a culture shock of some sort in California, where my experience with the anarchy of the park and the East Coast might make me an odd man out. I otherwise had no real anxiety about college, which, no matter what challenges it presented, would not involve mass near-drownings.

Despite the stress of the job, I felt a lot of pride over what we had accomplished so far. Though we struggled with the overcrowding and general recklessness of visitors, the Wave Pool had claimed no lives and we had managed to avoid any serious calamity. Only one guest had sued us. Dan Giachin had tossed a waterlogged buoy into a man's face and shattered his teeth. Dan's position was that the guy should have been thankful we saved his life. That was certainly one way of looking at it, though the man's lawyer didn't agree. We wound up paying for the guest's dental work. The full extent of our legal problems was still unknown to me and to most of our visitors. That would soon change.

I intended to study business at Stanford, but the university didn't offer an undergrad business degree, so I settled for political science. I was not yet sure what would happen after that. Julie, who had been head of Water World, had just graduated from college and was going into marketing full-time for both the ski area and the summer operations. It felt like she would be a lifer. Splinter and Pete were not. Splinter would soon wed Eloise, a park attendant, and move into electrical engineering. Pete was in graduate school. Our father never pushed us to pursue a career under any of his various business umbrellas. Of the two possible paths, I didn't know which one I would follow.

"Hey, look at that," Rich said, nudging my arm. We were sitting on his porch, which overlooked the ocean. I saw something bobbing and then another. Rich and I climbed over the railing and moved through the sand. There, washed up on the beach, were three inner tubes. All bore the Action Park logo.

"I guess people are taking souvenirs," Rich said.

I picked up a sand-encrusted tube, which had traveled an untold distance, like a message in a bottle, to find me.

It felt like the perfect time to move across the country.

I WAS CONSCIOUS OF THE FACT THAT THE RELOCATION MEANT A new window onto the world. The park, for all its charms, presented a very narrow selection of humanity, one that sought out ways to destroy, not nourish, brain cells. That world had given me a calloused exterior. It made me wary of people who acted first and thought never. Being park-smart had made me street-smart. It had also cultivated a sense of abandon, a freedom from structure. Stanford promised a different, cerebral perspective, one that might save me from Gene logic and return me to a normal outlook on life.

When I arrived, my freshman advisor told me there was a job opening on campus.

"Okay," I said, eager for the spending money my mother would never give me. She had demanded receipts for the food budget she was allotting. "Where?"

"Lifeguard at the pool," he said.

I braced for a repeat of the summer but it didn't come. The campus pool was meant to sharpen the skills of students who might one day become Olympic hopefuls. They dutifully signed in, then deftly glided into the water, barely displacing any chlorine-scented liquid upon entering or exiting. They were obnoxiously excellent. I wondered how they would fare with sentient and malevolent waves dragging them under.

The pool was my closest brush with elite collegiate athletics, which were serious business there. The easiest way to go from feeling reasonably fit and brimming with confidence after a summer spent saving lives to feeling socially inadequate is to step foot on the Stanford campus. All around me, students on sports scholarships mingled with one another. The swimmers were six foot four and had giant wingspans, forcing them to turn sideways to walk through classroom doors. The football players seemed to be molded out of concrete, their thick necks offering no slack for their shirt collars. In high school, I was one of the bigger guys at any given gathering. Here, I felt like a Keebler Elf.

Though Stanford was not one of the marquee football schools back then, its gridiron program was solid, with future NFL star John Elway as starting quarterback. A guy in my freshman dorm named Fred Buckley was Elway's heir apparent. Fred's father worked as a sports tout, someone who would advise gamblers on the best bets of the week. Making a living on sports betting while your son is a Division I quarterback struck me as odd, but there was never any hint of impropriety. Mr. Buckley's business was apparently cash only, though. He sent Fred Federal Express envelopes stuffed with bills on a regular basis.

It was Fred who first made me aware of the List.

"Hey, man," he said. "You heard about the List?"

I had not and told him as much.

"It's a list of classes for the players that are easy as shit," he said. As he explained it, the players were "dumber than a box of hammers" and needed these dubious courses in order for the football team to remain intact.

He had my attention now.

"There's this class called 'The Man and the Sea,'" Fred said. "It's just an old fisherman telling stories." There was a class on public speaking and another that spent the entire semester on just one question: Should Northern Ireland be part of Ireland or should it remain part of the United Kingdom? I had already signed up for a number of challenging classes in history, political science, and sociology. It was clear that many of my classmates were borderline geniuses, while I had barely squeaked in on good, but not incredible, academic accomplishments. If I could round out my schedule with courses meant for athletes with room-temperature IQs, I was not going to turn the opportunity down. (The vaunted List thrived until 2011, when the *San Francisco Chronicle* exposed the school for coddling its athletes academically. I was shocked it went undiscovered for that long.)

The straight classes made up for the scam courses. I attended psychology lectures by Philip Zimbardo, who devised the infamous 1971 Stanford Prison Experiment that cast students in the roles of inmates and guards at a fictional prison in the school's basement and then watched them devolve into animals. Zimbardo would have found the park fascinating. The political science class was taught by Condoleezza Rice, the future Secretary of State. I thought she was sensational, smart, and charismatic. I took as many classes from her as I could. Later, when I was told I needed an advisor in my major, I picked Professor Rice—long before George Bush Senior or Junior did.

I also took a journalism class from Professor Kendall Jackson, who lived below the freshman dorm as a kind of den father. One night, in anticipation of a Rolling Stones concert the following day, I decided to stay up all night with two East Coast guys I had met there, Adam Tracy and Eric Weintz. Adam was best known for having gotten wasted out of his mind the night before a major test for an advanced math course and somehow getting the highest grade of any student. The handful of classes he bothered attending must have made an impression.

The plan was to arrive at the concert at six o'clock in the morning to get good seats, which were first come, first served. We stayed up, drank, and blasted Stones music. After about a half an hour, there was a pounding on the door. It was Professor Jackson in a pair of pajamas, berating us for being boorish. I offered to turn the music down, acknowledging it was rude.

Prepared for a fight, he seemed disarmed when I capitulated. "You know what you are?" he asked me, pointing at my chest. "You are an elite thug."

This prompted Adam to burst into laughter, but I didn't quite get it. Was I supposed to be some kind of privileged kid? My entire high school experience consisted of homework during the school year and toiling from dawn until dusk in the summer. I had just bought a run-down Chevy Nova that might not last the semester. No girls would even look at me because I didn't have a varsity jacket. My mother wanted milk receipts.

I soon realized some of the blowback was from the culture clash. Stanford's student body was predominantly made up of incredibly smart people, with a small selection of super jocks. The geniuses were largely introverted. Athletes got a hall pass for acting out. I was neither, so my ability to cut loose and have a little fun seemed odd. I decided to lean into it. On Halloween, I walked a motorcycle up to the second floor and rode it through the hallways like in *Animal House*. To me, it was utterly harmless, but to the other kids, I was some kind of untamed New Jersey savage. They couldn't stop talking about it. At least not until a bunch of football players set a couch on fire and tossed it from a third-story window.

That Halloween was when I first met Cammie Buchanan. I was at a party on fraternity row and ran into her and a few of her friends.

She was a high school senior, eighteen, and beautiful in a classic Californian way, with blond hair and a bright, bubbly personality. We spent the night talking, and she told me she went skiing with her parents in Aspen during winter break. I mentioned that my family also went there and that maybe we'd run into each other. She asked if I was seeing anyone back home. I wasn't. Ginette, my summer crush, had been a seasonal romance, the sort of fleeting bond that often developed between park employees. As Cammie and I talked, I grew more and more smitten. At Stanford, there was no way of competing with guys like Elway. But Cammie seemed interested. We dated the rest of the school year.

"By the way," she said. "What are you dressed as?"

I had on a leather jacket, boots, and a kerchief. I went as an elite thug.

BECAUSE STANFORD STARTED LATER THAN MOST SCHOOLS, IT LET out later. This was unacceptable, as my father demanded I be on duty when the park opened for the season. As a result, I tried to take classes in the spring semester that allowed me to turn my final-exam papers in early. Thankfully, the same schedule that accommodated slow-witted jocks also catered to amusement park employees.

When I returned to the park, the place appeared to be busier than ever. Julie and her assistant, the former lifeguard Kip Merritt, had gotten to work setting up promotions with established brands like Subway, Burger King, McDonald's, and Pepsi. Now, when you went into a fast-food restaurant, there'd be Action Park displays on the counter and offers for discounted admission. If you bought Pepsi, there were similar offers on the side of the can. At the time, this kind of tie-in was reserved for the bigger parks, but Julie convinced their marketing teams that our swelling attendance and growing reputation would make it a mutually beneficial relationship. Coupled with the television spots, awareness of Action Park was at an all-time high. Traffic to the entrance was sometimes backed up for miles, honking horns and screaming drivers putting the parking attendants under siege.

This marked increase in the park's population was not the only adjustment I had to cope with upon my return. Now that I was a college student, my father declared me overqualified for corralling guests in the Wave Pool. This was upsetting. Despite my Stanford affiliation, the thing that most impressed people back home was still my Wave Patrol jacket. I insisted on keeping it.

With Julie having transitioned into marketing, her position as head of Water World was open. I got the promotion and immediately asked Julie for advice. Foremost on my mind was finding out what the head of Water World did. I had no idea.

"A lot of everything," she said. "It's the slides, the pool, and the new attractions. You're going to be busy." Then she cackled, the way someone does when they know something you don't.

There was no training for any of these roles. My father expected us to figure things out as we went along. I got to the park early to work on the schedule and make sure the water rides were ready for opening. To get around the property, I had a dirt bike. Immediately, guests started waving me down.

"Is everything okay?" I would ask, bracing for an emergency.

"Can I get a ride to Motor World?" they would respond.

"Take the Transmobile," I would say, exasperated. I pointed to the cart overhead, which ambled along in a jerky, halting motion, kids dangling precariously from its seats.

I also had a walkie-talkie, which crackled to life with activity from all over. "There's a car in Lot B driving erratically," someone said. "They are impaired." A pause. Then: "We need a stretcher."

"We're out of inner tubes."

"The air compressor doesn't work."

"There's a chlorine smell over here."

"A customer punched an employee."

"An employee punched a customer."

You could spend the whole day responding. I quickly learned to prioritize. I had no bandwidth to escort people to the nearest funnel-cake stand. Patrons who were not visibly wounded went ignored.

Maybe it was college and the feeling that I had one foot in adulthood. Maybe it was just a natural progression. Either way, I wanted to do something to contribute to the underlying fabric of the property and help address its operational issues. Julie was too good at her job. Her marketing was leading an increasing number of people to the park and to the Wave Pool. The lifeguards were struggling with an enormous number of saves per day, unable to keep up with the surge of bodies wading into the water from every direction. I decided to make a major executive decision in my new role, one that would make a bold statement about my commitment to quality and safety.

We would mandate that people take showers.

I initiated a new policy that required that people entering the pool area stop for a rinse. We installed a spigot and showerhead adjacent to the pool and directed guests to take a quick, prison-style wash. This served two purposes. It would slow their entrance into the water to something resembling an orderly fashion, and it would clean their bodies of the grime accumulated elsewhere in the park or, worse, at home. Less filth meant clearer water and less of a need for eye-scorching levels of chlorine.

While I was proud of the innovation, the shower did not have the desired effect. Unlike the water on slides and in the Wave Pool, which was warmed by the sun, the plumbed water was tapped from the mountain lakes and came out freezing. People yelped and jumped out of the way of the spray, shooting themselves into the pool even faster than before.

"Chaos," said Smoke, who was still a lifeguard. (The pump room now had a decorative throw rug.) "This is chaos."

I did not want to report this misstep to my father. I wanted to bring only good news. So I made another executive decision, one that Julie approved. I decided to bring in consultants.

I called Jeff Ellis & Associates, a nationally renowned "lifeguard firm" that offered training for lifeguards everywhere from oceans to public pools. They were a well-respected operation and full of Red Cross–trained and certified professionals that were among the best in the world. Dorney Park used them. If we could not limit the influx of people, then we had to learn a manageable way to ensure their safety.

Jeff Ellis was a blandly handsome man in his early thirties who wore the stern expression of a cop issuing a ticket. He was all business and suggested I call a meeting of all the lifeguards in the park. We met at the Wave Pool early one Saturday.

"Good morning," Ellis said, strolling back and forth along the edge of the pool like General Patton. "Today, we're here to talk about safety." He paused for dramatic effect. "First rule: You guys need to wear shirts at all times." Many of those assembled were topless, brandishing chiseled torsos.

"Why?" Smoke asked.

"Because people need to know that you are lifeguards," Ellis said.

"Uh," Smoke said. "The problem with that is people are just going to grab the shirts and use them to drag us down into the water with them. This place is full of panic swimmers. Some of us will die if we have to wear shirts. Not doing it." The other lifeguards nodded in assent. We were off to a contentious start. I hoped it would get better.

"What would you do," Chuck Kilby asked, "if there are five people drowning in the Death Zone?"

Ellis's frozen expression seemed to twitch a little. "I'm sorry, the *Death Zone?*"

We had continued to refer to the right side of the pool as the Death Zone because it was habitually overflowing with guests who jumped in and immediately found themselves underwater and in mortal distress. The designated seat next to it was known as the Death Chair. I didn't feel this was a detail we needed to mention to Ellis.

"What would you do," Chuck said, "if you saw multiple people going under, all at the same time?"

"That happens?" Ellis said. The guards sighed and shuffled their feet.

"How many saves have you made, man?" Smoke asked. "In total. How many saves?"

Ellis paused. "Most lifeguards don't make many."

"How many?" Smoke pressed.

"None," Ellis said. Smoke and the others broke into laughter.

"All right," I said. "That's enough for today."

The lifeguards began doing their laps in the pool. Ellis waited for the area to open to the public. When he saw the migration of people from the admission window to the water, his jaw grew slack. I could see the whites of his corneas through his amber sunglasses. There was nothing resembling a line. Patrons seemed to come from everywhere, spilling into the water so quickly and with such abandon that the stragglers had to circle the edge looking for even a single square foot of free space to occupy. The waves came on with a *thrrrrom*, knocking them over like figures in a foosball table.

Ellis swallowed hard. He scribbled on a piece of paper and then handed it to me. It was a list of guidelines. He said he would be back soon. I took the suggestions to my father's office, where we held my first official meeting as head of Water World.

"The first thing Ellis wants to do is make sure we tell people they can't jump in from the side," I said.

"Screw that," my father said, biting into a tomato sandwich. He grew beefsteak tomatoes as a hobby and considered them a food group unto themselves. Little seeds plopped on his paper plate. "We're not telling anyone what to do or how to get into the water."

"Okay," I said, writing a tiny note next to the item: *screw that*. "Second, we should limit the number of patrons in the pool so—"

"Screw that," my father said. "Don't you see? The minute you start putting limitations on how people choose to experience this place, you've lost them. When you go to a lake, is there a sign saying 'Enter Here Only'? Is there a sign saying 'Only Fifty People Allowed'?"

"But it's not a lake," I said. "It's a giant washing machine that's overflowing with people."

He shook his head no in two cycles, almost as though one rotation was to warm up for the second, far-more-violent shake. "Crazy. No way. What else?"

In the face of certain defeat, I threw one last Hail Mary. "It would be nice to have an office," I said.

"Yeah, you can have an office," he said. It was the first thing he had agreed to in the entire conversation.

"Yeah?" I said.

"Sure," he said, and then picked up the phone to begin yelling at Charlie.

The office was in a building the size of a work shed in the middle of the park. In fact, it had once been a work shed, one meant to store snowmaking equipment. It was better than the first location he proposed, one of the pump houses at the bottom of the Green Water Slide. To make it more welcoming, I set up a folding table and two folding chairs.

"Hey, college boy," Charlie said, his giant face looming in the window. "How much is the lemonade?"

I wasn't about to let the spartan accommodations get me down. A large part of my duties was sifting through job applications and conducting interviews to fill positions in Water World. I wanted more lifeguards to rotate in and out of the Wave Pool to avoid the rescue fatigue that afflicted those stationed there. Many of the guards worked seven days in a row. It was grueling, and new recruits had to be operating at peak performance mentally and physically to endure it. A few shifts at a public pool wasn't sufficient preparation. EMT experience was good. So was military service, especially if they had seen combat.

Many slots had opened up as a result of the new ride the park was pushing that summer, the result of my father seeing a Slip 'N Slide in a neighbor's backyard. The Slip 'N Slide was a popular outdoor toy composed of a thirty-foot-long plastic sheet, which people would wet down with a garden hose then slide across. Wham-O, the makers of the Slip 'N Slide, believed they were mass-producing innocent fun for families. Mostly, they were. But they did not account for variables like body mass, slopes, or the possibility that someone might lay out the slide near a tree or a rock. And while there was a recommended age limit, they neglected to mention that it could prove catastrophic for adults. Throughout the 1970s, the Slip 'N Slide caused several broken necks and paralysis, a surefire way to stop family fun right in its tracks. The manufacturers of the set took it off the market, began putting warning labels on the boxes, then pulled it from shelves again in light of the continued carnage.

"You know what we should do?" my father said. "Build a giant Slip 'N Slide."

He called it Surf Hill, and it was a sight to behold. It was as though someone had taken a slick Slip 'N Slide mat that was thirty yards wide and one hundred and fifty yards long and spread it out over a hill. The ten lanes all had a decline that leveled out until your momentum slowed at the bottom and landed you in a shallow pool. It was possible, however, to achieve uncontrolled speed, shooting down so fast you skipped like a stone over the water and crashed right into a padded wall, like the kind found in insane asylums, at the opposite end. There were eight standard lanes and two expert lanes, which provided a precipitous jump with an impressive hang time. Like many of my father's rides, it encouraged racing and competition and discouraged a sense of self-preservation.

He had designed it in conjunction with Dick Croul, the man who had invented the concept of the water slide as a public attraction. Naturally, Croul became a perennial source of innovation for my father's needs. He was a master with foam, which was then relatively new to the industry. Unlike steel or concrete, foam granted greater flexibility in ride design and safety. It allowed riders to get altitude and not crash into a hard surface. To build Surf Hill, Croul covered the side of the mountain with the foam, laying large rolls of it directly over the untreated dirt then coating it in a slippery vinyl paint. When gravity intervened and you fell, there was virtually no potential for injury. The three to four inches of foam absorbed almost all the impact. If we could not pad guests, then at least we could pad where they landed.

Foam's only downside was that it was easily damaged, tearing or flaking off like dandruff, and required constant repair. Rather than give it up as most other parks did, my father embraced it, using its malleability to craft unique rides.

Of course, foam could not account for the devious ride tweaking that had been perfected by our staff. Quickly, employees figured out that they could modify the two expert lanes by stuffing a garbage can under the wooden ramp at the end, which was on a hinge and could be adjusted. When you hit the elevated jump, you could fly up to thirty feet in the air. Like the modified Alpine carts, it was for employees only. I marveled at how nothing in the park remained impervious to tinkering. If something was safe, someone felt compelled to amplify the risk.

When some of the lifeguards and I became proficient on the ride, gathering speed and sailing upward, my father began summoning us. "Quick, quick," he'd say, directing us to perform like aerialists to impress potential investors he'd gathered. A few of us could even do flips in midair. We became something of a demonstration squad, showing off the potential of his vision.

Like the Kamikaze, Surf Hill also involved what I had come to regard as the physics of inadvertent nudity. Because people shot down the slide at high speed, the water acted as a power washer, stripping them of bathing suit tops and bottoms. Sometimes they'd even get back in line, or even all the way to the exit, without realizing they were at least partially naked. With ten lanes of people going down at once, it became a startling display of synchronized stripping.

One day I arrived at the bottom of Surf Hill and saw the snowmakers hovering over wooden planks, erecting something near the lanes.

"What are you doing?" I asked Charlie.

"Work order from your dad," he said.

"For what?"

"He wants a spectator platform," Charlie said.

By the next day, large crowds gathered in the bleachers. They had come to watch and cheer as guests flew through the air, reaching incredible heights. It was undeniably spectacular, but it was also clear that word had spread about the nudity. Soon, the snowmakers and other workers began taking their lunches there, using the wooden railing as a makeshift table.

A new and lurid phrase soon entered the park's vocabulary: Titty Hill.

Titty Hill joined the Wave Pool as a signature attraction. I fielded applications for both in my hobbit-sized office.

This was how I first met Laurie Zickler.

Laurie was a college student who wanted to make money before returning to school in the fall. Her long, dark hair framed stunning green eyes. She laughed easily and often. She was wearing a blue bathing suit that revealed a runner's figure. I tried my best to maintain a professional composure even though I was smitten, my knee nervously bouncing up and down underneath the folding table. Even the penmanship on her application was endearing. Cammie and I were no longer an item, which meant I was free to entertain a future with Laurie. The first five minutes had gone amazingly well.

"How do you like the place so far?" I said.

"I think it's possible to have too much fun here," she said, laughing. "Surf Hill is something else. Your dad owns this place, right?"

My father just built bleachers so construction workers could stare at underage boobs. I paused. "Uh, yes," I said.

"Well, it's great," she said. "The whole place. Like the Magic Kingdom or something."

"Yeah," I said. "It's pretty magical."

Shortly thereafter, I observed a guest shitting on a bathroom floor for the first time.

JULIE HAD PUMPED THE ADVERTISING TO THE MAX. THE PARK HAD commercials in heavy rotation, newspaper ads throughout three states, radio spots in both English and Spanish, and the fast-food promotions. There was a heavy emphasis on Surf Hill, and the lines ran long. My hopes of loitering with Laurie, whom I had hired, were out the window. I waved at her as she ushered people through the ride, smiling and shrugging at me.

The park had an overpopulation problem. My father had built it around the existing ski-resort infrastructure. That meant, for example, the bathrooms were located in the lodge, far from Water World or Motor World. As the park grew, he invested the profits in more rides, not more amenities. A new ride was fun. A new toilet or trash bin was not.

Garbage spilled out of receptacles, bees buzzing around the sticky puddles of spilled soda. People approaching the bins would see the swarm and panic, tossing their drink or half-eaten hot dog on the ground. By the time the maintenance workers collected the trash bags, they were so congested with concession food and drinks that they dripped slime. Employees had a name for this goo: "garbage juice." It leaked from the cheap bags as carts hauled them off, leaving a trail of sludge that would remain until it rained or someone hosed it away.

At the peak of the park's bloated capacity, Julie solicited and collected comment cards from guests to see where we might be able to improve our service. Many of them were laudatory, but others were not. Once assembled, they read like a haiku of criticism. Under "What Didn't You Like," they wrote:

> Rides are scary
> Bitch in paddleboats
> Lost my teeth
> Bees
> Lewd bathing suits
> Almost drowned and lifeguards laughed

When it came to complaints about lackadaisical employees, concession attendants were usually the prime targets. Park employees considered food workers a rung below the ride attendants, and the quality of the workforce often showed it. Lines for a slice of pizza could stretch for an hour. The concessions people brushed food crumbs from the counter onto the ground and let garbage pile up in the back until it attracted flies. Ketchup and mustard packets were everywhere, squirting all over the pavement when people stepped on them. The workers sometimes opened cheese packets with their teeth in front of guests. When supervisors asked them to maintain the area better, they protested. In their northwestern Jersey dialects, it sounded like, "It's naat my jawb."

We had no tolerance for such apathy, but my father had painted himself into a corner. He had tried to acquire some farmland near the park to facilitate expansion but didn't have the cash on hand to pay the asking price. Instead, he told the landowner, a sideburn-sporting farmer named Bud Kelley, that he could run the food and beverage operation at the park. Bud Kelley knew as much about food and beverage operation as he did about piloting a 747. He was a surly man, infectiously grumpy, and turned food handlers into glowering misers with bad attitudes who took no pride in their work. Our sausage and peppers had no sausage. Grease trays overflowed or caught fire. We constantly ran out of napkins, straws, and cups. It all overwhelmed Bud, who was used to caring for farm animals, not humans.

Ellen, who was now Pete's fiancée, had moved on from Motor World to all ride operations and general services, which was responsible for making sure the place was clean. In my father's world, being a relative or near-relative held no guarantee of preferential treatment. It was usually the opposite. It was impossible to keep up with the tidal wave of garbage, and her days were spent bravely attempting to stem the cascade of slop from completely overtaking the grounds. She carried a walkie-talkie to communicate with foot soldiers charged with rounding up trash. In need of assistance somewhere, she radioed her college roommate, Nicole Molina.

"What's your 20?" Ellen said. This meant, "What's your location?" When Nicole didn't respond, Ellen radioed again, this time a little more impatient. "What's your 20?"

"Signal C," Nicole said, meaning Ellen should switch to a private channel. Of course, every employee knew what this meant and also switched over so they could eavesdrop.

"What's your 20?" Ellen repeated on the private channel.

"I'M UP TO MY EYEBALLS IN SHIT," Nicole said. "WHAT DO YOU WANT?"

We found out that Nicole had been in a bathroom snaking out an unspeakable mess of backed-up human feces when the door locked behind her. She had to climb out through a roof hatch.

My own confrontation with this level of biohazard came when I entered a restroom and saw a father standing over his child, who was defecating on the floor.

"What the . . . what the fuck are you doing?" I said, temporarily forgetting the Snow White approach to guest interaction.

He pointed to the stalls. "They're all clogged," he said. "And I don't see any other bathrooms."

The kid finished and pulled up his pants without wiping. Other people apparently had the same idea, as several turds dotted the linoleum floor. I gagged and ran out, radioing Ellen to come and put a lock on the door until the bathroom could be cleaned up.

At the next all-hands meeting with my father and the other supervisors, I joined a queue of people with problems. One complaint was that the women's changing rooms were poorly lit, which forced guests to get dressed in the dark. Another was that the keys to the lockers for personal items kept falling off the bands intended to secure them to wrists or ankles, prompting people to hide them under rocks.

I patiently waited my turn and then tried to explain the situation, slightly embarrassed at the nature of my complaint. "People are shitting on the floor," I said. "We need more bathrooms."

I proposed shutting down the roller rink pavilion—by now a quaint and outdated activity—and turning it into a massive restroom area with enough facilities for everyone. It would be like a highway rest stop, with a devoted maintenance crew instead of overtaxed employees like Nicole. More important, we could build it in such a way that the maintenance crew could take a high-pressure hose to the walls and floor to power-blast any fecal matter off. As I described this, Ellen nodded so hard I thought she was going to break her neck.

I also told my father I had been to the other rest areas. In one, stall doors were missing. In another, sanitary napkins from the wall-mounted dispenser were scattered everywhere. It looked like the opening scene in *Carrie*. It all needed to be cleaned up and expanded. I made my case and then braced myself for the reasons why it wouldn't happen.

"Okay," my father said.

"Really?" I said.

"The Disney parks are spotless," he said. "We've got to make more of an effort to be spotless, too."

The irony of the situation was that my father was anal about litter and mess in the park, sometimes stopping employees and telling them to straighten their collars or water the sod, which remained one of his largest pet peeves. The recent surge in attendance had left us struggling to keep up with sanitation. It was probably better to have anticipated the problem, but once I presented it to him, he pledged to fix it.

I later found out that part of the reason people had an urge to shit on the floor was not entirely attributable to lunacy or a lack of convenient amenities. When Bud Kelley was hired, he bought a towering inventory of chickens to roast on the premises. He boasted that he had paid only fifty cents per bird.

"Why so cheap?" my father asked him.

"They're just a little expired," Bud said.

We were feeding people spoiled chickens and then had no place for them to empty their bacteria-ridden guts.

AS THE SUMMER WORE ON, JULIE RAN INTO AN IMPASSE WITH SOME of the tie-in companies. Great Adventure and Dorney had gotten wind of the promotions on the soda cans and were strong-arming Pepsi into keeping their deal with us limited. Great Adventure sold more Pepsi than we did, so they had all the leverage.

It didn't really matter, though. Word of mouth was what brought people in the gate. Besides, if a lack of advertising on soda cans helped shrink the crowds a bit, I could not complain.

I tried to work with the resources I had available. I could do little about the garbage or the poop, but I could still exert influence over my domain. I vowed to make Water World the most improved section of the park. I did not expect the lifeguards to listen to all of Ellis & Associates' suggestions, but there was undoubtedly room to mature.

With the understanding that Ellis was monitoring us throughout the summer, I headed to another pre-opening meeting at the Wave Pool. The guards were doing their laps. I asked Chuck Kilby where Jeff Ellis was.

He shrugged.

Ellis didn't come that week or the next. Without a word, he simply stopped showing up.

In abandoning us, Ellis signaled that he knew what the rest of us knew. The park was getting too big to control.

The snowmakers. Easily the toughest and most durable men I've ever known.
Charlie O'Brien is on the far right. The lion club was presumably from the old
Great Gorge resort zoo.

The dune buggies. Adults could opt out of wearing a helmet.

Chapter Seven

THE HANGMAN'S FRACTURE

"Since 1983, Action Park has been the target of more than 100 lawsuits, with defendants alleging everything from negligence on the part of ride operators to faulty equipment. . . . The park's most popular ride—the Alpine Slide—accounts for the most accidents, the majority of the lawsuits, and 40 percent of the citations against Action Park."

New Jersey Herald, May 21, 1986

"The phenomenon is, where there are accidents, the riding public can't wait to get on them. I don't know what it is— maybe thrill-seeking."

William J. Clark, director, Office of Workplace Standards, New Jersey Department of Labor, 1986

I t was Smoke who first told me about the drowning.

In 1982, the same summer that Surf Hill opened and marketing was fueling record attendance, a fifteen-year-old named George Lopez went under in the Wave Pool and drowned. No longer a lifeguard, I was not there, but the consensus among the Wave Patrol was that, following another rainstorm, some of the overflowing muck from the adjacent hill had again clouded the water, affecting visibility. Given that and the sheer volume of humanity in the pool, no one noticed Lopez failing to resurface.

Lopez's drowning rocked the guards. It marked the first time they had failed to save someone. Everyone felt a little more on edge, more conscientious. I decided to begin moving guests to the shallow end of the pool when the water grew murky. We stationed guards in the water with buoys, hoping their presence alone might encourage more respect for the waves.

My father's reaction was neither impassioned nor impassive. He simply regarded it as a tragedy as one would when hearing of a casualty at a beach. To him, Action Park was a natural structure, like the ski slopes or the oceans, and thus similarly prone to potential hazards. His reaction wasn't a lack of compassion so much as it was resignation.

The Lopez family did not see it that way. They sued the park and several of the guards on duty, including Tommy Smith, charging negligence. This, I knew, was not the case. The guards were never indifferent or lackadaisical. They were simply tasked with managing an entity that had outgrown their ability to police it.

A week later, I awoke in the condo to someone pounding on my door. It was Julie.

"Come now," she said.

We drove over to Motor World, where she parked in one of the adjacent lots. Inside the park was the typical commotion—Lolas buzzing along the track, the tennis-ball tanks spinning like tops—but off to the side of a building was a small group of people standing almost perfectly still, their body language heavy.

They were crowded around the entrance to the Kayak Experience, a ride that my father had installed just a few weeks prior. He bought it from a company named Inventex. The Kayak Experience combined elements of the Wave Pool and rafting, with fans agitating the surface of a one-thousand-foot-long circular water channel. People would paddle against the current in a kayak. You could have twenty of the single-person vessels going in the ride at once.

Jumping inside one of the kayaks when the whole thing was close to finished, I found it to be a fairly mundane experience and not up to the level of excitement of the other attractions. The water was choppy, but not in a white-water rafting kind of way. It just lapped against the boat, giving it only a slight nudge. It wasn't deep, either. You could stand up in it, though you weren't supposed to. If anyone bothered to conduct an exit survey of people coming out, it would have been the written equivalent of a shrug.

Despite being an expensive undertaking, it drew only a fraction of the attention of Surf Hill or the Kamikaze. Compared to those rides, which were simplistic but effective, the Kayak Experience was something my father usually avoided—a big mechanical thing that cost too much and didn't provide a quarter of the same thrill as a slippery foam mat worth just a few dollars. Not long after installing it, he bemoaned the decision.

Still only half-awake, I recognized a couple of the inspectors from the Department of Labor. One man had a police badge on his hip. I didn't understand what was going on. Following the Lopez tragedy, my heart began to flutter.

"What is it?" I said.

"Three people got electrocuted," Julie said. "One of them is dead. Don't talk to the press."

IN THE 1930S, AN INDUSTRIAL-ACCIDENT ANALYST NAMED HERBERT Heinrich argued that 88 percent of mishaps he analyzed were caused by a human decision to carry out an unsafe act. He also stated that reducing the number of minor accidents would minimize the number of serious accidents. The thinking was that, for every major mishap, there are three hundred near misses that go unobserved. To reduce the big disasters, one had to address the comparatively less catastrophic events. The theory came to be known as Heinrich's Triangle.

Of course, Heinrich wasn't thinking of amusement park rides. In a factory, averting minor accidents was good for employers, for employees, and for business. In the theme park industry, the manufacturing of thrills—the nagging possibility of danger—is what sells tickets. Heinrich would argue near misses needed to be eliminated. Park operators would argue near misses are the entire point.

Bob Krahulik, one of our lifeguards, illustrated this dynamic when he visited the State University of New York at Albany one weekend. Bob was scouting the campus with thoughts of possibly attending in the fall. He wore an Action Park T-shirt. He noticed people were staring at him.

"They came up to me in awe," he told me. "They asked if I worked there. They asked if I had scars." When he shook his head no, they showed him some of their own.

"Alpine," one said, pointing to a dark wedge of skin on her elbow.

"Lola," another said, his disjointed finger unable to extend completely.

Word-of-mouth became incredibly important to us, as it was for many businesses. But the way people spoke about Action Park was very different from how someone might describe their experience at Great Adventure or Disney. With those places, it was about the fact you said hi to Mickey Mouse and Pluto and came out with a cool hat. At Action Park, it was like describing how you were T-boned by a tractor trailer and narrowly escaped with your life. How you endured each ride was a story you passed on to family and friends.

This kind of early viral marketing was completely unintentional. In the days after someone rode the Alpine and suffered superficial wounds from the friction, they'd attract attention as their skin began sloughing off to reveal a scar. People would ask what happened. Action Park is what had happened. Human bodies were our billboards. We never hid what we were doing. The whole conceit of the park was that the operators assumed their own risk.

I don't know exactly when I first heard the phrases "Traction Park" or "Class Action Park," but, at some point, they entered into common parlance, even making their way into a few newspaper articles. Julie hated it, but my father was unfazed. He was elated that the place had gotten big enough that people were bothering to poke fun at it. When Julie told him people were describing Alpine gouges as the "Action Park tattoo," he immediately realized it was free advertising.

If our guests were sobbing as they showed off their contusions, it would have undoubtedly upset him. That they did it with a sense of pride, the same way a skateboarder displays road rash was, in its way, gratifying. It meant he was succeeding in his own unique brand of escapism. It was also a signal that people understood the mission statement of the park. When you laughed at your own injury, you did so because you knew you were, in some way, culpable, just as you would blame a sore thumb less on the hammer than on the person swinging it.

It was hard to define the parameters of safety, in part because nothing like this place had ever existed before. My father was in one corner, believing that none of it was any different from someone driving a car, riding a bike, or sledding. Their free will and skill determined the chances they took and whether they might need a bandage. A heavyset man with no upper-body strength should have been able to discern that he would not be able to hold on to the rope in the

Tarzan Swing after watching fitter people struggle with it. But Gene did not believe that man should be denied the chance to try. My father would not pass up a ride that required good judgment simply because some people might exhibit poor judgment. If he did so, he believed he would be failing the people who could rationalize risk, make a decision, and enjoy the resulting thrill.

In the other corner were guests who categorically did not understand this premise. They were going to a recreational destination, and those traditionally eliminated any kind of risk. They left their critical thinking at home. I believe this was why we continued to pull so many people from the Wave Pool who seemed astonished that their lungs were filling up. In their minds, that simply wasn't supposed to happen. While at the park, they forgot the reality that a body of water could take their life. There was a presumption of safety that was supported only by their belief that they couldn't get hurt at a theme park. It was a social contract that only they had agreed to.

As soft-tissue injuries grew, so did our reputation. In a way, it became an example of confirmation bias. Of course someone got hurt at Action Park, because they were at Action Park. But when something happened at another park, one with a flawless reputation, it was an aberration. Fights at our park were publicized and reviled as signs of loose management. Yet, when a teenager was stabbed to death during a scuffle at Disneyland in 1981, it surely was not Mickey's fault. When the Spin Meister at Six Flags hiccuped and bruised eleven patrons, sending two to the emergency room, the public waved it away as an unavoidable mechanical error. Such incidents passed through the cultural consciousness only fleetingly, even as the family of the Disney victim sued because employees had failed to call outside paramedics, relying instead on their in-house staff to treat the wounds. To the public, Action Park had become a dangerous place—for better or worse, depending on whom you asked.

However skewed the guests' perspectives may have been, it was clear that injuries and the resulting lawsuits were going to be part of the park's operating expenses. My father offered risk. People took him up on it. Some had regrets. To survive, he would have to invent a way to not be sued out of existence.

So, that's exactly what he did.

I WASN'T PRIVY TO MANAGERIAL OVERSIGHT THAT WENT INTO PRO-cessing the wounded. It is only now, decades later, that I have been able to assemble the pieces. What they reveal is a man determined to remain sovereign, never to allow Action Park to become a homogenized area that only simulated risk. The thrill was not in being bolted down to the Alpine. The thrill was in deciding how fast you wanted to go without being constrained by rules or seat belts. What broke the reverie was when someone sped into trouble.

As my father added rides and expanded the property, our once-favorable newspaper coverage—of the skiing in Vernon or the announcement of a new addition to our amusement utopia—began to change. Now, when New Jersey newspapers mentioned Action Park, it was in relation to an injury. Skiing or recreational accidents were not newsworthy. But here, as a result of man-made attractions, they became regular bulletins. The lawsuits piled up.

In 1980, Laurence Franzel sued after being thrown from a dune buggy and suffering a compound fracture of his left arm. He argued that our employees were not properly trained to safeguard the public.

In 1981, Alfred Sorge sued after fracturing his ribs on the Alpine. He had driven a charter bus to the park and decided to try out the ride. He argued it was defectively designed.

In 1982, Wilfred Juan sued after driving a speedboat and

colliding with another vessel. He argued that we did not properly supervise the ride.

In 1982, Israel Schwartz said he suffered "permanent disfigurement" after being allowed to use the Alpine Slide without supervision.

In 1983, Philip and Delores Shaw sued after falling near the Wave Pool entrance.

In 1983, William Sussie sued, alleging three drunk men crashed into him on the Alpine.

In 1983, Ruth Richards sued after a Lola car driven by a high school student with a fake driver's license struck her, breaking her nose and tearing cartilage in her knee.

In 1984, Logan Pemberton sued after breaking his left femur on a water slide and spending six months in a body cast. He claimed that a sharp turn meant the slide was defective.

In 1984, the father of three-year-old Cherie Fu sued after his daughter got her hand stuck in the Alpine brake while riding with him, severing a finger.

These were just a few of many.

As the park evolved from a small-scale operation, its growth led to the perception that the park had a Disney-sized pocketbook, prompting many of these lawsuits to be filed years after the incident took place. Legal consequences, once rare, became something for which my father kept a file folder on his desk. We logged 110 reported injuries in 1985 and 330 in 1986, the latter making us responsible for roughly half of all theme park accidents in New Jersey that year. That may seem excessive, as though scores of the walking wounded populated the park. But this was a place the size of several city blocks that hosted a highly concentrated population of fifteen thousand to twenty thousand people on some days, a swell that meant we were going to experience a certain number of medical incidents.

People had heart attacks they would otherwise have had at home. They choked on food. We were highly responsive, dispatching a staff of EMTs to calls of accident or injury anywhere in the park. If it was minor—a bruise, a small cut, a dislocation—they'd treat it on-site. More serious cases, such as someone being knocked out or breaking a bone, were herded onto golf carts equipped with stretchers and driven to the first-aid station.

This is where my father's preemptive actions began to take place. The park was required to report serious accidents to the state Department of Labor within forty-eight hours of the incident. State language was murky, though. What qualified as "serious" was open to interpretation. Was a broken bone serious on its own, or only if it resulted in an overnight hospital stay?

We were not alone in this regard. At a Jersey Shore outfit, Gillian's Island Waterpark, fifty-one people were hurt on the Serpentine Slide over a three-year period. Of those, only seventeen were reported to the state. In Florida, home to Disney World, only 10 percent of theme parks reported 75 to 80 percent of their accidents. Traveling carnivals hardly ever reported any. No one wanted their customers to feel imperiled. Unless states were aggressive in demanding reports, they often never left the parks' offices.

My father saw no reason to behave differently. We filed nothing that was not clearly mandated by law and, at times, stretched the definition of "non-serious" to include fractures. Major head, neck, and back injuries were noted, but anything else was often left to the discretion of EMTs and other workers dealing with guests. My father did not want the state to decide what was too adventurous for people. He believed they could decide for themselves, and that the serious injuries were often self-induced.

While the EMTs were treating an injury, a staff member would ask the guest what had happened. Inevitably, they would begin their story with, "I was horsing around," or, "I thought it would be funny if . . ." They might also admit to not knowing how to swim, or steer, or having ignored safety instructions. The staff member would nod, taking copious notes.

Wounds that required off-site treatment were directed to the office of Dr. DeLuca. Dr. DeLuca had what was probably one of the first urgent-care centers in the area, if not the entire East Coast. His office was on Route 94 and could easily be reached by driving along the property. EMTs would bring the injured party to Dr. DeLuca's on one of the first-aid carts to get their head examined or broken bone set. As a private-practice physician and someone who had a business relationship with my father, Dr. DeLuca was essentially Action Park's only in-network provider. As such, on the occasions when the park was found at fault and ordered to pay a guest's medical bills, it avoided the inflated expenses of an ambulance ride and an emergency room visit.

In building this conveyor belt for broken toys, my father was able to sidestep repercussions from the Department of Labor and the financial implications of major medical treatment. But that didn't mean that someone who had been knocked unconscious was no longer a legal threat. Often, people would decide they had not been sufficiently protected and decide to sue.

My father stifled some of these potential problems by enlisting a man named Eric Karg, who was the claims adjuster for the insurance company covering the park, London and World Assurance, Limited. A day or two after an accident, Karg would phone the individual and offer a nominal sum to cover medical costs and smooth over any lingering resentment. Someone who wiped out on the Alpine might agree to a $750 payout to let the matter drop. If you're a teenager, and you've been hurt worse playing sports or climbing trees, you took the cash. It was not unusual for guests to consider a broken nose part of the price of a fun Saturday. If Karg believed the park was in some way negligent, he would increase the amount. If he believed the patron was trying to scam us—the equivalent of spilling water on the floor of a business and then proceeding to slip on it—he would tell them to pound salt.

Karg couldn't dissuade everyone, however. In those cases, my father dispatched a lawyer named David Chaffin. David was a preserved hippie who wore his long, gray hair tied in a ponytail and carried a cane to support a limp, a morbidly amusing trait for someone representing Action Park. His services were needed often enough that he kept an office across the street from the property. He'd open a dialogue with the plaintiff's attorney by informing them that he was going to challenge the claim every step of the way.

The opposing lawyer would scoff, incredulous that a major business would want a legal skirmish. That's when David would introduce the statement the plaintiff gave at the time of the accident, the one that usually began, "I was horsing around," or "I closed my eyes on purpose," or "I don't know how to swim." He argued most all cases on the premise that the guest was assuming risk. If their assumption of risk involved goofing off, then the park was not at fault. At least, that's how a jury was likely to see it.

David made it clear that the suit would go before a jury. He didn't settle cases, which meant defense attorneys would be tied up for months or years in what they initially thought would be a quick phone call to get the park to admit wrongdoing. This insistence on not settling quickly made the rounds in the legal field. Action Park didn't do what big, liability-prone places are supposed to do, which is roll over. It became difficult for people to find attorneys to take on their case. "I'm sorry," they would say. "That place fights."

If a plaintiff and their counsel somehow cleared all those barriers and decided to pursue litigation, David flourished. He made sure park employees gave depositions like dullards, poorly dressed and slack-jawed. When they got to court, they were sharply dressed and well spoken, completely throwing off the attorney who had been counting on making the employees look stupid. When David deposed the opposing side, he exhausted them with questions. Depositions that should have taken an hour took a day or more. By the time someone got on the stand and saw David approaching, they were already hostile. Juries wondered why the plaintiff or their witnesses were so belligerent toward David, who had a warm presence and appeared undeserving of scorn. It made them less sympathetic, a fatal flaw in a negligence case.

David's theatrics became the talk of the sheriff's office, with bailiffs arguing about who got to sit in and watch the Clarence Darrow of Action Park ply his trade. David often jumped on an Alpine cart in the middle of the courtroom, demonstrating the brakes that allowed anyone to slow down to a crawl. "That's all you have to do," he'd say, "to avoid a problem." He parroted my father's belief about skiing and the responsibility bestowed upon the person on the slopes, raising his cane to punctuate his point. "It's called Action Park," he bellowed. "Of *course* you can get hurt if you're not careful!"

The variable nature of the rides, which long confounded regulators, wound up being a benefit for David, who would often argue that just because something like the Alpine had logged a number of accidents, it didn't mean that the trip taken by the injured had to follow suit. Each experience was so unique, he said, that none of them could possibly set a precedent. The only constant was how often people would operate it with recklessness.

Jurors who walked in expecting to be sympathetic toward the injured soon found themselves hanging on his every word, convinced the plaintiffs had wronged themselves. In one case, in which a man had flipped off his mat after hitting the landing pool at Surf Hill and had to wear a halo brace for months to heal what was known as a hangman's fracture in his neck—another half inch and he would have been a quadriplegic—Chaffin accused him of engaging in "horseplay." A judge agreed the man had been behaving irresponsibly. He found in favor of the park.

The legal theory that the rider, not the operator, was negligent held water most of the time. But whether juries would be as convinced in the event of a death was another matter entirely.

The family of George Larsson, who had died after taking a chance riding the Alpine in the rain, had sued, and that litigation had been dragging on for years. Because he was there after hours, it was hard for his parents to back their claim that there was inadequate supervision. No one could monitor a ride around the clock. Employees were told not to get on the track in bad weather.

That was the only fatality at the park prior to 1982. It was rarely anything other than bruises and broken bones. People taking a chance and coming up short, miscalculating the odds and paying for it. Lopez drowned, a possibility in any body of water. There was only one time in my memory that my father wondered if he had done something wrong: the Kayak.

HIS NAME WAS JEFF NATHAN. HE HAD COME TO THE PARK FOR THE first or second time with his cousin, Steve Langenthal, and Steve's wife, Janet. All three were on the kayak ride, wading in the water after getting knocked over and out of the boats. The next thing Janet and Steve knew, they were waking up in the hospital. Jeff didn't. He was pronounced dead by the emergency room staff. The only information we had was that he had experienced some type of cardiac event.

Of the people who were on the scene immediately after the

accident, I knew only Kevin Curley. "I got a code red call," he said. Along with other employees, he ran to the Kayak and saw three people unconscious and floating in the water. "We made a human chain across our arms to get them on a stretcher," he said. Curley thought it had been a lightning strike.

If the park had largely been leading a charmed life given the nature of the rides and their risks, the Kayak accident, coming so quickly on the heels of the Lopez drowning, broke the dam wide open. The town's building inspector wanted the ride drained and closed so he could look at it. The Department of Labor inspectors wanted to do the same. A police detective opened a file. The Sussex County district attorney said he was "monitoring" the situation. All of a sudden, there were questions about the state's jurisdiction over "sporting" rides and whether it had somehow dropped the ball. The Department of Labor quickly came out and insisted that the ride had been inspected five times before opening. The deputy mayor of Vernon, Nic Roseto, said that the state had no oversight of non-mechanical rides—things like Surf Hill. When the Carnival and Amusement Ride Safety Act was passed back in 1975, water slides weren't even in the state yet, let alone regulated. (They would finally be subject to oversight in 1983.) Whether the fans that produced the waves made something like the Kayak Experience or the Wave Pool something other than sporting became a crucial issue of semantics. Was the Alpine open to review because it involved a mechanical ski lift? No one knew. Everyone was quick to blame someone else. No one wanted to declare anything an accident if it wasn't or take responsibility if they didn't have to. The Kayak accident had provoked these forces into admitting that the park was a no-man's-land.

Donald Allen, a New Jersey policy maker, took the opportunity to begin pounding the podium. "Someone has got to start looking at

Action Park," he told the press. "The number of accidents has crossed the line."

Julie's main mission was to prevent our father from speaking to the media about anything relating to either incident. "The press already has their story written," she told me. "They're never going to write good stories about the park." She always stayed on message, getting out what she wanted to say even if it didn't answer the reporter's question. She was unflappable.

My father, however, couldn't help himself. He wound up picking up the phone when reporters called and went on the defensive, partially to protect the park's reputation and partially because he truly did not believe we had been negligent. He went back and forth with the coroner, Mary McPhillips, in the newspapers. McPhillips insisted Jeff Nathan's death was due to electric shock, or "rapid contractions of the heart due to electrocution." My father produced records from the company that built the motors for the fans—coincidentally, the same company, Flyght, built the Wave Pool fan motors—saying that there was no possibility that could ever occur. McPhillips hired an inspector of her own who found a damaged underground cable. My father said her inspector wasn't a licensed electrician and that the cable was fifty feet away from where the accident had occurred. The state inspectors who examined the ride had found an intermittent short in one of the motors, but it was impossible to discern whether that had directly led to the accident. It went on and on like this, the ambiguity causing everyone involved to arrive at different and contradictory conclusions.

I asked my father what he thought had happened. He kept repeating that the ride had been inspected many, many times before opening, not only by the state, but by his own contractors. He looked at the motor-inspection reports over and over, searching for any fine detail that would reveal whether it was a random event or the result of some kind of mistake. Unlike some of our more haphazard ride construction, the motorized Kayak had been handled with care. He had hired top electricians to do everything correctly. One of his employees had even written to Flyght an entire year prior, when the ride was still being planned, to make absolutely certain the equipment wouldn't pose an issue. My father took the idea of an underwater motor extremely seriously.

"I don't understand it," he kept saying. "I don't understand it."

It seemed odd to me that for all the park's potential hazards, a fluke occurrence had led to a tragedy. Jeff Nathan wasn't a daredevil. He hadn't tried to cross any boundaries. In my father's ski analogy, he hadn't run into a tree. It was like the tree had erupted in his path. This, I believe, is what bothered my father the most. If the blame couldn't be placed on the rider, then it had to fall on him.

That didn't happen. Not officially, anyway. The Department of Labor eventually announced that the park wasn't guilty of any wrongdoing. The Kayak had been properly installed and maintained. There was no violation of any safety law. A short circuit was a no-fault situation. We were, at least in terms of public opinion, exonerated. My father closed the ride permanently. Bulldozers came and buried it. The Nathan family sued and met David Chaffin in court. This time David's histrionics and persuasion were of little use. This time there was a settlement.

I AM OFTEN ASKED ABOUT TRACTION PARK, THE MYTHIC PROPERTY that often replaces Action Park in the popular imagination, a frenzied battlefield of moaning and groaning guests who were left to navigate an obstacle course of malfunctioning, hazardous attractions, a human mulcher masquerading as innocent fun. I have heard it compared to Vietnam or *Lord of the Flies*, that my father did not care if people were hurt, that we took no notice of them. It did not help that my father was often inscrutable in these moments of tragedy, rarely discussing them or lashing out in the newspaper in an effort to defend the park.

I think that, if he had confided in anyone, it would have been Father Boland. Many years later, I called him.

"How did my father feel when someone died?" I asked. I reminded him of George Larsson and Jeff Nathan and George Lopez.

"He felt awful, always, as anybody would who had kids themselves," Father Boland said.

"Sometimes I wonder," I said, "if we could have done better. How much is enough? But when you take chances . . ." I didn't finish the sentence. It felt like assigning blame.

"With the child from Sparta, George Larsson, I asked him. I said, 'Gene, have you talked to the family? Make arrangements to meet with the family.' And he turned to them and said, 'Any costs for the funeral, we'll take care of them. And I will well understand if there's an insurance case afterward.'"

"The other times?" I asked. "The other tragedies? What about then?"

Father Boland was silent for a moment. "When the park is a special place for people to enjoy, and then it isn't that . . ." He trailed off.

"He didn't always act contrite," I said.

"He found it hard to listen to criticism." Father Boland paused, searching for the words.

"Yes?"

"He was always heartbroken."

DANGER AND RESPONSIBILITY. ACCEPTABLE RISK. LIABILITY AND negligence. I think about these things often.

Jeff Nathan should not have died. He did nothing wrong. George Larsson was a tragedy. He bent the rules until they broke. George Lopez succumbed to the water, realizing any lifeguard's worst fear. There would be two more deaths, including another Wave Pool drowning in 1987, when an eighteen-year-old named Gregory Grandchamps went under. When people remember, I want to tell them the park admitted millions of people across decades, and we failed only a few of them. I wish it were none.

When an eighteen-year-old named Jim Higgins fell out of a car at Space Mountain in Disneyland in 1983, seriously injuring his head and back, no one called for the dissolution of the park. When it tallied six deaths in its first twenty-five years of operation, no one wanted it shuttered. At the Happiest Place on Earth, an injury was an anomaly. At Action Park, it was framed as inevitable. This was the consequence of my father's design. In promoting risk, we could not cry foul when it sometimes proved to be consequential.

Still, I wonder. When someone sailed off the Alpine, into the air and into rocks, should we have protected them? Should we have padded those surfaces—those trees—in case of misadventure? Should we have doled out helmets? At the Wave Pool, we could have counted people and restricted entries when capacity grew too cumbersome. There were always ways to make it safer.

But safe is not what theme parks sell. They sell excitement and the promise of a break from the mundane. Our problem—my father's problem, Action Park's problem—may have been that people assumed the thrills were an illusion, just as they were at other parks. People step into a park and experience a detachment from reality, doing things they never would dare in real life. On a lake, you would not ram a speedboat into another. Here, people thought that was the point. An admission ticket was like a waiver from responsibility. Admit one. Admit nothing.

The numbers spin in my head, arguing for and against. There were ten thousand injuries reported in theme parks across the country in 1984, a relative drop in the bucket compared to the tens of millions of visitors who entered their gates. Disneyland reported scant few. But what was their definition of serious? Was it like ours? And were we even a theme park at all? "This is not a fantasy land," Julie told reporters. "You stay with what . . . you can handle at the level of ability you can handle. Our guests are responsible for themselves."

With those two deaths, only days apart, we garnered more bad press in the summer of 1982 than at practically any other time in the history of the park. The weather had also been lousy, extended rainfall hurting our attendance. We closed down on two Sundays due to the heavy precipitation, a step my father reserved for nothing short of nuclear war. We steeled ourselves for even more of a decline. Our park had been stigmatized, possibly for good. Parents would prevent their children from attending. Teenagers would steer clear.

At the end of the season, we looked at the numbers. The previous summer, five-hundred thousand people had come through the gates. That summer, it was eight-hundred thousand, a number that surprised even my father. It was our best year yet. The accidents were not and never would be a deterrent.

A few days after Jeff Nathan died, a newspaper reporter approached a young man in the park to get his thoughts on the accident. The man did not know what had happened. The ride was closed, the reporter explained, because of a death.

The guest thought about it. He said he hoped it would reopen. "It makes it more challenging and daring," he said.

What would Heinrich think of that?

Guests being ejected from the Cannonball chutes, unaware that freezing mountain water is awaiting them below.

Chapter Eight

ACTION PARK AFTER DARK

"'We're trying to expand the park's image,' said Julie Mulvihill. 'We want to be able to attract senior citizens and
make it a nice place for the family to come and visit for the
entire day.'"

Daily Record, January 30, 1983

I n the Vernon of the early 1980s, if you were under the age of eighteen and looking for a job, Action Park was not one of your options. It was your only option.

It wasn't like that in the rest of the country. When a teenager was
searching for part-time employment, they typically headed for a fast-
food restaurant. Donning aprons and paper hats at chains like Mc-
Donald's, they would dole out Big Macs and Chicken McNuggets, a
new and addictive bite-sized menu item introduced in 1983. There's
a reason many of the kids in *Fast Times at Ridgemont High* slung fast
food: Handing out sacks full of salty burgers was practically an
American teen's first job by birthright.

But in Vernon, the closest fast-food restaurant was a twenty-minute drive away. Many of the nearby communities rejected the encroaching franchises, wanting to preserve their small-town charm. Even my father rallied against them, once standing up at a town meeting and wailing, "Hasn't anyone heard of mad cow disease!" He didn't want anything siphoning away his workers—or his concession sales, for that matter.

The Golden Arches did not cast a shadow in Vernon. We had a complete monopoly on teen labor. Then, suddenly, parents caught wind of the negative publicity surrounding the park, put down their newspapers, looked over at their kids, and told them to quit.

It happened during the summer of the McNugget. While sitting in my office shack one day, a memo crossed my desk warning that we were in danger of being understaffed. The size of our workforce had not kept up with our growth, and our lousy press wasn't helping. In the note, Julie said that the situation was dire enough that we might need to widen our pool of potential hires by interviewing senior citizens. I frowned. If you couldn't sprint to someone's rescue, or away from a raging forest fire, you were not park material.

Negative press was not our only problem. Like any summer operation, we offered seasonal jobs. Teenage enthusiasm was strongest in the busiest months from Memorial Day through late July but began to wane in August and into September. Kids heading off to college needed to leave their jobs early to prepare. Some wanted time off before high school got back in session. As a result, ride attendants simply stopped showing up, causing gaps at stations. This was unacceptable: an unattended ride could mean unprecedented idiocy. Guests could smell when there was a lack of supervision.

To resolve the shortage, I came up with an idea I knew my father would get behind.

"Let's bribe the kids," I said.

We began offering workers an additional twenty-five to fifty cents an hour if they stayed through Labor Day. It was retroactive, but you had to make it all the way to September to be eligible for the bonus. For sticking around, they got an automatic bump in pay that allowed them to strut around like senior staffers.

It worked well, but I wished we were able to sell the kids on the intangible benefits. At the park, they met students from other schools, widening their social opportunities and bonding over the shared experience of trying to corral unruly patrons. I saw more than a few listless workers, who probably hadn't given a single thought to college, watch as their co-workers saved every dime and spoke about their admission essays. The park became a snapshot of a bigger world they didn't know existed. That was a better reward than the quarter, though I doubt many of them realized that until much later.

Just because we found warm bodies didn't mean we could trust them to be responsible. Some were the same level of delinquent that we sometimes had to chase off the property. Two employees who quickly became short-timers were in Water World doing absolutely nothing one day. Spotting this, Topher, who was by then a manager, approached them and told them that guests often enjoyed a refreshing spray of cold water while waiting in line on particularly hot days. Kids and teens liked it, anyway. Adults didn't always seem to appreciate it.

"Grab the hose and wet them down," Topher said. "It helps take their mind off the heat. Can you do that?"

They nodded. Topher went to get lunch at a concession stand nearby. Within a few minutes, he heard screaming. Turning around and jogging back to the line, Topher saw the two employees roaring with laughter. They had not grabbed the garden hose but a fire hose. The force of the water was knocking guests over like bowling pins.

"Stop!" Topher shouted. "Stop!"

Even a normal-pressure hose had its perils. A man once sued us because an attendant hit him with a jet of water near the mouth of a slide, knocking him down the track face-first and without a mat. The park settled for $18,000. I told Topher to cool it with the hoses.

When employees misbehaved, I chalked it up to restlessness. A ride that seemed so exciting in the first few days on the job could foster ennui as they watched thousands of people come and go in an endless churn. The extra money didn't solve that problem completely, so I decided to go a step further and create a different kind of excitement, one that had roots in my father's approach to management. I organized a series of intermural sporting events in Water World that I dramatically dubbed the Water World Wars.

I divided the area into two teams, tasking each with paddling small rafts across the Wave Pool, racing down all the rides in a relay, and running a foot race up the hill, navigating the park like an obstacle course. The workers liked it so much they came two hours early and on their own time to participate. Because no one had ever showed up two hours early for their shift at Burger King, I felt we had accomplished something. Next, I planned a major contest between the three main sections of the park: Motor World, Water World, and the Alpine Center. Motor World and Water World were hugely territorial, with each faction believing they had superior athletes. The Alpine Center was more like Switzerland. They participated, but not with any fervor. After hours, we raced cars, had sprint races from the bottom of the park in Motor World to the water slides in Water World, and held softball games. Jimmy and I were the team captains and likely more invested in the outcomes than the participants. If there was a close finish, the two of us would scream and berate each other. As manager of Motor World, Jimmy was particularly salty that his squad never won a single softball game. He argued that the diesel fumes affected their lungs and made them weaker. Fresh air was considered performance enhancing.

When I saw the response to the park-wide competitions, I plotted something even more ambitious. The mountaintop parties I threw for the Wave Pool lifeguards had helped keep our top employees coming back year after year. "What if," I asked Julie, "we held a big Water World party for everyone at the end of the season?"

Julie was busy writing a note to paste over the employee time clock: DO NOT CLOCK IN IF YOU HAVE BEEN DRINKING. She looked at me like I had just suggested we expose everyone to the plague. "Absolutely not," she said. "I know what goes on at those parties."

Whatever Julie had heard, the reality was certainly far worse, but that wasn't the point. "It won't be like the mountaintop parties," I said. "It will be great for morale. We'll do it responsibly."

"I think the liability risk is insane," she said. "You cannot have kids running around the park in the middle of the night."

"This is going to help employee retention," I said, trying to appeal to her administrative side.

"Insane," she said.

Julie's management style was that of an authoritarian. Employees were on time and did their jobs because they dreaded her wrath and her ability to materialize out of thin air just in time to catch them arriving late or making out in the break room. I, on the other hand, felt you got more out of people if you gave them time to unwind and alleviate stress. We asked a lot of these kids for a few dollars an hour. We had to offer more than money, especially as they got older, obtained their driver's licenses, and began looking for jobs elsewhere. When their parents told them to quit because they read a story about a ride mishap, they needed to insist they loved their low-paying and potentially injurious job.

I didn't want to back down. More to the point, I didn't want to acquiesce to my older sister. Finally, I told her I would just ask our father. I knew he would side with me. It was a cheap but effective tactic.

"Fine," she said. "But you're responsible."

I breathed a sigh of relief, happy I didn't have to ask him about it. Not because he'd say no—he wouldn't—but because I felt he deserved plausible deniability.

THERE WAS ANOTHER REASON PARENTS WERE SOMETIMES HESI-tant to let their kids work here. We had developed a reputation for violence.

Scuffles were not an uncommon occurrence. Surly guests stewing in a mixture of beer and baking sun were often combustible. Hold a leering glance at someone else's girlfriend for too long, and it might invite a shoving match. Couples with relationship troubles might get physically abusive with one another, prompting security to intervene. Once, a man pulled a knife on an employee. A young attendant had caught him smoking weed on the Alpine chair lift and confronted him. The man produced a steak knife with a kind of stoned indifference, then got back on the lift. Police had to wait for the chair to come back before making an arrest.

In a crowd that could exceed fifteen thousand people on some days, these were relative nonevents. Only on occasion would things escalate to the point at which tear gas would have proven useful.

At approximately 3:45 p.m. on a Saturday—I know this because I saw the police report—a teenager was holding a place in line for his friends. When he finally got to the front, he waved the rest of his buddies over. This was a common practice among some attendees at the park and referred to as "making the line." Few guests dared protest, as a roaring band of aggressive teenagers could be intimidating.

On this day, a number of guests of Italian descent decided to voice their concern, alleging the offenders, who were Puerto Rican, were not "making" the line but cutting the line. Decked out in white muscle shirts and shouting enough to shake the gold jewelry around their necks, they accused the line-makers of selfish behavior. Words were exchanged. Ethnic slurs may have been uttered. The two groups moved closer to one another, trotting in unison like a troupe of stage performers. Some spread their shoulders out to appear wider, their heads tilting back so their necks grew thicker.

When they were nose-to-nose, the conflict ignited. It was like something out of *The Outsiders*. They began pummeling one another, grabbing fistfuls of shirts and putting their boots to downed opponents. Someone produced a bicycle chain and wrapped it around his hand, bludgeoning anyone who got close. The other guests gave them a wide berth, forming a circle of spectators. I grabbed my walkie-talkie and shouted for every security staff member we had, along with anyone else in the vicinity. Security guards and employees poured in, trying to restore order. Kevin Curley, who was fond of trading punches with belligerent guests, waded into the melee and began swinging his fists with a smile on his face.

We kicked out the brawlers from both sides, leaving only a few remaining to try to explain why they shouldn't be permanently banned. Some of those ejected loitered in the parking lot, tensions still simmering.

This was not the worst of it.

Moments earlier, a young employee had come to Topher and announced she had to quit. Topher asked why she was leaving. The girl explained that her mother felt the park was too wild and that she was concerned for her daughter's welfare.

"I'm sure this is all a misunderstanding," he said. "Why don't I talk to your mom when she comes to pick you up?" Topher did not want to lose an employee, but his motives were not entirely altruistic.

He would later tell me he had been thinking of asking her out. At the park, a supervisor dating a subordinate was not the human resources nightmare it would be today. This was mainly because we didn't have a human resources department.

The employee agreed and said her mother would be there around four o'clock in the afternoon. Her punctuality would prove unfortunate.

Soon after, the employee's mother pulled into the parking lot to pick up her daughter, oblivious to the fact that she was driving into a war zone thick with the coppery smell of blood and Brut cologne. Topher had practiced a speech that emphasized how safe the park was and how she had nothing to worry about. The fight had blown over just in time, salvaging his hopes of keeping the daughter employed long enough to gather the guts to ask her out.

As he walked toward the mother's vehicle, he noticed movement out of the corner of his eye. Suddenly, an Italian kid sprinted in between cars, a mob of Puerto Ricans carrying two-by-fours, retrieved from a nearby Dumpster, in hot pursuit.

Topher grabbed the girl and jumped into her mother's car for safety. As they piled in, a massive body slammed into the driver's side door, smearing blood on the window. A piece of wood snapped her side view mirror. The lone Italian jumped into her passenger seat, desperate to avoid being maimed.

"Drive, dammit!" the man screamed. "Drive!" The car veered out of the lot before the stranger jumped out, taking off on foot down Route 94.

The girl never even came back for her last paycheck.

Handling disruptive visitors was supposed to be the job of the park's security team, but people figured out relatively quickly that it was ineffectual. For a long time, the head security guard was a former police officer named Arnold. Arnold was in his seventies and moved extremely slowly. He carried two guns, one on his waist and one on his ankle. Few if any situations at the park would ever require a firearm, so Arnold was more of a fixture than an asset. I suspected my father had hired him as a favor to someone.

The day did eventually arrive when we needed Arnold. Someone near Motor World spotted a rabid raccoon, frothing at the mouth and terrifying customers. The situation was tense, as we didn't want the animal to disappear into the Human Maze, where he might cause a pandemic. A bunch of us jogged across the road and tried to back it into a corner without getting too close. When Arnold finally arrived, he drew his weapon and told us to stand clear.

Arnold and the raccoon were perhaps fifteen feet apart. He fired once, twice, and then four more times, emptying his revolver. Not a single bullet connected. The raccoon hissed in victory. It was then that we knew that Arnold would be almost entirely useless in a conflict. Someone finally put a cardboard box over the raccoon and probably drowned it in the speedboat lake.

I tried to communicate these problems to my father as best I could, but my ability to be his eyes and ears on the ground was limited to Water World. He needed a lieutenant, someone who could act as his sentry in the thick of the lunacy. For this role, he hired a park general manager named Adam Ringler. Adam had come from the ski operation and had impressed my father with his ability to keep tabs on the snow accumulation and make sure the hotline had the latest ski conditions. Adam segued into a role as my father's emissary, motoring around on a scooter and keeping him updated on weather, attendance, accidents, and anything else Gene wanted to know, all in real time.

"Predicting three thousand tomorrow," Adam would say. "High chance of rain."

He wore a white shirt with white shorts and a safari hat with a built-in fan. He also wore a massive set of keys that made him look like an old-time prison guard. Like a cat with a bell, you could always hear him coming. Julie called him Ring-Ding.

The only real adult in our midst, Ring-Ding rarely took anyone's shit, which became useful when we had issues with guests misbehaving. If we had to detain a patron until the police arrived, we kept them in a small holding area in the Hexagon Lounge. Usually, it was occupied by fence-jumpers. Our employees were notoriously oblivious to people lacking wristbands and one could spend hours in the park without paying or being confronted about it. I didn't take a hard line with gate-crashers aside from asking for the admission fee. If they didn't act like assholes, we'd cut them loose without any further hassle. But if Adam was around, he'd turn into Dirty Harry, playing bad cop to whomever was trying to let the offender off easy. It was a necessary injection of authority. Some of the guests became convinced we had the power to send them to Rikers Island.

THE PARK HAD BECOME A HUB OF ACTIVITY FOR KIDS HOPPED UP ON adolescence and beer. Their money was as good as anyone's, but my father felt the fights and rabid animals were alienating the family demographic that could add to our bottom line.

His solution was to emphasize attractions that catered to children and their parents. In the past, he had promoted classic car shows, antique fairs, and craft exhibits. He once hosted a park event in which we awarded a prize for the child who best resembled one of the little Hummel figurines. Hundreds of kids showed up in coveralls and wooden shoes, their cheeks reddened with makeup by their stage mothers. He hired street performers to entertain the kids and distract the older teens who might instigate conflict. One of these performers was a magician named Sebastiani, whom I once took to a Bruce Springsteen show in the hope that we might become friends. Instead, he used his sleight of hand expertise to pilfer a half dozen concert shirts from a souvenir booth. My father also enlisted Vernon high school students to march the grounds in military formation as the Action Park Marching Band. I found it hokey and told my father as much, but he just shook his head, as though I had a lot to learn.

"These kids aren't interested in being ride attendants, but they're still working here," he said. "Think about it." The band was a way of ingratiating himself with parents who still viewed the park with skepticism. It was always harder to voice opposition to the park and its development if it gainfully employed your children.

The band ignited his interest in live entertainment. Many parks had begun offering shows to keep parents occupied while their kids went on rides, with the themed spectacles of song and dance repeated multiple times daily. My father found out that the person responsible for most of the performances was a veteran stage choreographer named Allan Albert. My father contacted him and offered to build a soundstage above Motor World to host Allan's Broadway Revue, a greatest-hits compilation of show tunes.

Always well dressed, Allan spoke in a brusque, clipped tone and seemed slightly ill at ease around the uncivilized park clientele. My father called him "artsy" and loved having him around, in part because his fastidiousness was in sharp contrast to the demeanor of the snowmakers and the belligerent New Yorkers who visited the park. Allan was also an insane taskmaster, barking orders at his young charges like the teachers in *Fame* and weighing the female dancers twice a week to make sure they didn't succumb to the temptations of the concession-stand funnel cakes. It was less mentoring than psychological torture.

Full of hits from shows like *Grease* and *West Side Story*, the Broadway Revue was entertaining but was designed to be filler, something that anyone could drop in on at any time without feeling confused. We also added a country show and a rock-and-roll show so the performances could be spread around the park. You could hear the beat of the shows throughout the property. Families were enraptured. Delinquents were not. The latter largely avoided the Revue, repelled by its wholesomeness.

At one point, we brought in senior citizens, who ambled through the gates on walkers to take advantage of a package deal. For one price, they could have lunch at a nearby deli, take in one of our shows, and get a charter bus ride to and from their retirement home. Somehow, the highly underqualified food and beverage manager, Bud Kelley, wound up serving them bock beer, which was twice as potent as our usual beer. In the heat, the brew quickly went to their heads. By the end of the show, a dozen seniors were teetering over, the falls threatening to snap their brittle bones like saltines. Medics treated a few of them for bruises. Angry calls from the senior living facility followed.

While the Broadway shows were lively, they were passive, which was thematically out of place at Action Park. My father wanted to make visitors active participants in a spectacle, and he knew a competition was the way to do it. This was how we wound up with beauty pageants.

Everyone knew the template from the televised Miss America specials held in Atlantic City. These were battles of genetics, makeup, and charisma, and a thinly veiled excuse to have women in bathing suits parading around stage. Like any competition, they inspired viewers to root for their favorite contestant. Our entrants vied for a small cash prize and a sash that read "Miss Action Park."

My father's instinct was to get the crowd heavily invested in the outcome. To do that, he decided to introduce territorial tension. We might pit a contestant from the Bronx against a contestant from Brooklyn, with the emcee goading each faction on.

"Ohhh, the Polish are out in force today!" the announcer would say. "This poor Italian woman doesn't have a chance!" This would cause a small army of Italians to begin screaming and circling the Polish side.

"Hey, man," I told the emcee. "You really need to knock that shit off. We're going to have a riot." I knew this because we had literally just had a riot.

He didn't listen. When we promoted a battle for aesthetic supremacy between women of Irish and Puerto Rican descent, the crowd resembled an Irish Republican Army assembly. We crowned only two or three women Miss Action Park before we agreed it was best to abandon the idea. It wasn't fair to expect the winners to fight their way off stage.

Surprisingly, our biggest entertainment attraction wasn't the pageants or even recognizable performers like Chuck Berry, who made periodic visits. It was Jimmy Sturr.

One year, my father invited Sturr and his polka band to come and perform at his Polish festivals on the Great Gorge grounds. Sturr, who lived just twenty miles up the road in the dirt flats of New York, was the Elvis Presley of polka. He had a great blond mane that looked like a wave you could surf and flashy jackets that were so sparkly he resembled a holiday ornament. Sturr has won as many Grammys (eighteen) as Paul McCartney, Tony Bennett, or Yo-Yo Ma, though, to be fair, the polka field is probably not as crowded as the other music genres.

Julie initially dismissed Sturr as corny. There was never an era in which polka was cool, but my father insisted New Jersey's high concentration of Polish Americans was being underserved. He thought that community would flock to Sturr. He directed Julie to take out ads on polka radio stations and spread the word in polka newsletters. He hired a Motor World employee named Chris O'Keefe, who went by the nickname Puff for his wildly overgrown head of hair, to go to Polish neighborhoods and bars and stuff flyers under windshield wipers, earning Puff the modified name of Puffer the Stuffer. If there was a big turnout, my father promised to reward his dogged determination with several pairs of Gucci shoes, which Puffer desperately and inexplicably coveted.

The first time Sturr performed, five thousand people showed up, packing our parking lots with campers and Winnebagos full of Sturr devotees who followed him around the country the way the Deadheads followed Jerry Garcia. I attended the show, expecting to find the whole thing lame, but the crowd's enthusiasm was infectious. Before long, Smoke, Vinnie Mancuso, Bob Krahulik, and I were doing the chicken dance, a famous polka step.

Every time Sturr appeared, we made a killing in beer and concession sales. I cannot recall a summer in which he didn't play. He was our secret polka weapon. A proud Puffer the Stuffer would periodically strut around the park to show off his Guccis, carefully avoiding discarded ketchup packets like they were land mines.

Entertainment was only part of the plan to attract families. We also tried our version of Disney's Main Street, USA, opening a collection of quaint shops and small-town storefronts that overlooked Water World. Dubbed Cobblestone Village, its purpose was to bridge the gap between the winter and summer months by remaining open year-round. It had twenty-four shops in all, including a candle store, a deli, a Bavarian pretzel outlet, a photo lab, and an ice cream shop, where Laurie now worked. She soon developed scooper's wrist, a painful condition resulting from repeatedly digging into the cement-like concoction.

On a break one afternoon, the two of us walked over to Cinema 180, an expensive new theater my father added to the park with a giant 180-degree screen that exceeded your peripheral vision. It showed footage of Mount Saint Helens erupting and a first-person car crash, an immersive experience also available in Motor World.

Inside, there were no chairs. People had to stand for the ten-minute reels.

"It smells in here," Laurie said, wrinkling her nose. "Like puke."

Watching the disorienting car footage, we understood why. If people came into the theater shortly after gorging on pizza and pretzels from the nearby shops, they stood a decent chance of having their food come back up. Years later, I would see IMAX theaters and think that we had been ahead of our time in offering motion sickness as a form of entertainment.

Out in the fresh air, we dodged globs of melted ice cream on the pavement and discussed how we would navigate the next few years of college. Our time on separate coasts had gone extremely well. I had come back for holidays, and we had taken vacations together. We were determined not to be a park couple, a pair that thrived only in the intensity and intimacy of dealing with the teeming mobs and hysteria. Such relationships were commonplace here, like romances on movie sets. We agreed that we were more than that. I believed this even as I wrapped my Wave Patrol jacket around her shoulders.

We left Cinema 180 and discussed the recent expansion of Fantasy Isle, a child's play area in Motor World where Laurie had considered taking a job. We already had a kids' play park in Water World with a number of attractions, including a punching-bag forest. The objective was to run through the bags while your friends swung them, attempting to knock you stiff. We agreed this appealed to cruel children. Fantasy Isle had bumper boats and a less-imposing version of the Human Maze. My father planned to build a pirate ship featuring hidden treasure for kids to hunt. He also spoke of wanting a plank for pint-sized traitors to walk, plastic swords prodding them into a pool, but none of it ever came to fruition.

The jewel of the kids' area in Water World was a massive ball pit. A wooden enclosure held thousands and thousands of plastic balls in which kids could swim. One day, a father idling near the pit began screaming at the attendant, taking some perceived slight at her attitude. Whatever she said in response only made him angrier. In retaliation, he reared back and kicked the wooden enclosure as hard as he could. Made of relatively flimsy plywood by harried snowmakers, it collapsed under the force of his strike. The balls began tumbling down the hill, spilling like a bag of marbles. Attendants spent hours walking around stuffing them into bags and bins. We found balls under benches and tucked near rides for months afterward.

Cobblestone Village and the kids' areas endured for years, though they quickly became afterthoughts for most visitors. To a group of young adults, a candle store at an amusement park was just a speed bump in the way of their thrill-seeking. We had already cemented our identity as a wild place run by teenagers for teenagers. We were not, and never would be, known as a place for all ages.

I wished we had learned that lesson before the party.

THE BASH FOR THE EMPLOYEES NEEDED FUNDING. THERE WAS NO expense account, and even if there was, Julie never would have allotted a penny toward an after-hours affair.

Fortunately, the lifeguards had become very adept at canvassing the Wave Pool and the other water rides for money and possessions that guests had lost. The guards called it "scarfing," and it could be extremely lucrative for anyone diving at the end of a shift. On a busy Saturday or Sunday, one could pull out hundreds of dollars, mostly in singles and fives that people had stuffed into their swim trunks to spend at the concession stands, as well as the occasional dime bag of weed. Jewelry was set aside in case the owner came back for it. We'd even send out search parties for wedding rings if someone returned in a panic. But not many people bothered to come back in pursuit of a few missing dollars. Added up, the money was sometimes more than an employee might make in an entire week on duty, another reason the lifeguard job was so coveted. I pointed this out when some of them complained about not getting the extra twenty-five cents an hour.

When he moved up to head lifeguard, Bob Krahulik asserted himself as the gatekeeper for scarfing. No guard could dive for money without his permission. He'd act as a spotter, remaining poolside and directing employees to swim toward wherever he detected water-logged currency.

"Couple singles at six o'clock!" he'd yell. "Come on, man!"

In his benevolence, Bob divvied up the money with the diver. He set half aside for the mountaintop and Water World parties, and split the other half with the person who had fetched it. But Bob's oppressive rule didn't extend to the entirety of Water World, and other rides had different protocols. Some water-pump operators kept scuba suits in their cars. One guy in particular, whom I'll call Joey Lion, developed an utterly diabolical method for scarfing that I didn't discover until long after he had left the park.

Blond and muscular, Joey Lion was a big and intimidating guy who had a tattoo of a snarling lion on his bicep and the tense energy of someone who might break a bottle over your head at any moment. He was stationed at the Cannonball chutes. Not to be confused with the Cannonball Loop, these tubes were adjacent to the Tarzan Swing and spit people out of enclosed slides into a pool ten feet below. At the entrance, Joey Lion stopped people ready to jump inside and gave them a quick set of instructions.

"We can't allow you to wear jewelry," he said. "It's sharp and cuts up the foam surface inside." This part, at least, was true. The struggle to repair the foam cushioning the rides was unending.

Guests would ask what they should do with it, and Joey would set them up. "Make a fist and hold it really tight in your hands," he said.

The riders would oblige, taking off their gold pendants or chains and clutching them tightly. After going down the Cannonball tube in total darkness, they would hit a bank turn and then get shot out into blinding daylight and freezing mountain water kept cold by the shade. This disorienting series of events caused them to open their hands on impact, at which point the jewelry would go flying. If someone came back looking for their trinket, Joey Lion would shake his head, mustering all the fraudulent sympathy he could.

"Probably got sucked into the filters, man," he'd say. He portrayed the filters as black holes that devoured all matter. Retrieval, he said, was impossible.

At the end of the day, Joey would scour the pool and come out with a fistful of necklaces. His grift grew to enormous proportions. Once, at a house party, Smoke told me he stumbled into Joey's bedroom and saw a jewelry chest that was the size of a refrigerator.

"It looked like something you'd see at the Saks jewelry counter," Smoke said. "I think I saw diamonds."

In addition to being conniving, Joey Lion was also selfish. He kept all his stolen goods for himself, which left the funding for the Water World party entirely to Bob and his crew. Still, by the end of the summer, we had collected over a thousand dollars. I posted a sign above the punch clock in the break room with a time and date. The whole of Water World would be open for any employee looking to blow off steam and celebrate the end of the season—but only if they were still on the job. I could hear the excited chatter begin almost immediately.

"See?" I boasted to Julie. "It's all anyone is talking about."

"Remember," she said. "I have nothing to do with this."

After weeks of anticipation, the night finally arrived. The party was for all the staff, including some of the maintenance workers who were as young as fourteen or fifteen, but that did not preclude us from making sure the older employees were well hydrated. I delegated beverage duties to Tommy Smith and Smoke, asking them to buy beer. The night of the party, I saw Tommy standing over two large plastic garbage cans, dumping bottle after bottle of liquid inside until the cans became immovable.

"What is this?" I asked.

"Party punch," Tommy said. "Orange juice, pineapple juice, 7UP, and a little something extra."

As Tommy finished pouring, a swell of workers began circulating near the Wave Pool. They dipped plastic cups into Tommy's concoction, sipping it and making foul expressions. Behind him, Smoke had constructed a makeshift island in the pool, using the foam mats to support a fake palm tree and a beer keg. It had the charm of a high school stage set, only with much, much more alcohol.

I swam out to the "island" for one or two beers but avoided Tommy's swill in the belief that I was acting as a chaperone for the evening. I was getting older, growing further away from the next generation of workers. Some looked young enough to be in junior high.

Laurie and I wandered around on foot for the first hour or two. We talked about how big the park was getting. She wondered if I saw myself in a long-term role there, finishing college and then going to work for my father, like Julie had.

"I think about it," I said. "But I don't know for sure." In my mind, the park was a place for kids. When it stopped making me feel like one, I thought, it would be time to move on.

I asked her what she wanted to do.

"I think I'd like to be a teacher," she said.

"You haven't had enough of kids yet?"

She laughed. "Working here has been instructional."

We spoke about my father's determination to continue to expand the park. He liked Laurie a great deal, waving hello whenever he saw her and engaging her in conversation when she came over to the house for dinner. This meant she sometimes had park gossip that had not yet reached my ears.

"Your dad is thinking of starting a nursery," she said.

I cocked my head, confused. "For plants?" I said.

"For kids," she said. "Kids that are too young to roam around. Parents can come and drop them off. He'd like for me to run it."

I knew my father was after the family demographic at all costs, but the idea of an Action Park nursery sounded no safer than leaving children at home alone near a pile of matches and a barrel of gasoline. I imagined a state subcommittee panel assembled just to evaluate the fallout, but I kept my opinion to myself. Whatever made Laurie happy made me happy. She was a calming presence, not prone to courting danger. Laurie projected a bubble of normalcy, reminding me that the park did not define me. Here was someone who considered it a job, not a life philosophy.

As we talked, Smoke waved to us from Beer Island. We waved back.

As the night wore on, the kids grew looser. They sang and ran around, orbiting Tommy's garbage cans as cup after cup got dipped in and discarded. Couples splintered off and found dark corners for heavy-petting sessions. The park had a host of spots for this, like the pile of rafts near the Wave Pool, the rope climb in the kids' park, or inside the Cannonball tubes. Enclosed rides provided the most privacy. Other kids sat by themselves and just stared, so intoxicated that they seemed to have only minimal brain activity. I began to reconsider the wisdom of not setting a minimum age for attendance.

As Laurie and I continued walking, Smoke came up to us. "Hey, man," he said. "Cool party."

"It's going well," I said.

"Just thought you should know, I think some of these kids are fucking." He said this in the same tone you'd use to tell someone that they had a mustard stain on their shirt.

"What?" I said.

"Yeah, back behind the pump room," he said. "Definitely fucking."

I gasped, struck by terrifying visions of trying to explain to Julie—or worse, child protective services—how I had allowed an adolescent orgy in our amusement park. I ran to get one of the motorized Cushman carts and started making the rounds. Smoke had not been exaggerating. Heavy, borderline-pornographic make-out sessions were going on at the deck of the Wave Pool. Other kids were in the water. I exhaled, relieved they were just swimming. When they emerged, they were naked.

"Hey," I said. "Hey! Take it easy!"

The scene became increasingly carnal and disturbing. Farther out from the Wave Pool, I saw motionless bodies splayed out on the grass. Approaching them, I winced. Some had lost their shirts, others their pants. A few were passed out, drunk.

"Kid," I said, slapping one. "Kid, you okay?"

"Summunah," he said. "Summunah party."

I spotted Tommy. "What the fuck did you put in the punch?" I said.

"Orange juice, pineapple juice, 7UP," Tommy said. He stopped, as though he needed a moment to remember. "And fifty percent grain alcohol." Tommy had served them a recipe from his college fraternity.

I got back on the cart, breaking up fornicating teenagers wherever

I spotted them. As it got closer to midnight, parents began pulling into the parking lot to pick up their kids. I swallowed my panic and waved, directing them to stay in their cars. Smoke and Tommy began dragging some of the bodies over near the lot, piling them up like sacks of animal feed.

Knowing some of the older kids would be too inebriated to drive, I told them to stay in the park overnight. On cue, they collapsed on the ground, dozing. I spent the rest of the night clearing the Wave Pool deck of couples and making sure Tommy didn't refill the garbage bins. Older siblings who wouldn't rat drove many of the kids home, but a handful of employees would certainly smell rancid enough to raise suspicions. I braced for disaster.

The next morning, I avoided Julie, who was rumored to be after my head. My father asked how the party went.

I had already received calls from some parents about their kids appearing tipsy. I played dumb, never hinting that we had gallons of moonshine on hand and let the parents believe they had gotten hold of the booze on their own. Fortunately, the truly hammered had remained there overnight.

"I think it was great for morale," I said.

If he knew, he didn't say a word.

THE FOLLOWING SUMMER, WE HAD A SHARP INCREASE IN THE NUMber of applicants, many of whom had heard about the Water World party. This drove Julie into spasms.

"Never again," she said. But we brought it back every year, minus the bins full of rubbing alcohol. The employees loved it.

I couldn't blame them. Under cover of night, the park took on a much different atmosphere. The crowds that piled in during the day were gone, leaving its walkways clear and the rides empty. The lights we used to illuminate Motor World at dusk bathed everything in an artificial glow. The din that rose from tens of thousands of people swarming toward one end and then the other was muted. There was no screaming over line-cutting, no fighting, no splashing, no hysterical reports of disaster on the radio. There was only silence. It made me feel like I did when my father first broke ground there, that he was building a park just for us kids.

Many times, I found myself pulling into the parking lot late into the night and piling out with Laurie or my friends, unlocking the fence in front of the admission window, and running inside. We divorced ourselves from being sentries. We wanted to be guests.

In Motor World, we turned off the governors that limited the speed of the cars and pushed the Lolas up to seventy or eighty miles an hour, taking sharp curves around the track and veering dangerously close to one another. Jimmy and Kevin Curley took the Lolas out on Route 94. Had anyone in an actual car plowed into them, the Lolas would have crumpled like aluminum cans. They were not street legal. But they were nimble, able to weave in and out of traffic, and there were never many cars on that stretch of road late at night. Still, I never climbed inside one. It was Jimmy who inherited my father's reckless side.

Surf Hill was a different story. All of us sought out increasingly creative ways to take the jump. Smoke and Tommy built tiny rafts made of two-by-fours and mats and shot themselves off the lane and into the sky. We also rode inner tubes three people at a time, hoping some kind of inviolate law of physics would get us farther and higher up in the air according to how dangerous our makeshift vessel was.

During one of these midnight excursions, I watched as Smoke went down in a tube, soaring so high he seemed to be eclipsing the moon. The landing was less romantic. He plummeted down to the foam mat with such force that it dislocated his shoulder. As he writhed in pain, I ran over and helped him to his feet.

He was in agony but functional. I persuaded him to put off surgery until after the summer. He thought I was just worried about him, and I was. But we also couldn't lose a lifeguard.

On a different night, I was contemplating going down the Kamikaze when I noticed a small band of strangers bouncing around near the bottom. Afraid it might be security, I slowly walked down the hill. As I got closer, I could make out faces. It was Nicole Molina, Ellen, her sister Erin, and Ginette in a pack and headed for Motor World. In the center, laughing louder than all of them, was Julie.

Startled, I stopped. It was like seeing the pope at a Megadeth concert. I wanted to yell and chastise her, playfully, but resisted. She looked over at me, then disappeared with the others into the night.

The park seduced everyone, kids and seniors, polka fans and daredevils. Julie never had a chance.

The Super Go-Karts. Not highway-approved.

The Aqua Skoot, from the mind that brought us the Bailey Ball.
Employees tempted fate by riding it while standing up.

Chapter Nine

THE FLOOR BENEATH OUR FEET

"Most people spend their lives trying to dodge trouble. The best fun in the world is dodging trouble you've made for yourself."

James Bailey, co-founder of the Barnum & Bailey circus

My father always had an interest in magic. When we were younger, he would perform card tricks at the kitchen table during breakfast, blowing our adolescent minds with disappearing aces and recovered kings. Later, when my brothers got older and started having children of their own, he would gather the grandkids during family getaways to his vacation home in Aspen. By then, his illusions had grown more elaborate.

"I'm going to turn into a rabbit," he told them.

The kids were skeptical. They were old enough to know their grandfather could not turn into an animal but young enough to think, *well, maybe*. He ushered them into a spare bedroom and told them to examine every inch of the place for signs of a rabbit or anything else suspicious. He had them check that the window was too high up to accommodate his escape. There was nothing.

"Okay," he said, ushering them out and shutting himself in. "Come back in five minutes."

They milled about. After a few minutes, they opened the door. There, in the middle of the room, was a rabbit. My father was no-where in sight. They were amazed. They looked everywhere for him. Soon, the rabbit consumed all their attention. My father would rejoin the family a short time later. He did this often. To this day, some of them don't know how he managed it, or what became of the rabbits that had temporarily replaced him.

I could have guessed what happened to the bunnies—my father was a meat-eater—but didn't learn the rest of his methodology until later. There was a trapdoor in the closet, a place for additional storage, that was obscured by clothing. That was where he hid the rabbit, and then himself.

My father's sleight of hand was legendary in the family, but it was also well known across New Jersey, where his misdirection took on a different form.

When the injuries at the park began to pile up, I'd hear people make jokes about how he must be paying out the nose for liability insurance. Who would insure a park designed by an amateur with no previous water ride experience? That served beer? That was effectively run by area high school kids?

When anyone wanted a real answer to that, Gene would say he was covered by the prestigious firm of London and World Assurance, Limited, which never seemed to raise an eyebrow at anything he wanted to do. He gave the state proof of insurance whenever they asked.

London and World, I would come to find out, was surprisingly affordable. The cost of premiums was zero, and their office space had extremely low overhead.

That's because London and World didn't actually exist in any conventional sense. He had conjured it out of thin air.

Like his grandkids, the state was amazed by the illusion. But he didn't see the trapdoor until it was too late.

I LEARNED OF THE INSURANCE FRAUD THROUGH MY STANFORD classmate Adam Tracy in March of my sophomore year. Adam was from Rye, New York, and kept up with the East Coast newspapers.

"Hey, Andy," he said. "Your dad's in some shit."

"You'll have to be more specific," I said. Adam handed me the newspaper. On page three was a headline:

RESORT HAD NO INSURER, STATE SAYS

"For fuck's sake," I said.

"This is the death park, right?" Adam said. "What do they mean, he has no insurance?"

"It's not a 'death park,'" I said. "There have been mishaps. It's no different from swimming in the ocean." *Oh, my God. I am turning into him.*

"They're saying he made up his own insurance company."

"It's a mistake."

I got on the phone with my mother, who explained that my father was "having some difficulty" with insurance regulators. "The state," she said, "seems a little vindictive."

"Put Dad on the phone," I said.

"Heya," he said, as if I had caught him on a lazy afternoon.

"What's going on?" I said.

"It's all a big misunderstanding," he said. "Don't worry about it. How's school?"

My father's stoicism made it impossible to gauge the seriousness of any given situation. It was always difficult to know what to be worried about because nothing appeared to worry him. It wasn't that he didn't consider the consequences of his potentially troublesome actions. It was that the consequences bothered him so little, their threat seemingly so remote, that he was never distracted by them. This was a man who once went on a trip to Las Vegas with his Mayflower men, hopped on a real live bull, and rode it until he was flung to the ground and into unconsciousness. Getting trampled was not something he feared because it was not an option he weighed.

With help from Julie, Topher, and the newspapers, I absorbed the details of his latest maneuver. For the past year, the New Jersey State Commission of Investigation (SCI) had been looking into allegations that London and World was not actually an independent insurer but one of Gene's own companies. No one knew who urged the commission to conduct the inquiry, but a prime suspect was Tom Kean, the governor of New Jersey. Kean, a Republican, was apparently irritated after Gene threw his support behind an opposing candidate during the 1981 gubernatorial election and may have decided to retaliate by sending the SCI after him. (Kean would later come to the park for a photo op and go down the Alpine at an apparent speed of a few inches per hour. Maybe it was his version of a victory lap.) It was also no coincidence that the SCI became concerned about the park's insurance status following the two deaths the previous summer. As I feared then, we had attracted all the wrong kinds of attention.

Asked to submit records of his various businesses, my father passive-aggressively sent over an entire moving truck full of documents. It took them three months to comb through it all. The SCI was looking for evidence of London and World's existence, but could find no trace of it. There was only a post office box in the Cayman Islands.

My father was cryptic on the topic of London and World. "Just because they can't find it doesn't mean it doesn't exist," he said, as though it were common for insurance companies not to have telephone numbers.

For those who knew him, there was little mystery as to why my father had done something so brazen. He hated insurance. Period. Premiums had skyrocketed in the late 1970s, jumping 400 percent after a number of people injured at ski resorts won the resulting lawsuits. My father considered insurance a substantial waste of money that served only to line the pockets of the insurers, with no apparent benefit to him. If an insurer did need to pay out a claim, his premiums, deductible, or both would go up. The state's mandated amount of two million dollars in coverage for the park would have been incredibly expensive, even more so because of our spotty safety record. He theorized that it would be much cheaper to field claims himself and pay settlements out of his own pocket when needed, which wasn't often with the tenacious lawyer David Chaffin in his corner.

So, after the first couple of years of the park's existence, he opted out of conventional insurance. In this way, he avoided premiums, but it also meant that every time someone slid down the Alpine and stumbled off with weeping skin, the park was vulnerable to litigation. Every bump, broken bone, concussion, dented nose—he was liable for everything. It was now clear to me why he fought claims so aggressively, why David Chaffin was a bull terrier in court. A large settlement could have wiped out the park financially.

Tipped to London and World's curiously ethereal quality, the state's insurance department asked for proof that my father had paid insurance premiums. He could produce only one check. It was dated 1978 and did not appear to have been sent to London and World. Instead, it was cashed by New Jersey Financial and General, another one of his companies, which effectively meant he had paid himself. He did, however, give the Department of Labor certificates of insurance, which were required to obtain a permit to open a ride. They were signed by Joe Dasti, a former Mayflower employee. That was alarming because Joe Dasti did not work in the insurance industry. Someone at the SCI remarked that the certificates appeared to be homemade. Since Gene owned the company, that was a perceptive observation.

Not only were London and World's existence and ownership shadowy, the company was not authorized to do business in the state of New Jersey. This was a clear violation of my father's lease terms with the Department of Environmental Protection, which owned a large swath of the mountain. If an injured guest had received a large judgment that Gene could not pay out of pocket, the state could have been open to liability. London and World had no assets to back up any substantial claims, no reservoir of funds if someone wound up paralyzed. The exposure was enormous.

My father, once again, ignored the pleas of both Julie and his lawyers that he avoid speaking to the press and tried to explain, in a very rational tone, that he had done nothing wrong. It just made everything worse. He said he had paid all valid claims. He insisted any gaps in coverage were handled by Dover Insurance, which was licensed in the state. When contacted by newspaper reporters looking to corroborate my father's assertions, a representative for Dover said they only agreed to handle claims exceeding London and World's coverage. Dover seemed unaware that, since London and World offered no coverage, anything would have exceeded it. He had, in effect, taken out insurance for his quasi-fictional insurance company.

He refused to apologize. "There is basically no difference," he said, "between self-insurance and having a high deductible."

The self-insurance paper trail acted as a crowbar for the SCI, which proceeded to submerge itself in his escalating history of audacious behavior. The commission's report included mention of the snowmaking systems being fed with the help of a dam at the top of the mountain, which no one at the DEP had authorized. (My father argued they only had jurisdiction for concrete dams; his was made out of dirt and, therefore, immune to oversight.) The state was also annoyed that he was slow to pay the share of the ski-lift revenue that he owed them under the lease agreement. My father's explanation was that they had never sent him a bill. While this happened to be true, it was not what the state wanted to hear.

Things quickly began to unravel. A battalion of lawyers who had active lawsuits against the park modified their complaints to note that the rides on which their clients were injured were only approved because of an insurance certificate from a company that was owned by the person seeking the ride permit. The Larssons were among those who thought it made the park even more at fault.

In perpetuating this scheme, my father had somehow managed to embarrass and anger at least four major state agencies. The state held a three-day hearing to discuss its findings, which turned into a kangaroo court, with no one defending him. Someone from the DEP who examined the dam said it was "hazardous" with "the potential for loss of life" if the water escaped the barrier. (It held up for decades.) They said he created the illusion of insurance, and that he had cheated them out of resort revenue.

It was incredibly surreal to see state employees discuss my father like he was a career criminal. For my entire life, he had done things his way and redefined rules that didn't suit him. Time and again, he emerged triumphant, no worse for wear and hardly in need of a defense attorney. His behavior in this case was all pretty typical of him, playing with semantics and outmaneuvering opponents who were not as crafty. Usually, people recognized they had been outplayed and moved on.

This was different. Now he had outsmarted the state government, and they were, as my mother said, a little vindictive. It's never good news when a state holds a multi-day meeting to argue that you're out of your mind.

The unmasking of London and World forced him to obtain actual insurance from an actual insurance company to remain in operation. He paid back most of what he owed to the state from the allegedly underreported ski-lift income. But the damage was already done. The opposition to development in Vernon now had the backing of the state. After years of my father forcing the town to submit to his whims, the pendulum was now swinging the other way. Officials grew quiet, withdrawing to consider their options. All my father could do was wait.

One day, Julie was driving to our house and passed a lawn sign with a drawing of my father. It was a cartoonish depiction of him trying to hoard more of Vernon's real estate. Enraged, she pulled over and yanked the sign out of the grass. When she got back home, she told Gene about it. He just laughed.

"You can't worry about what people think," he said. "This whole thing is going to blow over. It's not like we're the mafia laundering money up here. It's crazy. You'll see."

That is what some people would call misplaced optimism.

UNDER SUCH SCRUTINY, IT WOULD HAVE MADE SENSE TO SHOW CONtrition, lie low, and work to mollify the park's reputation for mayhem. It was 1983, the year of the insurance scandal, and probably a time to embrace gentler rides.

It was categorically not the best time to reintroduce the Cannonball Loop.

Like a pharmaceutical drug with serious side effects, the Loop's human trials had not been encouraging. Though it had been at the park for years, it had never been open to the public. Yet my father would always refuse to tear it down, believing he could crack the code of its deficiencies and turn it into a marquee attraction.

Merely by existing, it had become part of the park's identity. The very top of the Loop loomed over the skyline and was the first thing people saw upon entering. They would congregate around it, as if summoned by its insanity, craning their necks up at its formidable height and looking awestruck in the same way people must have looked at mushroom clouds during early atomic testing. Because it was always shuttered, rumors spread that someone had died riding it or had been stuck in it for hours. It became an urban legend, like the rumor that a combination of Coke and Pop Rocks would explode in your stomach.

"I don't think it should ever be open," Julie said. "Ever."

Julie did her best to temper some of my father's most radical impulses. She rarely succeeded, but it was important to her that she make the attempt. Her role was to make him question his decisions. My role was to do what I was told. I knew trying to talk him out of anything was a waste of air.

Predictably, he waved off her concerns, telling us changes had been made. From a distance, it looked no less terrifying than before. Up close, I saw where he had instructed the snowmakers to make a major modification. Someone had finally alerted him to the concept of centrifugal force and the need to shore up the loop at the bottom so that riders would remain tight to the slide as they moved around the circle. He had the entire thing cut apart and reassembled to shorten the loop, reducing its height. That significantly reduced the chances of a guest smashing their face into the opposing wall. This was progress.

There was more. A hatch had been installed on the bottom of the loop that could be opened to rescue anyone who failed to clear the circle and got trapped in the chute. It seemed to me that this didn't necessarily make the ride safer; it only meant that we could now fetch unconscious bodies more efficiently. To demonstrate, he dispatched Pee-Wee Lazier, a diminutive Lazier family member less than five feet tall. Pee-Wee was able to disappear into the exit easily, crawling in on all fours and coming out through the hatch to give a thumbs-up with an elfin hand.

My father gathered some of the employees around and began waving a one-hundred-dollar bill. He was in full carnival barker mode. "I need three people to clear the Cannonball Loop!" he announced.

Like impoverished urchins, ride attendants mobbed him, waving their arms in the air. A handful of greedy daredevils trudged up the steps and disappeared into the Lovecraftian structure. I braced for the familiar *tonk* sound of a passenger smashing their nose into the opposite wall of the Loop, but it did not come. Tightening the circle had worked. A state inspector signed off on the ride. We celebrated like bad students who had barely gotten a passing grade.

My father had Julie get the word out that the Loop was going to be one of the big attractions for the summer. Amid people calling for his head, we ran print notices declaring that the ride would soon open. It was therefore possible to read an article about the amusement park run by a maniac on one page of the newspaper and see an ad for that same park's giant death circle on the next. I suspected some editors did this on purpose.

The optimism proved to be short-lived. A few days later, during another test, a ride attendant came tumbling out with a bloody mouth.

A fall from the top of the loop wall to the bottom had knocked out his teeth. When two more attendants went down, they came out with bloody forearms. This seemed inexplicable. A snowmaker crawled inside the hatch and came back out nodding to himself.

"Here's your problem," he said. He held up two teeth. "These were stuck in the foam."

My father paced back and forth, clearly feeling he was closer than ever to rendering the ride consistently survivable. He asked some of the engineers orbiting the park for their input. Postmortems of the fateful test runs were prepared, in much the same way that NASA spent months exhaustively analyzing a failed shuttle mission. It soon became clear what we had been missing.

The attendants who had traveled through the Loop safely were of average height and weight. The young man who had misplaced his teeth was not. The engineers determined that there was a sweet spot for the kinds of bodies that could be shot through successfully. Too heavy and they'd pick up too much speed, risking disfigurement. Too light and they might not have the momentum to make it all the way around the knot, also risking disfigurement. The solution was to place a scale at the bottom of the stairs leading to the mouth of the slide. Attendants would weigh prospective riders and assess them for an ideal physique. We had to body-shame patrons to keep them from getting hurt.

"I'm sorry," an attendant might say. "But you are too skinny to have fun."

Every time an engineer told him it would be best to simply disassemble the Loop and scatter its parts to the four corners of the globe, my father would redouble his efforts. Telling him he could not do something, or that there was no solution, had no bearing on his behavior. That intractability empowered him to open the park and turn it into a success. He would not be defeated by a guest-eating tube.

"We're opening it," he said. "And that's that."

Before introducing the Loop to the public, my father made one conciliatory gesture. He had Father Boland come by and bless it. Other rides would receive his benediction, but the Loop was most in need of divine supervision.

THANKFULLY, THE LOOP DID NOT FALL UNDER THE RESPONSIBILITY of Water World. It was operated by the employees of the Alpine Center, who dutifully weighed guests at the bottom and shooed away children deemed too small to ride safely. Back from my sophomore year at Stanford, I returned to my post as head of aquatic attractions. Though I was concerned about my father's future, he had taught me never to let anything distract me from the task at hand. As if to reassure us, he acted as though nothing was troubling him.

He let this veneer of stoicism slip only once. He invited me to come watch a fireworks display from his office on the Fourth of July and told me to be there by nine o'clock. I got sidetracked by another brawl, this one involving a group of crazed bodybuilders tossing lifeguards into the water. Security and police brought the situation under control, but Laurie and I arrived at his office late, my work shirt half-torn from the conflict.

"I told you nine o'clock," he said. My mother and grandmother were there. So was Julie.

"Yeah, right, but—"

"Nine means nine," he said, irritated. "Your grandmother has been waiting an hour for you!"

He continued to dress me down like the marine captain he was, barking at a subordinate. Unable to articulate that the need to dampen a riot trumped the fireworks, I just slumped in a chair.

That holiday weekend marked the opening of something called

the Aqua Skoot, another of Ken Bailey's ideas. The Aqua Skoot was more pragmatic than the Bailey Ball in the sense that it had no potential to roll someone across a busy highway, but it still wasn't entirely safe. On the Skoot, guests sat on a cart that was propelled down a thirty-two-foot-high tower made of metal rollers, like the kind found in airport security. They would pick up speed at a steep, downward angle, which then flattened out and shot them across the water like a skipping stone.

The problem with the ride was that it was dependent on the patron holding their torso upright. If they messed around and leaned back too far, their head would slam into the metal lip near the last roller, which would effectively scalp them. The Skoot lacked the foam encasement that made rides like Surf Hill, while not necessarily idiot-proof, at least idiot-resistant. The overhang at the bottom also attracted bees, which built nests there. It was therefore possible to tear off part of your head, then attract stinging insects with your panicked flailing. In our new, ambiguously insured world, I had reservations about the Aqua Skoot.

As with most of the rides, the attendants knew how to go down safely (and to swim away from the bees). Not satisfied with this absence of peril, however, they began riding the carts standing up. Then one of them struck upon the idea to take the backboards used by the EMTs and use them in place of the carts. They would strap new employees to the boards before sending them down headfirst in what amounted to a demented initiation. Their bodies secured to a flat surface, the employees could easily become trapped once they hit the water, sinking until they unhooked themselves from the straps. Drowning was a distinct possibility.

"Did that occur to you?" I asked them. "Do you know how dumb this is?"

I may have called them shitheads, which was uncharacteristic of my otherwise affable management style. I had always struggled with the tension between being a participant and being responsible. Another time, I might have gone down the Skoot on a board with them. The insurance debacle had changed my mind-set. I told the EMTs to begin taking inventory of the backboards and not to let them be checked out like library books.

The Aqua Skoot remained open that summer. The Loop did not. Only a small number of people were able to clear it successfully. Bloody noses persisted. Grit collecting on the slide scratched up people's backs. Worse, the vinyl coating on the interior foam kept bubbling up from the force of bodies sliding across. It would absorb water, increasing friction and necessitating constant repairs. (Foam was our everlasting nightmare.) When people did make it through without incident, the ride had so disrupted their equilibrium that attendants would tell them to lie down for five seconds before attempting to get up. From a distance, it looked like the Loop was spitting people out unconscious.

We had also come to realize that body mass was not the only factor that made each trip different. A slick bathing suit could increase momentum. So could the addition of suntan lotion, as Smoke proved during his early runs. Each variable resulted in a different ride. As hard as we tried, there was simply no way to make skill a factor in success. Each rider was little more than dead weight subject to the laws of physics. Anything could happen to anyone at any time. Unlike the exploding Pop Rocks, the Loop was no myth. It was the closest any theme park ride had come to Russian roulette.

My father still refused to tear it down.

THE INSURANCE SCANDAL GREW MORE SERIOUS AFTER THAT SUM-mer. The SCI had no authority to fine or penalize my father, but they were more than willing to hand their findings over to the state's attorney general, who decided to pursue a criminal complaint. Since I was back at school for my junior year, I once again found out about this through Adam Tracy.

"Your dad's being indicted, man," he said. Adam was quickly becoming the Tom Brokaw of terrible shit happening to my family.

There were 122 counts in total. My father was the alleged "central figure" of a "complex and massive conspiracy to defraud various state agencies." The state's Division of Criminal Justice spent months putting their case together, ultimately listing more than two hundred acts of fraud, theft, and embezzlement, with some forgery thrown in. My father held a press conference denouncing all charges.

"I'm shocked," he said. "Shocked and outraged." He insisted none of what he was accused of doing could have hurt anyone but himself. He said he had taken a substantial risk in taking on the legal claims, painting a picture of significant responsibility rather than one of heedless neglect. Rather than express remorse, he called it a "brilliant insurance program." He did not believe he had done anything wrong. In a sense, he hadn't. Not exactly. Self-insurance grew to be an accepted form of coverage in the years to come, particularly for businesses seeking health benefits. But, in 1983, it was a bit too forward-thinking.

"Your dad is out there," Adam said.

It would be a long time before I learned that many of my Stanford friends referred to my father as "Uncle Vito" behind my back, believing he had ties to organized crime. I found this ridiculous. Still, he was looking at a high-profile trial, with prosecutors saying there were more than one hundred thousand documents to review. There was talk it could be the longest criminal trial in the state's history. If convicted, he was facing twelve years in prison. Admittedly, it was a little mobster-ish.

After Adam debriefed me, I called my mother. "Dad doing okay?" I asked.

"He works all the time," she said. This was my father's way. One of his attorneys later told me that some defendants facing trial and conviction roll themselves into a ball, essentially shutting down. My father never brooded, never got depressed. He also never risked an unoccupied moment, purchasing a limo and hiring a driver so he could work on the ride to and from his office at the park.

I knew he was downplaying the seriousness of the situation, but I decided to go along with it so I wouldn't upset my mother. I couldn't imagine my father going to prison. Then again, I couldn't imagine him going on trial for crimes committed in the course of running an amusement park, either.

"We're a law-abiding family," I told her. "They'll see that."

Someone began banging on our door. I hung up the phone and opened it. It was Jimmy. "The cops are looking for me," he said.

JIMMY HAD FOLLOWED ME TO STANFORD AND WAS A YEAR BEHIND. By this time, I had moved out of the dorm and into temporary student housing on campus known as the Trailers, which were pre-fabricated homes with three bedrooms. My roommates were Adam, Fred Buckley, and Eric Weintz. Since we each wanted our own space, we decided to build an addition. We got some lumber and assembled the room, a rather patchwork job that probably wouldn't have passed any kind of code inspection, but that somehow no school official noticed. The snowmakers would have been proud.

After a week or so of living together, I came to regret the arrangement. Adam, Fred, and Eric were all good guys, but as roommates, they were absolute pigs. Dirty dishes and a rancid bathroom were the least of it. Someone threw a bowling ball through a television, thinking it would be funny as a kind of avant-garde art piece. They tossed smelly clothes on the sofa and chairs. They left food to rot in the refrigerator. It was like living in the concession area of the park.

I tried berating and shaming them. I tried rotating weekly cleaning duty. I tried every trick I had learned managing the workers of my father's uninsured utopia. Nothing worked.

When two of my friends from Newark Academy, Evan and Gary, came to visit as prospective students, one of them accidentally dropped a beer bottle on the floor.

"Shit, Andy, sorry," Evan said, and started to pick up the shards. The floor was already covered in empty pizza boxes. I had seen enough. "Leave it," I said. I chugged the rest of my beer and threw the bottle against the wall, smashing it. By the end of the day, we had finished an entire case and broke each bottle into pieces. If they wanted to live in squalor, I wasn't going to interfere.

My passive-aggressive stunt coincided with spring break. I went off to visit Laurie, leaving the trailer full of broken glass, hoping the brutes would get the message. When I got back three weeks later, all three of them were there. Not only had the broken glass been left untouched, but someone had nailed a giant ham to the wall. My mother had sent it to me as a gift.

"That's my mother's ham!" I yelled.

It had arrived in my absence and was left to rot for two weeks in the sweltering unit. Someone had stuck every eating utensil we owned in it. It was crawling with maggots.

"This is disgusting," I told Adam. "We're living like animals."

He shrugged and continued to stare at a basketball game on the television that didn't have a bowling ball in it, absently flicking maggots from the sofa cushions.

Knowing they would not lift a finger, and unwilling to become their chambermaid, I remembered my father's fateful game of poker on the houseboat and decided to make an alternative proposal.

"We'll play poker," I said. "Whoever loses has to clean the fucking place up. Unconditionally and immediately."

This intrigued them. They agreed. I had never played with such concentration or ambition. Fred Buckley lost. We celebrated, relishing Fred's misfortune.

"I'm not cleaning anything," he said. "I'll hire a cleaning service."

When the crew arrived and saw it for themselves, they demanded a higher fee. Fred forked it over without hesitation. No price was too great to avoid having to deal with a biohazard.

All of this meant I was not in the mood to have Jimmy come to the door looking for sanctuary from authorities. I spent my summers taking care of lunatics. I didn't want to do it on my own time.

Jimmy sat down, popped open a beer, and explained. He had been riding my motorcycle with a friend of his named Ernie on the back. The two decided to take it off the slow-moving roadway and onto the pathway reserved for pedestrians and bicycles. He was going pretty fast when a campus cop pulled up behind him and signaled for him to pull over. These weren't rent-a-cops or mall police. Stanford had actual law enforcement patrolling the grounds. Jimmy either didn't know this or didn't care. He tore away from the blaring siren and forced the officer to give chase. It ended with Jimmy abandoning the bike and leaving Ernie to be interrogated by the cops. Ernie made it sound like he had been beaten and starved before giving up Jimmy's name. He later admitted they had just asked him politely.

I told Jimmy to live with me for a few weeks until they got tired of looking for him. We had one suspected criminal in the family, so why not two? My only condition for harboring a fugitive was that he pay me for the bike.

Jimmy's presence and the ambiguity of our father's fate caused me to regress into a park-oriented philosophy of life, one in which self-preservation was an afterthought. Without realizing it, I devolved into Aqua Skoot levels of recklessness.

One night, thunderclouds forming overhead, we brazenly swiped an entire half keg of beer from a fraternity house. We didn't want to go back to the Trailers, in case someone had seen us, so we made our way to an area not far from campus known as the Dish. This was an undeveloped parcel of land with several hundred acres of rolling hills and meadows and a paved walkway for hikers and joggers. At the top was a large satellite-communications dish made of metal trusses and mesh.

Rain and wind cut through our clothes, soaking us. Adam and I charged up a hill, trying not to let our knees buckle under the weight of the keg we were both holding. Jimmy and the others followed, panting. When the hill leveled off, Adam dropped the keg. I kept going.

I made it to the dish long before anyone else. The bottom was low to the ground. I reached up and gripped the edge, then pulled myself up and into its concave surface. Hunched over on all fours, I crawled along, careful not to lose my footing on the slick mesh. Jimmy yelled something. My foot gave, and I felt the toe of my sneaker lose its grip. But I didn't fall. I kept moving until I reached the upper edge of the dish. I balanced on the narrow lip as the rain came down and the wind blew my shirt collar against my chin.

Seeing I had made it, Jimmy and the others followed me up, keg in hand. We sat up there, letting the rain pelt us, balanced precariously between an amazing view and total disaster. I supposed I wanted to know, if only for a moment, what it felt like to be my father.

The Cliff Dive at Roaring Springs, my father's most ambitious project.

Chapter Ten

AFLOAT

"The cliff divers who jump near the Roaring Springs are simply customers jumping from rocks—not a diving board— into deep water. A bad landing and, well, it hurts."

Asbury Park Press, September 15, 1984

A father and his son were passing by a bubbling grotto. The man was perhaps in his forties, his son no more than ten. In the heat of the summer, the water rippled and danced, reflecting the light of the sun. It was early, and no one else was around.

The man knelt beside the water, cupping his hand and letting the liquid pool into his palm. He brought it up to his lips and sipped it, smiling at his boy. "Mmmm," he said. "That's terrific. That's nature, son." He dipped his hand in again, this time offering some of the water to his child, who lapped it up. Satisfied, the two went on their way.

The water was not natural. It was full of chlorine. It was also not particularly healthy. Topher, who told me this story, had seen a turd floating in it some days prior. But the aesthetic of it—the waterfall, the clear pool, the atmosphere—made it easy to mistake for the real thing. The grotto was part of what my father called Roaring Springs, a massive installation on the side of the mountain meant to mimic the swimming holes of years gone by. Twin lanes carried guests in inner tubes along powerful water currents resembling the strong flow of a wild river. Their thrills, while considerable, paled in comparison to those on offer at the Colorado River Ride, which sent guests in rafts down a rushing water chute and through underground tunnels that carried them into darkness then back out into the sun. There were ledges to jump from and giant water slides leading into pools. Stone steps led people around the area. Water fell from above and ran across the landscape, immersing visitors in the oasis.

Roaring Springs was my father's magnum opus. Instead of trying to beat nature at its own game, as he had with the Wave Pool, this would be an homage to its beauty and grandeur. It was his exclamation mark, a sprawling testimony to his imagination—like the Loop, he had doodled much of it on a napkin—and drive to offer something unique and different. Six Flags could have their roller coasters. We had a chunk of Americana. It was like an interactive Norman Rockwell painting.

Roaring Springs opened in the summer of 1984, just as the unresolved criminal charges delivered that spring were still looming large over my father's head. The timing was not coincidental. He refused to shy away from his mission to see the park expand. He was introducing the biggest, most expensive, most elaborate addition to the property in its history. It was as if he wanted to tell his adversaries that not a single bead of sweat was forming on his brow. It was also a great distraction, a project so enormous that he couldn't afford a moment to think about the possible consequences of his insurance missteps.

At the same time, the margin for error in our operation had

narrowed to a tightrope's width. Frenzied patrons acting foolishly would only give my father's critics further ammunition against him. I was determined to navigate the introduction of this attraction, and its new set of perils, with an eagle eye, flushing out potential hazards and making sure people understood their responsibility to take care of themselves. The eight acres of Roaring Springs could be a statement announcing that people had finally begun to interpret the park as my father intended, as a place where one could assume risk, but only if they chose to embrace it.

I wanted to go the entire summer without a catastrophe. I believed it was possible. Yes, I did.

ROARING SPRINGS WAS BORN OUT OF MY FATHER'S DAYS AS A BOY Scout. When he was younger, his troop took frequent day trips to a spot just south of the Delaware Water Gap. An expanse of land sitting on the New Jersey side of the Delaware River, it was known as Van Campens Glen, or, simply, the Glen. The Glen contained natural waterfalls with rock formations and all kinds of beautifully uneven terrain. Years later, he began taking us there. We would run and play and submerge ourselves in the refreshing, chilly water. It didn't seem as though we were in New Jersey but a place and a time far removed from the trappings of modern life.

Although locals knew of it, the Glen still felt like a family secret. It was located off a bumpy back road and marked by an abandoned farmhouse. From there, a series of narrow paths ran through the woods and led to a river that had cut through the rock, leaving a gorge. We followed the river a few hundred yards downstream to the main event: a waterfall that cascaded down into a small pool about the size of a hot tub. From there, the water went down a rock slab, creating a natural slide that fed into a pond. Overhead, cliffs jutted out from the rock. Older kids would leap from them, though it was treacherous due to the pool being such a small target. Our mother never allowed such attempts. This was a place to commune with nature. We were not to risk paralysis.

When we got older, and the trips grew less frequent, my father kept his memory of his many visits there. He wanted his own version, one where there would always be a new family set to arrive. He would augment it with slides and other attractions, a perfect amalgamation of nature and modern design.

The idea was clear in his head, but a doodle on a paper napkin would not be enough. He needed an artist's hand to execute it. That job fell to Roy Scovill, an engineer and mason who came recommended to him by mutual associates. When Roy came out to have a look, he saw that workers had already begun digging. Roy was confused. My father had told him there was not yet any finished design.

"What are you doing?" Roy asked.

"Figuring it out as we go," my father said, too impatient to wait until he finalized his plans.

Roy measured the topography of the area and began drawing to Gene's specifications. "A waterfall here, a slide here," he'd say, peering over Roy's shoulder. Roy drafted an enormous blueprint that married Gene's desires with the logistics of carving a set of pools into the side of a mountain. The slides, waterfalls, and cliffs would all have to look organic despite being crafted and shaped by concrete.

Roy could do all of this because he was a master of gunite, a cement-based material that could be sculpted to form slides and pitted bowls for inner tubes to tumble into. It came out of a spray nozzle at incredible velocity, so Roy worked on the mountain's face like an airbrush artist. He toiled in the expansive landscape of Gene's Glen day in and day out. We would often see him walking through the park covered in gunite, clean only around his mouth where his ventilator had been strapped.

I did not visit the site often, as I was preoccupied with my duties on rides that were already operational. We had just opened the Speed Slide, which plunged guests down a one-hundred-foot, near-vertical drop at speeds of up to forty-five miles per hour. Rich Szuch agreed to test it for the one-hundred-dollar bounty and reported free-falling for the first twenty feet before his body made contact with the surface. In response, I installed a guard over the slide that prevented riders from bouncing off. This had its own problems. Instead of stripping them of their clothing, the water pressure rocketed into their ass with such force it effectively gave them an enema. Patrons would exit the slide and run to the nearest bathroom.

When I was finally able to break away to see Roaring Springs taking shape, it was a wonder. A platform called the Cliff Dive allowed for a freestyle fall into water twenty feet below, where crowds would cheer jumpers on as they plummeted into what resembled a sunken Colosseum. The twenty-foot cliff was called Big Mo. You could also jump from a less formidable height of fifteen feet from a cliff dubbed Little Mo. If you found that too imposing, you could reach the large communal pool on an air slide that started above the cliffs and ran along the right of Big Mo. We called it an air slide because it ended abruptly, allowing guests to briefly soar before hitting the water.

To the far left of the Dive, lined up in a row, were entrances to three Rapids attractions, two of which would be ready in time for opening. River Ride 1 sent guests on inner tubes down a roaring circular track before moving them through an underground tunnel in the middle, a crater the workers began calling the Toilet Bowl. River Ride 2 was tame in comparison, funneling visitors down a bumpy and twisty path. The Colorado River Ride, which would open later, was the crescendo, sending people on a simulated rapids excursion in sturdy, green rubber rafts, the water pressure creating a powerful current. The grotto, peaceful in comparison, let people wade through the water without any specific mission in mind. Two relatively calm and wide slides let families descend into the pool together. A more conventional water slide ran through the entire area and partly underground. If you didn't want to be in motion, you could luxuriate among the waterfalls or on an island in the main pool that had a cave for privacy. All of it was fed by an elaborate water system designed by our pump man, Ron Dyno, who kept the plans for everything in his head. My father worried about Ron; without him, we'd never figure out how all the plumbing worked.

As the rides evolved, we needed to test them before a soft foam surface—courtesy of Dick Croul—could be applied. If the design wasn't quite right, we didn't want to have to tear the foam out. The rough gunite, however, would have ripped a rider's bare skin off in chunks. Invited to test the Toilet Bowl, I retrieved my hockey equipment from storage—it still stunk—and geared up before repeatedly going down the literal drain and letting workers know where they needed to modify turns. Without trying, I had matured into our only expert ride consultant, instinctively knowing when a design might induce trauma.

When the Department of Labor asked to evaluate the area, no doubt concerned about the whole insurance company debacle, my father waved them off. He explained that Roaring Springs was not a ride but an enormous swimming pool. They could no more inspect it or approve it than they could the Glen. Eager not to share responsibility for anything that might happen there, they backed off.

The cost of labor and materials must have been enormous, easily the park's biggest investment to date. My father visited the site more and more frequently, growing argumentative with Roy and interrupting his ranting only to pee from Little Mo. (My father could and would pee anywhere.) The prolonged planning and construction tested the limits of his patience. As the opening grew closer, he could no longer contain his excitement. As Roy applied the finishing coat of epoxy to areas needing to be waterproofed, my father ordered the pumps turned on. Water poured over the places that Roy had caulked before they had a chance to fully dry.

"Don't do that!" Roy said.

"It's open," my father said. "It's time."

OPENING DAY AT ROARING SPRINGS WENT WELL. ONLY TWO TOES were broken.

That summer was my last before graduation, and my father had promoted me to all-rides operations manager, meaning Roaring Springs fell under my purview. No longer would Water World be my only concern. Now I could be blamed for almost anything that happened in the park.

For the Cliff Dive, I pulled some of the best lifeguards over from the Wave Pool. Smoke, who was by then a manager in Water World, helped me maintain a balance of competent guards between the two areas. The water at Roaring Springs was the deepest in the park, fifteen feet with a dark bottom that made it difficult to see what was going on beneath the surface. I needed workers with experience under pressure and the ability to navigate the pools like Navy SEALs, able to dive and swim to the appropriate depth in case someone went under.

The water was not the only area of concern. In his desire for a natural aesthetic, Gene refused to allow handrails along the paths. "No railings in nature," he said. Only a few loose ropes strung along poles aided people in keeping their balance.

Thanks to promotional efforts in newspapers and on the radio, the line to get into Roaring Springs hugged the perimeter of the area, stretching hundreds of people long. Once they entered, the guests sprinted in all directions, not yet familiar with the terrain we had laid out. The steps were either rocks or poured concrete shaped to look like rocks—all slip hazards, particularly for people running from one attraction to the next in bare, wet feet. It was easy to stub a toe or stumble. One walkway had a stream running through it and a small hole that allowed light and water to drip down into one of the underground tunnels. Catching themselves in the hole, two people broke a toe. The EMTs dutifully weaved in between the crowds to assist the fallen and carry them away.

My hopes of a spotless record had evaporated on the opening weekend. It was one of the few times I can remember being uncontrollably livid with my father. Not confused, or frustrated, but boiling with anger at his stubborn insistence and myopia. I stormed into his office.

"You cannot leave a hole in the middle of a walkway!" I shouted. "People are getting hurt. What is wrong with you?"

"We'll take care of it," he said. From his office, he could see the throngs of people flocking toward the area. He saw only their joy.

"When?" I said.

"When things settle down." To shut off the water and seal off areas on opening day was unthinkable.

I went back, picked up a rock, and wedged it into the hole.

From the main path, I could see people stepping to the precipice of the Cliff Dive for the first time. They sometimes leapt without looking, screaming as they plunged an unexpected twenty feet. Similar shrieks came from the air slide, where people tumbled down the snaking channels without knowing how far they'd go or how deep the water would be when they touched down. They were accustomed to slides emptying into shallow pools they could stand in, not the deep pools here. We put a sign up warning people the Dive was for "expert swimmers only," an over-exaggeration we hoped would discourage people who could not swim at all. Unfortunately, we had many patrons who didn't speak or read English. Although several of our radio spots targeted a Spanish-speaking audience, we had no Spanish-language signs, an inexplicable oversight. As a result, some guests didn't understand the warnings. Others, like the gold-chain-bedecked teenagers, knew full well what they were doing, launching themselves off the Dive and trying to land directly on the bobbing heads of their friends.

Not everyone was so reckless. Some people would approach the edge and look down, hesitant. The hundreds of people gathered below would shout encouragement. You could see the potential diver's courage ebb and flow as they shuffled back and forth, deciding whether to jump or not. When someone walked away, the heckling was unmerciful.

"Chickenshit!" they'd roar. "Pussy!" To show weakness in Action Park was to invite mass scorn and a sense of shame that followed you all the way out to the parking lot.

When the Colorado River Ride opened, crazed guests, unsuccessful in their attempt to maim a buddy at the Cliff Dive, opted to stuff three or four people in a raft. With their extra mass and a current fueled by three huge water pipes, they rocketed down into a cave, where water sprayers were waiting to douse them. Emerging from the darkness, a sharp turn nearly capsized them. As if this was somehow not perilous enough, people decided to begin jumping from one raft to another. They often missed, knocking their heads, elbows, or knees on the concrete. (We never covered it in foam, foolishly believing people would remain in the rafts.)

When vessels abandoned by their occupants spilled out at the end of the ride, they became bouncing projectiles, plunging down on top of people who had already been emptied into the water. Attendants who were supposed to collect the rafts would often be immersed in their portable radios or asleep, oblivious to the pileup until people began shouting profanities at them.

We had one incident that weekend which terrified all of us. In the Toilet Bowl, guests on inner tubes would descend into a hole in the middle and shoot through a tube underground. The tube was lined with the unpredictable foam, which soon began to rip, jutting out and creating a space big enough for a body to become lodged inside. The tear caused a human clog, the force of thousands of gallons of water wedging people in place between the foam and tube. We scrambled to turn the water off, then listened as the riders screamed at us, complaining they had nearly drowned in the congestion of bodies. Fortunately, no one was hurt.

I went back to the condo that weekend feeling pretty good about two broken toes.

That feeling wouldn't last.

THE SEASON HAD STARTED WITH A LOT OF RAIN. IT AFFECTED ATtendance, particularly in Motor World, which we often had to close in inclement weather. Other parks suffered as well. But because of Roaring Springs, total attendance increased 15 percent over the previous year, setting another record. My father was right about people wanting to experience the simplicity of a swimming hole. It was both big and intimate at the same time, and the area played host to a constant flow of humanity that only kept growing. This was why, despite my optimism, I knew a call would come.

It happened late in August, weeks after Roaring Springs had opened. I was headed for lunch when the walkie-talkie on my hip crackled. "Code red at the Roaring Springs air slide," a voice said. "Code red." Code yellow was a broken bone or a rabid animal attacking guests. Code red was something worse. It meant a life-or-death situation.

I turned my bike around and gunned the engine until I reached the entrance to Roaring Springs. The pool under the air slide and Cliff Dive had been cleared, and lifeguards were in the water in a search-and-rescue formation. They would line up, dive down, then come back to the surface before lining up a little farther over and going down again. Two EMTs stood by, an empty backboard propped up between them. I climbed down and saw Smoke emerge from the water, shaking his head.

"Someone went down," he said. "He came off the slide. We saw him go under, but we can't find him."

My hope was that it was yet another episode of a guy playing the rescue game, hitting the water and then swimming underneath the surface so he could emerge somewhere out of sight to fool the lifeguards into thinking he had drowned. That happened in the Wave Pool constantly. Yet the lifeguards didn't seem convinced that was the case here. There was real concern in their eyes.

I pulled off my shirt and set down my radio. The water was murky, thick with body oil and suntan lotion. I plunged deep beneath the surface, the dark gunite on the bottom making it difficult to see anything. I skimmed along, letting my fingers trace the concrete and hoping I wouldn't brush up against anything unexpected. I swam in a zigzag pattern, overlapping my own path. I wanted to be sure.

I looked to my left, where only a few feet remained before the wall.

He's probably splashing around in one of the grottos right now, I thought, *laughing at the panicking attendants.*

I swam toward the wall. Nothing.

Kids do this all the time. This will turn out to be a joke.

Satisfied, I began to turn around. I would find the offender and banish him permanently. I would sit with the guys and drink beers, and we would all shake our heads at how hard our hearts had been beating. We'd tell the story at the mountaintop party, and it would be a good one.

Then I saw him.

He was curled up along the back wall. His body was listless but moving slightly, animated by the water current. I swam toward the figure, hoping I would notice some indication he was alive. Between the black bottom and the murky water, he was hard to see. Only the red of his bathing suit stood out. I reached for him, grabbing a forearm and propelling myself upward. Breaching the surface, his shoulder met mine, and I tucked my left arm under his armpits, signaling the lifeguards with my free arm.

"Here," I said, spitting water as it sloshed against my chin. "Over here."

They hit the water, freeing his weight from my arms. They rushed him toward the EMTs, who started CPR immediately, pumping his chest as they carried him out on the backboard. I was doubled over, exhausted, sucking gulps of air into my lungs that I felt guilty for taking. I kept hoping to see his chest rise, to see him coughing out water.

Come on, I mouthed. *Come on.*

The EMTs loaded him onto a stretcher and then placed him on one of the golf carts to be rushed away. I asked one of them if he had a pulse. She shook her head.

WHEN SOMETHING TRAUMATIC HAPPENS ON A JOB WITH A POTEN-tial for tragedy, workers are usually afforded some kind of counseling. In law enforcement, it's mandated. You can't go back out on the street without processing a life you either took or failed to save. No one thinks of these things for theme-park employees.

The lifeguards on duty that day were gutted, but no one asked for time off. The drowning happened late in the season, and they figured it was better to just stick it out through Labor Day. Plus, there weren't any replacements. I could never simply hire a lifeguard who had been toiling at the community pool and expect them to last a day at either Roaring Springs or the Wave Pool. Setting aside time for grief could open up the potential for another tragedy, and everyone knew it.

I hovered around the lifeguards, offering reassurances that it wasn't their fault. The press coverage made that difficult. It ran the usual gauntlet of criticism. The accusation that we were somehow flippant about safety in deep bodies of water was especially frustrating. There were lazy and lackadaisical employees at some of the rides—just like there are slothful, doughnut-eating cops—but our lifeguards were like a SWAT unit. The park spit out underperformers.

"Don't read that stuff," I told Smoke, who was uncharacteristically sullen. "They have no idea what it takes to do this job."

He nodded his head. "Donald DePass," he said. "That was his name. Donald DePass."

Officials looking into the drowning believed the twenty-year-old DePass had inhaled water when he hit the pool. Guests fell ten feet from the lip of the air slide, and the impact could have taken him by surprise. It was just a theory, though. There was no more information available. In Smoke and the others, I saw the same agony over ambiguity that had upset my father with the Kayak accident. We needed to know the how and the why, but those questions were impossible to answer. As far as his family knew, Donald DePass could swim. Tens of thousands of people had gone down the air slide without incident. There was no reason he shouldn't have been able to resurface. He just didn't.

I kept waiting to have dreams of seeing his red shorts in the water, of touching his lifeless forearm and surfacing with him, bracing for the shocked faces of the people watching nearby, but I didn't. I couldn't take time off. I discussed it with no one aside from the guards. It felt as though someone else had retrieved him. I suppose it was necessary compartmentalization.

I told my father that we needed to drain the pool at the end of the air slide and the Cliff Dive and paint the bottom white instead of black to make people more visible to the lifeguards. I didn't bother asking him to do it immediately, though I would have preferred that. It would take a week, at minimum, and there was no chance he would shutter the area for that long so close to the end of the season.

He didn't challenge me as he normally would. He just nodded.

We braced for the inevitable lawsuit. Word eventually came down that the DePass family would not sue us for negligence. They were Jehovah's Witnesses. For them, Donald's drowning had been God's will.

We put up more warning signs around the park, hoping to dissuade people from taking uneducated risks. At the air slide in Roaring Springs, we tasked employees with broadcasting instructions to those in line. "You must know how to swim," they blared. "This slide empties into a large, deep pool. You must use caution."

At the Wave Pool, a banner read: WAVES CAN BE TIRING. For rides with long lines, we played safety notices on cassette tape or through megaphones.

The following week, I saw someone reading the EXPERT SWIMMERS ONLY notice near the Cliff Dive. He was wearing a tank top, sandals, and a bracelet with "CFS" scrawled on it. I watched as he stuck his gum on the sign and jumped off and out of sight.

"How deep is the water here?" someone else asked me at the Wave Pool.

"Ten feet on this end," I said, pointing to the deeper portion.

The man looked at me for a moment. "How deep is ten feet?" he said.

I EXPECTED THE NEWSPAPERS TO DWELL ON THE DEPASS ACCIDENT, but they quickly lost interest. That was probably because the state's legal case against my father was growing more salacious. It now included more of the office staff, including his secretary, Mary Meyers, a bookkeeper named Debra Evers, and Michael Teschner, a German real estate broker from Aspen who had facilitated some land deals for my father. Evers and Teschner had signed documents presenting them as officers of London and World. Gene felt terrible that others had been caught up in his divisive insurance strategy and hired lawyers to represent them. I doubt any of them had a complete understanding of what was going on. As with many of his operations, he doled out information piecemeal.

Everyone pleaded innocent, including my father. Some members of the county legislature came to his defense, saying the attorney general was looking to make a name for himself. Eventually, Meyers, Evers, and Teschner entered what was known as New Jersey's Pretrial Intervention Program, designed to save the state the cost of a trial for first-time offenders, and accepted supervised probation for their involvement. Prosecutors left Gene to dangle.

It was hard to conceptualize the possibility of my father going to prison. In some sense, I felt that what amounted to a foolish bit of hubris was probably deserving of a fine but not incarceration, particularly given the hall passes doled out for more serious white-collar crimes. His insurance scheme had not hurt anyone. There was grumbling that the state would not have permitted some of the rides to open had he not presented false proof of insurance, but that didn't hold up to scrutiny. Had he not invented London and World, the park would have been exactly the same, only with my father begrudgingly enlisting an insurance company to oversee its potential liabilities.

My mother seemed unaffected by it all, though we knew she was troubled. I think she had to believe, as we all did, that if he had been clever enough to operate his own insurance company for six years, he was likely clever enough to escape any serious reprimand for it. We wanted to believe the rabbit was going to appear. What none of us wanted to say was that he had lit so many fires without getting burned that the law of averages could kick in at any moment. This seemed like a plausible time for that to happen.

I left for California and my senior year that fall having no idea whether I'd be called back to see him on trial. I woke up some days thinking Adam Tracy would shove a paper in front of my face, a sensational headline blaring across its front page:

EVIL DEVELOPER SENTENCED
TO 20 YEARS OF HARD LABOR
Glen Smocovich named new Action Park operator

There was no time to dwell. I focused on my classes. I wrote letters to Laurie, whom I continued to see on breaks, and who lifted my spirits by telling me that the state prison system wouldn't want to deal with my father, either. Again dressed as an elite thug, the only costume I had, I celebrated Halloween by making a tremendous amount of noise with my friends during a party at a sorority house. The din prompted one student to open her dorm-room door and begin screaming for silence. She took one look at the prop pipe in my hand and vanished. Apparently, I was too convincing a criminal. Like father, like son.

One weekend, we rented a Winnebago so we could drive to the

Rose Bowl in Los Angeles to watch Fred Buckley play his first game as Stanford's starting quarterback in a big showdown against UCLA. Arriving on Friday, we parked the Winnebago at a friend's house and split up, which proved problematic when I promptly got lost. At a bar, I spotted Jim Cohn, a friend from my freshman year who happened to be the Stanford band's drum major and head baton-twirler. Confident Jim could get me to where he was staying, I proceeded to drink more beers. Oblivion followed.

When I woke up, I was staring at rafters. Sitting up, I realized I was on the bare, hardwood floor of a gymnasium. All around me were dozing bodies. Seeing Jim, I waved him over.

"Where are we?" I said.

"You drank a lot, huh?" Jim said.

This was apparently where the band was staying: UCLA's basketball court. I had no money and my friends had my ticket to the game. I pondered what my father might do under such circumstances. Normally, I would do the opposite, but on this occasion, his brand of impulsive behavior seemed appropriate.

I asked Jim for a band uniform and a set of cymbals. After following the band out to the field and trying to march in formation, I managed to sprint for the bleachers and spent the entire first half looking for my friends. When I finally found them, I enthusiastically recounted my exploits, expecting them to be impressed.

"Haven't you been here the whole time?" Adam said.

"You're dressed like an idiot," Eric said.

A few weeks later, I got a call from Julie. I started to tell her about the marching band, but she interrupted me.

"Well," she said. "Things are pretty much finished."

"That means what?" I said.

"He entered pretrial intervention," Julie said. "He's getting three years of probation."

"That's great news," I said.

"But," she said.

"But?"

"There's a two-hundred-forty-thousand-dollar fine."

Two hundred forty thousand dollars was a lot of money for a theme-park operator who constantly reinvested his profits in new rides and paid out guests who got mangled on them, but it still seemed like he had gotten off easy. My father pleaded guilty to a number of charges, including submitting false documents to the state, doing business as an unauthorized insurance company, and using a corporation for criminal activity. He refused to plead guilty to fraud because, he said, he did not defraud anyone. The state admitted that he hadn't gained anything personally out of the scheme. The judge acknowledged that Gene had no prior criminal history and had not caused harm to anyone. My father emerged from the courtroom a happy man. "Someone tried to make a mountain out of a Mulvihill," he said to the gathered throng of reporters. I wished his lawyer knew better than to let him near a microphone.

"So it's all over," I said.

"Yeah," Julie said. "But."

"But what?"

"One of the terms of the agreement is that he can't operate the resort. He has to give it up."

"What do you mean, give it up?"

"He cannot operate the resort. The state wants him out."

"Can they do that?"

"They're doing it," she said.

The state owned much of the land the park was on. Like any landowner, they could oust a tenant for violating the terms of their agreement. It was not all of the park, but a crucial stretch that encompassed many of the ski slopes, the lift chairs, the Alpine, and the entire top of the mountain. They wanted an independent party to operate the resort and park, paying rent to both Gene and the state. If he refused, they would pull the lease entirely. Laurie was right. New Jersey simply did not want to deal with Gene Mulvihill anymore.

The state was effectively evicting Action Park.

German brewmaster Otto Binding and his beer-guzzling dog, Daisy.

Chapter Eleven

THE DRAFT

"A fire caused an estimated $100,000 in damages to a water slide ride at Vernon Valley Action Park Wednesday, but injured no one, park officials said. Park spokeswoman Julie Mulvihill said the fire started when a hot piece of metal from a welder's torch dropped from the 100-foot slide tower and ignited some bales of hay beneath it, setting a year-old fiberglass water slide ablaze."

Daily Record, May 24, 1985

For four years, I had been fortunate enough to attend one of the best universities in the country. I was taught by world-class professors, advised by a future Secretary of State, rubbed shoulders with elite athletes, and immersed myself in an unfamiliar culture. I was exposed to new ideas. I felt worldly.

I couldn't make the graduation ceremony. I was needed at a barely legal amusement park.

Normally, I returned to a hive of commotion, with new attractions erupting out of the ground. This time things seemed to have shifted into a lower gear. The Cannonball Loop, having briefly reopened, was shuttered again. In an unprecedented decision, the Carnival and Amusement Ride Safety Advisory Board urged the Department of Labor to shut it down, declaring it too unpredictable. It was the first time the state had taken such a measure.

Passing the molten tower of wood and fiberglass that used to be our Speed Slide, I approached Julie and asked her what was going on. I saw no new attractions, just repurposed ones. She explained that the park was adding relatively few rides this year because money was scarce.

Gene's reputation, never unblemished under the best of circumstances, was tarnished further by his pretrial intervention. Though he never had to serve a day in prison, pleading guilty meant he was a convicted criminal. While on probation, he could no longer vote in elections. (His record would eventually be expunged, but not until years later.) His friends remained his friends, but his professional pursuits were another story. Investors curious about a possible ride or land development would hear his name and bolt.

Bob Brennan tried to make the situation palatable. Bob had no qualms about associating with Gene and continued to celebrate Action Park and Great American Recreation in his First Jersey Securities stock offerings using creative language. Following the conviction, First Jersey wrote that GAR was under "imaginative leadership." Bob was a loyal friend.

I knew my father was relieved, but the looming eviction felt oppressive. The state had softened its stance somewhat, no longer insisting he relinquish control as operator, but was now insisting he appoint a "fiscal agent"—a glorified babysitter—to oversee his accounting. I had no idea if this would be the last summer Action Park was in operation.

Yet my father forged on, smiling and upbeat, waving off the state's aggression like a martial-arts master deftly sidestepping a mugger. It was as if he knew something the rest of us did not. It turned out, he did have money to spend, obtained by the superior salesmanship of the sharks on Brennan's team, by one of Gene's former stockbrokers named Owen Davis, and by other investors who still believed in him. His latest investment opportunity, he argued, would provide an immediate return.

He was able to do this because the money was not for a ride, which had caused so many of his recent problems.

Instead, he was going to open an authentic German brewery at the park.

MY FATHER'S FASCINATION WITH GERMANY WAS THE STUFF OF FAMily legend. His mother was 50 percent German. In college, at Lehigh, he had frequented a bar overflowing with Germans. He went there to unwind, hoisting thick lagers in glasses so heavy your wrists ached if you held them up long enough.

When he started traveling to seek out rides, he made detours to Oktoberfest, the annual festival in Munich celebrating its history of beer brewed to exacting standards. He spoke of how the festival ignited something in him and how much he wanted to host something similar in New Jersey. While anyone could throw a German-themed festival, it was virtually impossible to do it with authenticity. He didn't want tents that looked like the tents the Germans used. He wanted their *exact* festival tents. He didn't want folding chairs. He wanted the same wide benches that brought people in tight, thighs and shoulders rubbing together. He wanted pretzels made by a German baker using German flour. Instead of importing it, he wanted beer brewed on the spot and served in glass steins instead of paper cups. Guests would gulp down the authentic beer to satisfy their thirst, dance to an authentic German band, and gorge on succulent roasted chickens. Like the Glen, Oktoberfest was an experience that he didn't want to keep to himself. He wanted to reproduce it for the masses.

We were already one of the biggest beverage dealers in the state. Pepsi, which sponsored us, ran like water at Action Park. That deal had been in place for years, and it wound up being highly favorable when Coca-Cola introduced the notoriously unpopular New Coke that summer. Pepsi heckled Coke incessantly over its failure, and theme parks that served Coke hung their heads in shame throughout 1985.

Normally, you couldn't screw up serving soda. Beer was another matter. We got ours from local distributors, and it had the watery flavor of a baseball-stadium offering. Guests drank it out of necessity in the summer heat. It wasn't awful, but there was nothing unique about it. A brewery would change that.

Michael Teschner, the real estate broker from Aspen caught up in the London and World saga, was a German national who was a friend to the entire family. He agreed to take Gene over to Germany and introduce him to the owners of a brewery that they could disassemble and ship over wholesale. Gene arrived after flying all night, got in the sauna, and then drank a few beers during the meeting with the brewery owners. Because of the sauna, the brew went right to his head, and he did most of the negotiating while slightly drunk.

Fortunately, German brewery owners don't talk business while totally sober, either. With Teschner's help, he was able to negotiate for every delicate copper instrument, vat, and utensil; they even threw in a bakery for good measure. He insisted that the brewmaster, a sixty-eight-year-old German named Otto Binding, come to New Jersey to oversee the installation and early operations. Part of a family of brewers, Otto had fifty years of experience and was said to have the equivalent of a bachelor's degree in brewing. He was also rumored to have been Adolf Hitler's personal brewmaster. Otto consented, but only if his dog, a twelve-year-old dachshund named Daisy, could accompany him.

My father shipped everything. The brewery. Otto. Otto's daughter, Ursula, and her husband, who were both bakers. The bakery. The dog.

Slowly, the facility began to take shape on a small plot of land in Cobblestone Village. Wooden fermentation barrels nestled next to manufacturing equipment that was the zenith of German precision. The stainless-steel vats were ten feet wide and twenty feet tall. The oak kegs were constructed from Czechoslovakian wood aged exactly eight years. The barley and hops were organic and imported from Europe. The only domestic component was the water. We were effectively building one of the first microbreweries in the country.

I was of two minds about this development. On one hand, having a brewery at work promised to be a luxury few recent college graduates would ever enjoy. I would never run out of beer, day or night. On the other hand, consumption of beer in the park had traditionally led to nothing less than anarchy. More than one reporter had observed the contradiction in erecting participatory rides, which required a fair amount of manual dexterity and good judgment, and serving beer, which stripped both of those things away. It was like a car dealership offering you drinks before a test drive. However, alcohol was mandatory at a theme park. A policy of dry beverage stands would certainly put us out of business.

We spent time watching Otto as he readied the facility, the flow of hops and yeast mixed and heated with the utmost care. He sported his lederhosen, well-worn and stained from his efforts, day in and day out. He also sampled his wares regularly, checking the beer as it completed the various stages of production. He sometimes offered a little to Daisy, who lapped it up enthusiastically and would often whine when she could not imbibe.

Otto was fanatical about the operation and conditions of the area. Everything had to be in line with *Reinheitsgebot,* the strict standard of German purity that made no allowances for mistakes. If someone entered, he would yell at them to take their shoes off. "Keine schuhe!" he said. "Keine schuhe!" Otto spoke almost no English, but his intent was understood. There would be no contamination of his operation. Not even Daisy was admitted entrance. It was the cleanest area in the park by a wide margin.

Otto was also unaccustomed to my father's schedule, which typically involved getting an idea and then having it ready in a matter of weeks or days. Otto could not be hurried. He shook his head and wagged a finger, "Noch nicht," he said, the words wafting through a plume of the garlic bulbs he ate for breakfast. "Noch nicht." Not yet. Unlike ales, which could ferment and be ready in a matter of days, Otto's lager took six weeks or more, and there was risk it might not be ready in time for the festivals later in the summer. Knowing this, Gene had gotten him started early, even before the glass in the building's windows had been installed. At night, bats flew in the openings, driving Otto into a rage. He feared their droppings would ruin the brews.

My father dispatched Jimmy to work in the brewery, expecting him to cleanse his palate of cheap American swill and to shadow Otto and an assistant named Stefan, who would take over once Otto left to go back to Germany. Jimmy brought along a helper, a friend of his named Jim Bineau. At the beginning of that summer, Jim weighed no more than one hundred and fifty pounds. By the end, he was easily two hundred. One glass of Otto's beer was as substantial as a small meal.

While he made a lighter lager, Otto mostly served up a thick, dark brew that made Budweiser look and taste like water. It felt like a beverage you should hoist up before pillaging a village on a horse. My father dubbed it Old World Classic Beer, prepared in the Vernon Valley Brauhaus. He planned an extensive Oktoberfest homage, which would feature live music and allow people to experience an authentic German festival.

For weeks, I regularly walked past the brewery, wondering when Otto would be ready to offer a first taste to those outside his staff. When he finally was, some calamity or another pulled me away, and I missed it. Once I was finally free, I ran over and caught up with Jim Bineau, who motioned me inside and poured me a glass. I brought it to my lips and took a sip. It was unbelievable, smooth but not too sweet. My father had succeeded. The *Reinheitsgebot* was alive and well in New Jersey.

Suddenly, Otto burst in. "Nein!" he screamed. "Nein!" I thought he was upset that I had tasted his creation without permission. He pointed at the ground. I was still wearing shoes.

AS THE BREWERY RAMPED UP OPERATIONS, THE EMPLOYEE SHORT-age that had long plagued the park grew considerably worse. We had exhausted our supply of laborers from the area high schools, where we had held employment drives. Statewide, a prospering economy meant there were more seasonal employment opportunities than seasonal employees. We tried wage increases and extoled the virtues of working outdoors. It made no difference. We still had holes in our schedule and a lack of maintenance workers. Garbage began to rise in the bins, spilling over onto the walkways.

The problem grew so bad that, in a moment of desperation and out of loyalty to a friend, I agreed to Smoke's suggestion to set up a glorified night club on-site to keep employees happy, a kind of all-season-long Water World party. This quickly devolved into underage workers sipping fruit-flavored alcoholic drinks and watching wet T-shirt contests. I had to hire bouncers to keep them out.

My father's solution to the employee shortage was more pragmatic. He called a friend of his named Robert Pickett, who was a board member of an organization that provided educational and employment opportunities for low-income kids in Newark. Normally, no one from Newark would entertain the idea of employment at our property because of the lengthy commute each way. Yet there was an entire population of underprivileged teenagers there who were using their idle time to get themselves in trouble. What if, my father proposed, he gave those kids jobs at the park and arranged for a bus to take them there and back?

Pickett loved the idea. So did Kenneth Gibson, Newark's mayor. Gibson held a press conference to announce the plan and his office was soon deluged with applications from teenagers. The city got four hundred requests and chose fifty to fill the vacancies in our maintenance department. The first day, the new employees boarded a bus at 10:30 in the morning, arrived at the park at noon, and then promptly disappeared out of sight.

As the all-rides operations manager, I was also in charge of maintenance. My radio was always buzzing with pleas to come and collect garbage or address a messy bathroom. Expecting the Newark kids to answer the radio when I needed to dispatch a crew, I was met with silence. Later that day, when I decided to break for a basketball game—a common activity to ease the stress of a fourteen-hour workday—I noticed they were all on the court.

"What are you doing?" I said.

"Playing basketball," one said.

"You guys gotta work," I said.

"What're you doing?" One of them nodded at the basketball stuck under my arm.

"You never mind what I'm doing," I said, suddenly on the defensive.

Later, when I was able to corner them and insist that they perform their duties, I handed them each a dustpan and a broom. They held them upside down, feigning ignorance.

"We don't know how this is supposed to work," one said, smacking it against the ground.

"It's a kick pan," I said. "You sweep debris into it."

"Hmmm," he said, letting the chute at the bottom dangle from its hinge. "I think this one is broken."

"Let me show you," I said, and began sweeping trash into the pan. When I looked up, they were gone. The Newark kids were far from dumb. While many of them worked diligently, others knew this well-publicized work program meant job security even if they spent the entire day on rides. In retrospect, I didn't see what else you could expect when you bused kids into an amusement park.

One morning, Topher arrived in Roaring Springs to see a small platoon of the Newark workers marveling at the Colorado River Ride. They wanted to ride it while the park was still empty.

"Fine," Topher said. "But you cannot chain yourselves together on the tubes." Chaining was the great thrill and danger of the ride, and one we had increasingly discouraged. It involved guests linking the tubes together and traveling as one unit, with the people at the end of the line breaking off from the built-up force of the chain and soaring into the woods. This tactic had resulted in a serious knee injury for one of our employees, Wendy Towe, who had lost her athletic scholarship as a result.

Topher told them the woeful story of Wendy Towe to scare them straight. They nodded.

When Topher returned, the kids had done exactly what he had told them not to do. When the last kid in the chain let go, he shot off and cleared the wall, slung into the sky like a clay pigeon. Landing in rocks, he let out a yelp. He was taken to Dr. DeLuca's urgent-care clinic, where he received several stitches to his testicles.

With the Newark experiment flailing, we met to see how to salvage our workforce.

"The answer is foreign labor," my father said.

The Irish and French, he explained, were using travel subsidies from the state to transport workers over to the United States to fill employment gaps. They were effectively foreign-exchange students, except they were finished with school and wouldn't have to rush back to class in the fall. Soon, he said, a plane would be depositing dozens of them in New Jersey, practically air-dropping them right into the park. They would stay in an area known as the Swamp, where we could repurpose a number of older and ramshackle houses, whose only current residents were snakes, as employee dorms.

I was not sure exactly what to expect of these workers. New Jersey seemed like a long way to come for a job. Smoke imagined they might be IRA extremists on the run. The first worker I met was a charming eighteen-year-old named Ann Murphy, who smiled when she spoke and seemed delighted to be there. Her brother, Liam, had a kind face. I told Smoke I could not imagine either one had ever planted a bomb for political purposes.

Collectively, the Irish contingent may have been the best thing ever to happen to us. They had no family in New Jersey and no need to work specific hours because of school or personal obligations. They all happily toiled for fifty or sixty hours a week. The park became their entire life, and its influence was felt immediately. Late for work one day, Liam borrowed a roommate's car and sped down Route 94. Misjudging a turn, he managed to flip it completely upside down. Unhurt, he climbed out and walked the rest of the way to the park. The police eventually knocked on his door and arrested him for leaving the scene of a crime. Liam had no concept of such an offense.

"In Ireland, we call that common sense," he said.

Ellen, by now my sister-in-law, got her father, the state trooper, to intervene, saving Liam from deportation.

We marshaled the Irish forces at a crucial time, as they helped cover the gaps in our scheduling sheets, but we were still short. Fortunately, I had set into motion a contingency plan. Before graduating, I mentioned to my Stanford friends there would likely be summer openings at the park. Openings where they could run a department.

I did not tell them the department was sanitation.

BECAUSE MOST OF MY COLLEGE FRIENDS WERE FROM THE EAST Coast, it wasn't hard to persuade them to make the drive to see Action Park, which I had spent many a night portraying as a wonderland. I promised them free housing and unlimited access to the brewery that would soon be open.

Like rats to cheese, Adam Tracy, Phil Altinger, Brett Saderberg, Rob West, Doug Krouse, and Steve Sokil all made the trip, trickling in steadily over a period of weeks. For years, I had painted pictures in their heads of the park and its casual hedonism. After setting them up in vacant condos, I ushered Brett and Phil outside and showed them a large truck used to collect the garbage.

Phil fired up the truck, a relic from the ski operation, and headed off with Brett. I don't think a whole day passed before the stench of the job and the searing heat caused them to come undone. Short-tempered Phil took offense to something Brett said and the two got into a fistfight, which resulted in Phil rubbing Brett's face against a carpeted floor until his skin began to slough off. This prompted people to ask Brett if he had been on the Alpine. Their undoing forced me to move Adam to garbage along with Benji Bressler, my friend from high school who had recently popped up looking for work.

"You're going to be here," I said.

"What?" Adam said. "I thought you said we'd be in quality control."

"This is quality control," I said.

"Are those maggots?" Benji asked, peering into the back of the truck.

"The important thing to remember is the beer," I said. "Now please start collecting the trash."

Not long after Benji started, he radioed me and asked to switch to a private channel.

"There's . . . severed . . . head . . . fuck . . . Andy," he said, the radio squawking and erasing words.

"Please repeat. Over," I said.

"There's a fucking severed deer head over here!" Adam said, interrupting. "This is disgusting!"

There was deer hunting on the mountain. I assumed someone made off with a kill and left part of it behind. Regardless, Adam was the same man who had nailed my mother's ham to a wall and left it to rot. He had waived his right to be outraged. "Collect and return to base," I said. "Collect and return to base."

Retrieval was just one part of the job. Disposal was another. Awkwardly, I had to explain that the local garbage outfit would only come early in the day if we paid them $150 in cash. We relented because we could not have garbage trucks in the park while it was open.

"That sounds like mob stuff," Adam said.

"Probably," I said. I didn't know for sure and didn't want to know.

"Uncle Vito," he mumbled, then ran off before I could respond.

Because toiling in the summer heat was clearly stretching their patience, I decided to introduce them to the park outside of working hours. Adam was fearless, sailing down the Alpine until his skin began to crust over. At Surf Hill, he stood at the foot of the lanes, looking up like a man staring defiantly at Mount Everest. He had no qualms about risking a Stanford education by incurring head trauma. I had made the mistake of telling him we sometimes put garbage cans under the plywood jumps to increase the incline and get more airtime on the mats. It was only for experienced park people like Smoke, who had honed his skills over many a drunken night, but Adam would not be discouraged.

"This is nothing," he said, and began to hike up the slope, mat and garbage can in tow.

"Look at Posh Rye go!" Phil said. In journalism class, we read Jim Carroll's *The Basketball Diaries,* which referred to Adam's cozy hometown of Rye, New York, as "posh Rye." Adam became Posh Rye for far longer than he cared to be.

"Only go halfway up," I said. At the midway point of the ride, using the can was ill-advised but manageable. There wasn't enough distance before the jump to gather the momentum needed to rocket off. But Adam walked all the way to the top, flashing the victory sign at us.

"What's going to happen?" Benji asked.

"He'll be fine," I said. I did not believe my own words.

Adam got down on the mat and began his descent. He picked up speed and was sledding down at a rapid clip when he hit the ramp propped up by the garbage can. It was like thrusters had been engaged. He was easily fifteen feet in the air.

"Holy shit," Benji said.

For a moment, it seemed as though he paused, going no farther. Then gravity took hold, correcting the false beliefs instilled by intoxication and bravado. Posh Rye plummeted back down, his shadow growing larger over the slope of the lane. Normally, instead of hitting a flat surface, you hit an angle and continued safely downward, releasing energy. But Adam soared over the slope and landed squarely on the flat portion all at once, his arms and legs splayed out like a chalk outline at a crime scene. By some miracle, he seemed woozy but otherwise intact.

These excursions placated them somewhat, though soon trash was piling up. At the same time, I began to hear the Stanford crew using a cryptic signal on the walkie-talkie. "Signal H," Adam would say. "Signal H." I thought it meant another severed deer head. It took me more than a week to figure out it was a call to drop everything and go have beers in the middle of the day at the Hexagon Lounge.

"You fucks," I said, confronting them in the Lounge. "You can't drink on the job."

They shrugged, indifferent. "It gets hot," Benji said. "We need to take breaks."

"I'll tell you something else," Adam said, feet on the table. "Those Newark kids don't do shit."

THE WEEKEND OF THE NEW JERSEY OKTOBERFEST MADE THEM ALL believers.

Using his German connections, my father flew in a forty-piece German brass band called Musikverein Ellhofen. It would have been much easier and cheaper to hire a local group to emulate the sound, but that would have been like buying knock-off beer equipment. He hired waitresses who did not have German accents but did have authentic heaving beer-maiden bosoms that made my mother roll her eyes. At least a couple of them I recognized from our Dolly Parton lookalike contests.

He had the Old World Classic brew delivered ceremoniously to the Fest Haus tent, the giant wooden kegs put in carriages pulled by rented Clydesdale horses, just as they were in Germany. Otto rode in one of the carriages with Daisy beside him, his arm up in what might have been a wave but looked suspiciously like a Nazi salute. Ahead of the horses was the German band, marching in formation and scoring the parade, their Alpine horns erupting in unison.

In front of it all was my father, decked out in lederhosen, proudly twirling a baton as de facto bandleader. When the kegs arrived, the snowmakers dragged them to the stage under the tent. Armed with a wooden mallet, Wacky Joe struck the brass tap and the crowd erupted. We had anticipated five thousand people for what was doubling as the grand opening of the brewery. It was at least that, maybe more.

The maidens began filling up one-liter glass mugs with the lager, passing them around to outstretched hands. My father had bought tens of thousands of the authentic German steins, which guests could purchase and take with them. He told Michael Teschner to have them emblazoned with the Vernon Valley Brauhaus logo. The mugs read BERNON BALLEY.

Teschner never owned up to the mistake. "The B is the way Germans print a V," he said.

My father was already circulating, beer sloshing in his hand. Accompanying him was my mother, dressed in a traditional dirndl, replete with puffy sleeves and an apron. There were few times I had seen him this happy. He toasted the German band, which was on stage playing a cacophony of festive, up-tempo music. People in the middle of the tent began dancing and moving, the massive mugs sometimes dwarfing their grip. Those that were shy idled in the margins, clapping and laughing. Some spilled out beyond the shade of the tent and into the direct sun, sweating out the beer that kept flowing. It was August, a strange time for Oktoberfest, but the incongruity didn't matter to anyone.

The smell of meat was everywhere. My father refused to let Bud Kelley ruin everything he had built with his rancid chickens, so he persuaded Tommy DiMaggio, a chef with whom he had gone into business on a restaurant in Aspen, to come to the park. In Colorado, Tommy had grown accustomed to feting celebrities like Steve Martin and John Belushi—Belushi apparently liked to snort cocaine in the kitchen—and operating the hottest place in town. Here, Tommy supervised an entire steer on a spit. Dozens of chickens spun on a rotisserie, their skin turning a dark and crispy brown. In the midst of this gourmet menu, I spotted one of the snowmakers, his bloodline rumored to be incestuous, off in a corner. He was roasting groundhogs over an open flame.

Elsewhere tables were set up with German Black Forest cake. This was one of the few things my father outsourced, tasking his secretary, Mary Meyers, with ordering two hundred cakes, each of which was divided ten ways, for a total of two thousand slices. Mary wound up ordering two thousand cakes, not slices, for a total of twenty thousand servings. Black Forest cake took up space in every available freezer for months. We debated whether to hand it out when people bought park tickets.

Soon, employees began migrating over, turning their work shirts inside out and walking over to the festival tent as soon as their shifts were over. It was a standing rule that none of my friends ever paid for a drink or food. Ann, Liam, and the rest of the Irish workers materialized, their usual house parties in the Swamp canceled for the greener pastures of the festival tent. We were soon joined by staff from Water World and Motor World, the latter covered in grease. Smoke and Steve Sokil, both shameless lotharios, had been bonding already. Sokil was a professional lifeguard from San Diego. They compared lifeguarding approaches, Sokil the polished pro and Smoke the gritty veteran. It was like an FBI agent trying to find common ground with a beat cop from the city.

As the night wore on and the floodlights illuminated the festival tent, my father began dancing, twirling my mother and smiling at the hordes of people surrounding him. He was completely in his element, having arranged for thousands of guests to have some of the best times of their lives. He did not appear to have a care in the world. At the sight of a reveler driving a Lola car over to the tent, security in pursuit, he raised his glass. Much later, I would learn he usually lost money on these celebrations, the cost of the concessions and entertainment outweighing revenue. He put them on, year after year, not because they were profitable but because he enjoyed watching people have fun.

As he toasted Jimmy and Otto, I raised my beer back at him, my knuckles sore from pressing against the thick wall of the stein. If this was our last summer here, I thought, it would be a good way to go, among family and among friends.

The party never really stopped. Later that summer, we held an Irish festival. On that occasion, my high school friends—Rich Szuch, Chuckie Baby, Fast Eddie, Benji Bressler—partied while the Stanford crew was on duty.

During the festival, Rich broke away and scrambled to the precipice of the Cliff Dive in Roaring Springs, a bravado fueled by Old World Classic. He insisted he could do a flip off the platform. Some of us protested. Smoke, who had the day off, tried to talk him out of it.

As he stripped off his clothes, I advised Rich to take Little Mo, the smaller of the jumps. Glassy-eyed, he nodded. We were standing below with other patrons, giving into their mob mentality, screaming for him to leap.

"Backflip!" he screamed.

"No, no backflip," I said. A front flip was manageable. A backflip required dexterity he didn't possess, even while sober.

Suddenly, he was in the air, a majestic man in flight. The crowd cheered.

Midway through the descent, he tucked his knees into his chest and directed his feet toward the sky. Because he had chosen Little Mo, there was not enough time to complete the flip. When he hit the water, he was virtually horizontal, his face and chest smashing into its surface. He did not make a splash when he hit. It was more of a plunk, as though someone dropped a cement block from the platform.

Stunned sober, Smoke and I rushed into the water. Rich's motionless frame was floating facedown. We got him to land. Medics appeared and strapped him to a backboard as a precaution. He began to stir, mumbling incoherently. He was certainly concussed, but it was hard to know how much of his disorientation to attribute to the impact and how much to the potent Bernon Balley beer.

We followed the ambulance to the hospital. As the doctors evaluated Rich for possible head trauma, we sat silently in his room. Chuckie Baby stared at the floor. Ed and Benji smiled at the passing nurses.

"That was a bad one," Smoke said.

"No one backflips off Little Mo," I said.

As we wondered if Rich would ever walk again, another problem creeped in. It was past lunchtime, and we were very hungry. We had been at the hospital for hours already.

"I don't have any money," I said.

"I don't either," Smoke said.

"None," Benji said, though no one asked him because he never had any money.

We eyed Rich's clothing, lying on the hospital bed. I patted it down and found his wallet. Inside was a twenty-dollar bill. I looked at Smoke and the others.

They gave me a solemn nod. We would be back to check on Rich, but we needed to keep our strength up. While he was getting an MRI, we went out for pizza and beer.

Over pepperoni, I decided it might finally be time to grow up.

Yours truly on the Aerodium, a skydiving simulator possibly more dangerous than the real thing.

Chapter Twelve

FLIGHT RISK

"The diesel-driven engine that powers Action Park's 'Fabulous Flying Machine,' a ride from West Germany with winds that can lift people in the air, will be turned on tonight—but not for thrill-seekers. Instead . . . the township planning board will be there to determine what effects the ride might have on a nearby neighborhood in the form of noise, vibration, or pollution."

Daily Record, July 17, 1987

My father beckoned me into his office.

"What's going on, Dad?" I asked. I expected he would want to discuss a contract or zoning issue. Now out of college in 1986, I was working for him in a far more mature capacity, navigating the labyrinth of his condominium business at the resort. I was a grown man with a grown-up job. I knew this because I was wearing pants.

"I'm thinking about something new," he said, picking up what looked to me like a water gun. I braced for a light spritz of water.

"Come on," I said. "I don't want to have to dry—"

Kuh-tunk. The paintball pellet whizzed past my head, leaving a gelatinous purple splatter on the wall.

"Dad, what the hell is—" *Kuh-tunk, kuh-tunk.* Another paintball pellet slammed into the door. One got me in the thigh. I gasped, and zoning permits flew out of my hands.

"Does it hurt?" he asked, with real sincerity.

"Yes!" I bellowed, running out of the room. "Yes! Why ask me that! Of course it hurts!"

I could hear him laughing, long and loud, all the way down the hallway. "We needed to see how much!" he said.

For much of the 1980s, paintball had been illegal in the state, the victim of language in the New Jersey Gun Control Act prohibiting any kind of design that too closely resembled an actual firearm. You needed a permit to own one, making a recreational paintball area a logistical nightmare. When the state finally eased regulations, courses began popping up everywhere. My father brought in a paintball advisor along with a small armory of weapons to test out. Apparently, the salesman told him that it wouldn't hurt to get hit by a pellet, which the two of them decided to test at my expense. This was what it was like to be in my father's orbit. Supervising real estate deals did not prevent me from getting shot with paint.

The paintball attraction eventually became a reality. Unfortunately, as with the beauty pageants, it was too easy for participants to group themselves into factions and declare war on one another. A promoted Bronx vs. Brooklyn face-off began as a tame contest and devolved into a melee, with guests pistol-whipping each other once they had run out of pellets. One participant aimed his gun at a fallen foe and put two in the back of his head—*pew, pew*—like a mob hit.

Despite its surging popularity elsewhere, paintball joined the list of attractions that wore out their welcome very quickly. Examining the splattered obstacle course, I was again confronted with the question of why people behaved the way they did—why they would be well behaved on rides elsewhere, but would wreak havoc on our grounds. When my father installed another Alpine Slide in Colorado, it didn't produce injuries at nearly the same rate as the one in Vernon. Nor did a second Motor World location he operated in Pennsylvania's Pocono Mountains. It was inexplicable. We seemed to be ground zero for aberrant behavior with no discernible reason why.

I began to ponder this mystery at a distance, because I was now a former employee of Action Park.

WHILE THE PARK REMAINED A FAMILY ENTERPRISE—JULIE STILL running marketing, my father still in charge—not all of us wound up a permanent part of the operation. After graduating, Jimmy got into the night-club and record businesses in New York City before settling into a successful career in real estate. (Adulthood did not completely eliminate his wild streak. I once watched as he was thrown through a glass door in Manhattan, having angered a bar patron.) Splinter was an electrical engineer. Pete's adolescent sadism belied a sharp mind—he was able to retire at thirty-eight after a successful career in private equity. Topher, the youngest, was still milling about the grounds in management. He would eventually follow in our father's footsteps as an entrepreneur involved in several start-ups before coming back into the fold.

There did not appear to be a long-term role for me. Like my father, I wanted to manipulate landscapes and bring a personal touch to real estate, selling and eventually developing properties. But the park was immutable to everyone but him, shifting in design only under his watch. If I stayed within its borders, I risked a kind of inertia. Being trapped on the mountain in a perpetual state of adolescence, once my foremost desire, became a concern. I thought it was better to be apart from it, at least for a bit, and find my own footing without chlorine stinging my eyes and throat.

The separation did not last long. For one thing, I was still working for my father, making normalcy impossible. For another, I was working out of his offices near the grounds. The proximity meant that I often found myself fielding questions about operations from managers who knew I was well versed in the finer details.

"I don't work here," I would say. "I work over there," pointing to the office.

"Just come and look at this foam situation," they'd say.

During the week, I behaved like an adult, sifting through sales contracts and learning the real-estate business. On weekends, I would patrol the park grounds, scouting for operational gaps. I existed in a weirdly ethereal space between consultant and nonemployee—between the child I was and the adult I was trying to become.

Part of that separation anxiety may have been a feeling that the park wouldn't be around much longer. As part of his plea deal, my father was supposed to hire an outside financial advisor to run the resort. This person would also be responsible for handling the cash flow, making Gene little more than a silent partner.

Somehow, no one stopped to consider what it would mean to usher him away from the property like a drunken uncle at a wedding. Even without the state land, he still owned significant parts of the area, including the ski lodge, the brewery, Motor World, and the parking lots. It would be impossible to run the business without giving people a place to drink or park their cars, both luxuries he could refuse to host on his portion of the land. The state couldn't do anything to force the issue, either. The notion of a fiscal agent appointed to oversee the resort and its accounting was ridiculous—my father's byzantine bookkeeping would look like a dead language to outside eyes. And shuttering things entirely was out of the question. It would have a devastating effect on the local economy.

The two sides were in a stalemate, and Gene knew it. Even though there was a court order to oust him from the grounds, he kept building attractions and working on construction of a sports club called the Spa, as though nothing had happened. People found it mystifying. He behaved like a man with a fifty-year lease, not a man who had received his notice to vacate the premises.

This was because he had a plan to win. It involved outsmarting everyone. And it also involved major appliances.

The plot began with Robert Littell, a member of the New Jersey General Assembly. A political ally of my father's in Sussex County, Littell agreed to sponsor a bill that offered an alternative solution. Instead of kicking Gene off the state-owned land, the bill proposed that the state allow him to buy the nearly thirteen hundred acres outright. The state would normally balk at such a deal, but it was so desperate to sever its ongoing business relationship with my father that it was open to the idea.

After a few months of haggling, and with the help of a lobbyist my father hired, the bill passed the State Assembly and was approved by the State House Commission. Governor Tom Kean signed it under protest, realizing there was no other solution. The DEP, which owned the land, was equally annoyed. The bill rendered them powerless. Now the land would be his in totality.

Thinking they were clever, Kean and the DEP built a provision into the deed mandating that the portion of the land considered environmentally protected only be used for conservation, recreation, or fish-and-game purposes. One would think they would have realized that it never paid to try to outmaneuver my father. He agreed, but insisted that if the commercial prospects of the land were limited, he should get a discount. Instead of paying well over $1.6 million, he bought it for $837,667.

In a blink, Gene's opponents went from celebrating his imminent removal from Vernon to agonizing over headlines that he would now own and control even more of it than before—at *50 percent off.* As he built camping cabins—technically "recreational"—on the property, they bemoaned the possible erasure of the barred owl, a species that lived on the land. They pointed fingers at Littell, who had come in at a crucial time to mediate a deal between the parties. It smacked of cronyism.

It was soon discovered that, in addition to being a politician, Littell was also an appliance salesman. Gene had bought a stove, refrigerator, and microwave for every one of his hundreds of condo units from him.

"The man's got every right to be in business," my father said. "What, he's not allowed? It's all legal."

While my father's definition of legal could often be debatable, this time he was right. It was all legal, which made his enemies steam even more.

It wasn't the Maytags that angered them. It was that there were supposed to be repercussions for Gene. Instead, he now had it all: the slope, the park, the top of the mountain. I expected to read of spontaneous human combustion within the town's limits. The anger and resentment were palpable.

Going out for a drink at a bar called the Hay Loft, I noticed a local eyeing me with a mixture of suspicion and malice. He bumped into me once, which I could have written off as an accident. Then he did it again, which I could not. When he did it a third time, we came to blows. He blasted me in the face with a punch that nearly broke my nose. We exchanged no words. I could only infer that my blood-line was offensive to him.

After the scuffle was broken up, I drove home, careful not to leak blood on my car seat. As my nose continued to swell, I wondered how Gene and Vernon could somehow heal the divide. They were in a kind of codependent relationship. Gene needed land. Vernon needed industry and jobs. There had to be common ground.

I was soon proven right, though I didn't expect the common ground to be thousands of pounds of radioactive dirt.

IN APRIL 1986, THE WORLD WAS AGHAST AT THE NUCLEAR MELT-down at Chernobyl, where human error had allowed for a cata-strophic power plant disaster. At roughly the same time that people were literally melting in Russia, the state of New Jersey quietly and discreetly decided to rectify a radiation problem of its own. Several tons of contaminated soil had been found by the Environmental Pro-tection Agency in a residential development in nearby Essex County. The contamination was left over from an old watch manufacturing company. It was enough to fill five thousand drums. The soil was lousy with radium, a naturally occurring product of uranium. As radium decays, it emits radon, a radioactive gas toxic to humans that can cause lung cancer and other terminal unpleasantness.

This dirt—which officials described as "mildly radioactive," in the same way one can be mildly pregnant—needed to be disposed of, and quickly. Without consulting anyone in Vernon, the state decided it was best to ship it to a ninety-five-acre area off Route 94 that con-sisted of an abandoned quarry and an old dairy farm. The DEP said it would all be perfectly safe, the dirt transported and dumped with the utmost care. Vernon, they said, had nothing to worry about.

Upon hearing this news, the town began to worry plenty, assailing the head of the DEP, Richard Dewling, as well as Governor Kean. If this corrupted soil was so safe, they reasoned, there was no reason for the DEP to sneak it in without holding any public hearings on the matter.

Vernon's residents had good reason to be wary. The communications antennas erected between the nearby mountain ridges had been a perpetual source of concern since the 1960s. Townsfolk believed that the radio frequencies given off by the powerful dishes and antennas—which were owned by RCA and represented the town's only significant industry outside of the ski areas—caused a host of health issues that plagued the area, from cancer to neurological disorders. Medical and environmental professionals largely dismissed this theory, though state research into the concern revealed Vernon had a much higher rate of birth defects than surrounding communities in the state. This was all anyone needed to hear to confirm their suspicions. They believed the dishes were fundamentally altering the population.

Though the theory was tenuous, I thought it could explain much about the behavior at Action Park. Perhaps people careened into trees because satellite dishes were messing with their brains.

At any rate, the antenna concern meant Vernon was already on edge. They did not want this radioactive dirt contaminating their drinking water by leaching into the aquifer located just below the quarry. Consequently, they redirected all the energy they normally reserved to combat Gene toward this new, even more sinister threat.

First, they marched to the house of Governor Kean, who wisely refused to come out and confront citizens screaming for his head on a pike. They made plans to form a human chain across the road, blocking the trucks driving in with the soil. Residents said they would simply "forget how to walk" and go limp in the middle of the street. We began to brace for a civil war.

One day, on one of my regular patrols at the park, I noticed a number of people lying on the ground in Roaring Springs near the Colorado River Ride. Having heard of the plan to create a human speed bump, I thought perhaps some protestors were practicing. Upon closer inspection, I realized they were not moving. Quickly, medics and ambulances arrived and roused more than two dozen glassy-eyed people from the ground. We discovered that an ozone generator used to keep the water clear had been turned off so attendants could remove a woman who had injured her shoulder. Turning the machine back on—normally done before the park opened—released a toxic cloud of built-up ozone gas, felling twenty-eight people who were idling nearby.

"The thing about that," Smoke said, watching the last of the medics leave, "is that we're now putting people down nice and easy. No pain. They just go to sleep."

"Stop it," I said.

No one was seriously hurt—a few passed out, and some were nauseated—but the DEP was not happy. It fined the park $10,000 for the accident and criticized us for failing to report it. The Occupational Safety and Health Administration fined my father another $960. He grumbled over this amount.

We did gas twenty-eight people. To me, $960 seemed like a steal.

The soil issue was so all consuming that Vernon barely batted an eye over the mass sedation. The controversy had transformed the town. After the Supreme Court of New Jersey ruled the soil could be transferred, residents made good on their promise and began standing in front of the entrance to the quarry. Some spoke openly about arming themselves with rifles and shooting any DEP-manned transport that dared to come into the community, a plan met with shockingly broad approval from locals. Some of the townspeople who didn't endorse such drastic measures looked to Vernon's mayor, Vic

Marotta, to quell the uprising. Marotta addressed Kean and the assembling militia, telling the Governor that Vernon's faithful would be nonviolent unless the state made a false move. At that point, any blood shed would be on Kean's hands. This rural oasis was now floating the possibility of violent retribution and doing it with the endorsement of public officials. The theory of antenna-induced derangement was starting to make a lot of sense.

My father seized the moment. He stood with the townspeople, sharing their outrage. When activists needed a place to rally, he opened the gates of the park. Thousands of people streamed in, brandishing shirts and signs emblazoned with their slogan of choice: HELL NO, WE WON'T GLOW. In the heat of summer, he offered them water, soda, beer fresh from the Brauhaus, and shelter under the massive Oktoberfest tent. More than eight thousand people were in attendance, almost half the town's population of 18,561. He also hosted Vernon Aid, a Live Aid–esque concert down near Great Gorge with proceeds going toward the cause. Naturally, Jimmy Sturr headlined.

"We will not allow this travesty to occur!" my father shouted to the gathered throngs like William Wallace on horseback, a polka tune playing in the background. "This soil could harm us for generations to come!"

Vernon was livid, and Gene was livid right alongside them. He did not want his customers irradiated. They did not want to grow a third eye. The two warring parties had finally found their common goal.

After months of gatherings and threats of civil war, Kean and the DEP finally relented. The state would not send the soil to Vernon but would instead ship it to a remote part of Nevada, where it would be diluted with "clean" dirt and dumped.

For a time, it seemed as though the controversy would be a way for Gene and Vernon to understand they were not so different after all. I think my father respected Vernon for finding its backbone. They had taken a stand against the steamrolling. It seemed a truce had been declared.

Years later, I asked Vic Marotta, the former mayor, why the DEP was so intent on dumping the contaminated dirt in Vernon despite knowing it would cause a revolt and quite possibly generational illness. He asked me to remember the timing of the news. It was right after the agency had been forced into the land deal with Gene against its own wishes.

"You're saying," I said, "that they tried to send five thousand drums of radioactive dirt to contaminate the entire area *just to spite him?*"

"Correct," he said.

In the DEP's eyes, nothing less than a nuclear disaster would even the ledger against Gene Mulvihill.

THE SPRING OF THE SOIL CONTROVERSY, I DECIDED TO DO SOME traveling. If the dirt wound up in Vernon, this would at least buy me enough time to purchase a Geiger counter, or possibly to convert one of the buried skate-park bowls into a fallout shelter.

I headed for Ios, an island in Greece. Ios was hedonism unchecked, attracting young men and women with an opportunity to live out the remainder of their juvenile inclinations before adulthood took full hold. It was like the park but without the responsibility. Also, a hotel room could be had for four dollars a night.

I went with Benji Bressler and Andy Buckley, Fred Buckley's brother, who later became an actor and played David Wallace, Steve Carell's supervisor, on *The Office*. (His first job was in a commercial for the park, which somehow ran for years despite its unauthorized use of a Bob Marley song.) We flew into Santorini and awaited a ferry to take us to our primary destination the following day. That night I went on a small bender that put my brain through the booze equivalent of the Cannonball Loop.

A day or two later, we were firmly entrenched in Ios and had found the hotel's restaurant. Benji was elsewhere, sleeping one off. Midway through breakfast, I looked up. Sauntering down the hotel stairs was the most beautiful woman I had ever seen. She walked with poise and self-assurance, deeply tanned legs carrying her down the steps, a bright yellow dress making her impossible to ignore. She began walking toward me, smiling. It was not the smile of a stranger being polite. It was the smile of someone who appeared to recognize me. I had never seen this woman before. I would have remembered.

"Hello, Andy," she said.

"Hi," I said, thoroughly confused. "Hello, there."

"Where is Benji?" she asked.

She knew Benji, too? "Uh, sleeping in," I said.

We talked for a few minutes and then we went to get Benji, who acted like he had known her forever. I got her name—Katrina—as Benji made arrangements to meet up later on that night. When she left, I collapsed in a heap of confused infatuation. "I do not know this woman," I said. "How does she know me?"

"You do know her, dummy," Benji said. "You were just too hung over to remember. We met her on the beach the other day. I told her we'd meet up when we got to Ios."

Benji went on to explain that Katrina was from Austria, had caught his eye, and that I was not to interfere with their courtship. Benji was one of my absolute best friends, which is why I felt I owed him the respect of telling him I categorically did not give a shit who met whom first. I was totally infatuated.

"What about Laurie?" he said.

After four years of bicoastal living, Laurie and I had recently broken up. I wanted to see a little more of the world, while Laurie was intent on making her mark in education, eventually becoming a superintendent. We later became friends. Her scooper's wrist persisted, however.

Though it's no source of pride, Katrina and I didn't get a chance to know each other all that well before my pants disappeared. We went out to a bar called the Red Lion, the same place our group had been the evening before and where we had made fast friends with a band of Irish guys who had labeled me The Generous American for buying them unlimited beers—easy enough when beers cost twenty-five cents a pop. As I chatted with Katrina, they burst in, spotted me, and proceeded to drag me away so they could once again drink on my tab. While I liked these guys, their timing was awful.

They began to hoist me in the air like I had just won an Olympic medal. As I dodged lighting fixtures with my head, they started warbling an Irish tune. The lyrics are lost to time, but one line in particular proved fateful. It went something like, "And off comes pants." The Irish took this as stage direction and proceeded to try to pull my pants down in full view of the bar, including Katrina.

I resisted, but there were too many of them, and Benji was too busy laughing and being spiteful to be of any help. They succeeded in tearing off most of the fabric, leaving only tatters. The bartender took pity on me and gave me a towel, which I pinned to my torn crotch with a clothespin like a cloth diaper.

To avoid further disruption, Katrina and I headed for the beach. We talked until morning. She told me she was a graduate of the University of Vienna, had interned for a bank, and had taken a job there. I tried to explain what my father did and why people were trying to give him radiation poisoning.

Katrina narrowed her eyebrows. "So, like a fun park?"

"Yes," I said. "An amusement park." I drew the Alpine Slide track in the sand, explaining how people sailed down and sometimes flew into the woods.

She paused. "You are a Gypsy?"

"No, no," I said. "We're a normal family."

"I don't understand," she said. "Carnies."

I tried to change the subject. "I think we should get married," I said.

"I think you are a drunken idiot," she said.

I managed to convince Katrina I was neither a transient nor an alcoholic. We spent three days entirely by ourselves, though it was not entirely romantic. I soon came down with a mystery illness that left me bedridden, but she cared for me while my friends remained too drunk to tie their own shoes. By the time we were both ready to depart, we decided it would not be goodbye. Back in our respective homelands, we called each other frequently and spoke for hours until I got my first phone bill and discovered it was five dollars a minute to reach her in Austria. I persuaded her to come see me.

She arrived in New Jersey, and at the sight of the park, her eyes widened. "This is spectacular," she said. Coming from a culture so reserved, the histrionics on display there were the stuff of alien planets to her.

One night, I took her out to a bar with Chuckie Baby. Some drunk pushed her. Before I could even react, Chuckie Baby had broken a bottle over the man's head. And not just any bottle, but a large Sapporo beer bottle the size of a bowling pin. He was, if nothing else, a loyal friend.

Katrina was not amused. "I am not sure," she said, "I could live here all the time." I wasn't sure if she meant New Jersey or the country.

My father, always so fascinated by different cultures, was intrigued by the fact that Katrina was from German-adjacent Austria and took to her immediately. He wanted to know everything about Austria: its customs, its traditions, how its citizens spent their free time. He told her about his other, non-carnival businesses, like the condos and a wine cellar he was thinking of starting.

"You know," my father said. "If you decide to stay, that would make me very happy."

"Thank you, Gene," Katrina said.

"We're a little short in the quality-control department," he said.

"Dad," I said.

"I'm kidding," he said, but he actually wasn't.

I visited Katrina in Vienna, and she soon told me she would be coming to live in America.

"I think I will take the job in quality control," she said.

I was over the moon. "You are going to love it here," I said.

Within a few days of starting work at the park, she came back to me, her hands filled with packets of ketchup picked up off the ground. "Quality in Austria is very different than it is in America," she said. "This place is run by children."

KATRINA'S ARRIVAL AT THE PARK CAME JUST IN TIME FOR HER TO witness my father destroying all the goodwill he had generated with Vernon. He was now driving them to the brink of madness with the help of airplane equipment.

He called it the Aerodium, and it was literally a propeller—the same type used in DC-3 planes—situated in the middle of a vertical wind tunnel twenty feet high and eighty feet in diameter. Powered by a 700-horsepower engine, it screamed with enough force to take a multi-ton aircraft to cruising altitude in the sky. My father used it to simulate skydiving, the gust from the propeller able to blast people wearing special suits sixty feet in the air. The propeller was covered by a steel netting so guests would not be pureed if they came crashing down. Pads surrounded the bottom to catch wayward aerialists.

As with many of the newer rides, my father had seen it at an amusement convention. Because he considered it a temporary structure, he didn't ask for any site approvals. Initially, he put it up near the Alpine Center. That's when the noise complaints came rolling in. Condo owners living just twelve hundred feet from the site were aghast at this throbbing machine that could make the dishes in their kitchen cabinets rattle. They complained, at which point my father pointed out the sales contracts they signed prohibited them from making any issue over noise coming from the park. This led to even more wailing.

To placate them, my father hired a sound engineer and had him design a makeshift noise buffer for the engine. Following the engineer's instructions with economy, the snowmakers stacked up a series of trailers on four sides of the unit. It acted as a muffler for the din, turning it from a throaty and china-rattling nuisance to a low growl.

His ingenuity impressed Katrina. "He finds solutions," she said. "Almost like he does not need to obey any rules."

The townspeople were not fully mollified. They continued to inquire about this strange device and begged for its removal. When pressed by a reporter, my father said the mayor had given him permission to install it. Vic Marotta had, in fact, done no such thing. Vic stormed into Gene's office and threatened to punch him in the nose for dragging him into the controversy. My father set the record straight, and the town approved the Aerodium with a temporary permit good through Labor Day.

The Aerodium brought with it the newest character in his menagerie. He was leasing it for $40,000 a month from Scott Albuschkat, a German inventor and flight enthusiast who had built the Aerodium and painstakingly disassembled it into three large segments for international transport. Scott had a handlebar mustache and hooded, sunken eyes that appeared to glare at you even if he was in a good mood.

My indifference toward Scott upon our first meeting quickly turned to suspicion. Scouting the park in the winter during a snowstorm, he borrowed my expensive winter boots and then claimed they had gone missing.

"The boots, they have disappeared," he said.

"Where would they go?" I said. "Can you please look for them?"

"The boots, they are no more," he said, like we were in an Ingmar Bergman movie.

Scott often stood by as Gene attempted to explain the Aerodium to bewildered state inspectors. At most parks, they could check for loose bolts on roller coasters. Here, my father explained, we would be blasting people up to nearly twice the height of a telephone pole with a giant plane propeller. The inspectors wondered if they needed to get the Federal Aviation Administration involved.

"No, no, Gene," Scott said, after the confused inspectors had left. "Cannot do sixty feet. Too dangerous."

"Come on," my father said. If the machine could blast people sixty feet in the air, then that's exactly how high up he wanted them to go.

"Much less," Scott said. "Ten feet is safe."

"Thirty," Gene said.

"Ten," Scott said.

Gene wavered when he saw Scott's crew in action. Clad in wind suits that acted as sails, they spread their arms and legs out to be lifted, then collapsed their limbs when they wanted to come down. They performed all kinds of aerial maneuvers, including flips and rolls. Their expertise made it safe to throttle the engine all the way up. It was an incredible sight, their bodies hovering just outside of the wind tunnel and in full view of people passing by. At those altitudes, even the mandatory helmet wouldn't do much good if things went south. Seeing this changed his mind.

"Okay, ten," Gene said.

As spectacular as they were, the aerialists had little choice but to perform. Scott had brought over several Germans to help operate and demonstrate the Aerodium. To guarantee their loyalty, he seized their passports and refused to allow them to leave until the season was over. Soon, I began to hear of an alternative pronunciation of his name: Scott Albershitter.

One of Scott's employees was nicknamed Chickenhawk. He had the skill of a circus acrobat, effortlessly moving between routines while suspended in the air. He was also prone to excessive drinking, stumbling around at night in a daze.

"The guy can fly," Chuck Kilby said, "but he can't walk."

Despite being indentured servants for Scott, the Germans maintained a sense of humor. One night, Chuck was patrolling the grounds after the park had closed. Nearing the Aerodium, he heard the engine growling and then saw a man come shooting out of the exposed top and fly off into the woods.

"Holy shit!" Chuck said. He gave chase. When he got to the victim, it was nothing more than an empty wind suit. The Germans appeared behind him, laughing their brains out.

The Aerodium posed no real danger for Scott's experienced men, but the general public was another matter entirely. Without some modest training, they would not know how to react to the current. As Scott explained, "It is like throwing people into the water who cannot swim."

Since we literally did exactly that every day, my father was unmoved. Still, he decided it was best to have riders sign a waiver absolving us of any liability. Even at a reasonable ten feet, we logged a broken arm and a dislocated shoulder barely two weeks after opening.

Despite the mishaps, the Aerodium drew crowds, due in part to people spending their summer close to home. A rash of terrorist attacks—TWA Flight 840 had suffered four casualties after a bomb was detonated over Greece, of all places—had put many off air travel, making destinations within driving distance preferable to flying across the country. Like Surf Hill, the ride attracted more spectators than participants, which was good. Capacity was low, with just one person being able to go in at a time. My father built a five-hundred-seat spectator platform so people could watch. Curious kids would wander over, fascinated by this display of humans in flight. They watched in awe, but they always clasped their tiny hands over their ears to try to drown out the terrible scream of the engine.

"Try owning a condo here, kid," I wanted to say.

I went up in the Aerodium several times, hovering a few feet off the ground before getting the hang of it and going up a little farther with each attempt. The feeling of being completely detached from the ground—from anything—was sensational. Soon, Katrina wanted to give it a try. She put on the suit and spread her limbs, letting the air current carry her upward. The German controlling the propeller was supposed to throttle the airstream according to a person's weight. Katrina, being light and tall, required far less air pressure than someone heavier, but the attendant wasn't paying attention. He increased the force instead. Katrina shot up like a bingo ball being siphoned through a tube. At the same time the worker eased up on the throttle, she instinctively tucked her arms and legs in. She plummeted, landing on her head over the net covering the propeller, missing the crash pads completely.

"Unngghhh," Katrina said.

I wailed in horror. I had grown numb to seeing my friends rendered unconscious, but now the park had killed the love of my life. We summoned medics, who took her to the first-aid station. Luckily, she was alive, though her neck throbbed with pain.

"Now I suppose I am a carnival person, too," she said.

Showing support for my future wife after meeting in Greece.

The bungee jump, a.k.a. the Snapple Snap-Up Whipper Snapper.

Chapter Thirteen

FREEFALL

"If all this excitement isn't enough—why not try a sport that was recently banned by the New Jersey Legislature! Yes, bungee jumping is available from a 70-foot tower at Action Park. (Bungee jumping from a crane was banned this month after a few serious accidents at the Shore.)"

The Courier-News (Central Jersey), August 17, 1992

In 1988, a year after Katrina came to live in the States, we were married. She had moved from quality control to real estate sales to owning her own mortgage business. Despite her run-in with the Aerodium—her neck pain would become chronic, throbbing for years afterward—she was in the process of getting her pilot's license. In time, she would have a PhD in psychology. She would also become a marathoner, a mountain biker, a triathlete, a renowned choir singer, and thanks to the birth of our daughter, Alex, an amazing mother. The breadth and variety of her pursuits amaze me to this day. It is little wonder she had second thoughts about marrying a carnival worker.

My parents attended the ceremony in Austria, where we exchanged our vows in German. My mother presented her mother with home-grown tomatoes. My father created a minor international incident by overtipping at a restaurant, which is considered rude there. Afterward, we all traveled to Munich for the real Oktoberfest, where Mac Harris had too much to drink and head-butted someone. It was a beautiful time.

Back in New Jersey as newlyweds, we decided to brave a cold winter night to go out for dinner. Returning to our condo, we drove past the resort. Illuminating the night sky were flashing red lights.

"I'm going to pull in," I said.

I stepped out of the car. Ambulances and police cruisers were parked near a maintenance shed at the foot of a ski trail known as the Bunny Buster. Though the resort was closed, the lights were on and the lifts were running, both indicative of the snowmakers working. It was close to the end of the ski season and the beginning of summer operations. Perhaps the Germans were having more fun with their wind suits, scaring the night workers.

That wasn't the case. Walking closer, I saw people writhing on the ground near the shed. Paramedics were loading others into the ambulances. A toboggan was nearby, its front crumpled like a discarded aluminum can.

I climbed back into the car, my mouth slightly agape. The red lights flashed on our faces. I did not know it at the time, but I was looking at more than just the site of an accident. I was looking at the beginning of the end.

HEADING INTO THE 1990S, ACTION PARK WAS INCREASINGLY IN need of capital. Theme parks were massive endeavors that often relied on corporate backing with deep pockets and long-term financing.

My father found it difficult to find lenders who would embrace his colorful history, the park's perilous attractions, and his lack of long-term planning. A big park might have a forecast for the next five years. He worried only about the next five weeks.

Absent major funding, his solution was to keep the park growing and generating cash. He would use its profits to prop up his other businesses, or vice versa, redirecting money from venture to venture in a complex web of accounting. It was surprisingly volatile, which I didn't realize until I began working in the office. Sometimes phones would stop working. The lights would go dark, the bulbs flickering out as though we were in the middle of a storm. My father would materialize. "All a mistake," he'd say. "Just a misunderstanding." And, soon, the bills would be paid, and things would begin running as usual.

Cash flow would sometimes come from unexpected places. In 1988, he purchased the nearby Playboy Club Hotel for what was considered a bargain: $11 million. The Club had struggled to maintain its flirtatious aesthetic in a rural ski area and passed through the hands of a revolving door of operators who tried to keep it afloat. My father resisted overtures to buy it until the price was right. Eventually, it came up in a foreclosure fire sale, and I was soon tasked with selling off the renovated hotel rooms that we converted into condo units.

To help fund the acquisition, my father persuaded representatives for Pamela Harriman, a socialite and the future United States Ambassador to France, to invest. He then sold the attached golf course, the only real item of value, to a Japanese billionaire named Eitaro Itoyama, conducting the transaction on his preferred business stationery of a cocktail napkin. After enlisting Bob Brennan to feign interest as a rival buyer, Gene persuaded Itoyama to purchase the course for a staggering $20 million. It was worth closer to $8 million. We later heard that when Itoyama's lawyers saw he had committed to such a purchase on a handwritten contract, they tried everything they could to get him out of it. They were not successful. Gene's verbiage, while possibly stained with salad dressing, was airtight.

My father used these proceeds to keep the park churning, leaving the comparatively worthless Playboy Club to stagnate, never quite realizing Harriman had sunk most of her children's trusts into the flailing hotel. Her stepchildren wound up suing her for losing their inheritances. A *Vanity Fair* story framed it as a giant con and called the Club a "fetid sinkhole."

"How was I supposed to know she spent all her money?" my father asked.

When he was flush, he would walk the amusement trade shows with vigor. One year, he jumped on a contraption on the show floor that spun the rider in what amounted to a human gyroscope. In the middle of twirling around, he let out a load groan and demanded to be extricated. When he disembarked, he began stumbling around, holding his stomach in agony.

"Arggh," he moaned. "This ride's defective!"

When the attendant asked him what was wrong, he unbuttoned his shirt, revealing a large and fleshy protrusion over his stomach.

"My belly button came out!" he cried.

The owner of the ride nearly collapsed in panic. Amos Phillips laughed so hard he nearly sucked the Band-Aid covering his eye into his head. The bump was a hiatal hernia, a small bulge of the intestine that resembled a golf ball near his belly button. He'd had it for years. It was painless, and he never wanted to put his various responsibilities on hold long enough to get it surgically corrected.

What my father found most interesting about those conventions was how serious people in the theme-park trade could be, bloviating about capacity and admission margins and construction costs. He made a beeline for the idea men and other entrepreneurs who were as caught up in the excitement of operating a park as he was. When he found them, they usually became fast friends.

One of these men was Stan Checketts, a Mormon from Utah who had a boundless imagination and a keen mind to bring his ideas to fruition. His booth had video of someone making a dramatic leap from a tower and dangling like a yo-yo from a heavy elastic cord. It was a bungee jump. In 1992, virtually no one in America had seen anything like it.

"This works?" my father said. "Can you really do this?"

Stan assured him it did, and he could.

"Okay," Gene said. "I'll take one." He said this like he was ordering a chicken sandwich. Then he just kept moving through the convention, his eyes scanning the booths for something else he could impulsively pluck from the selection of attractions.

Stan would later say he crossed the aisle to ask someone if Gene was for real. "If Gene said he wants it," the man said, "then it's as good as done."

The practice of tying oneself to a cord and plummeting off a high-rise platform had origins on Pentecost Island in the South Pacific, where young men undergoing a rite of passage would use tree vines to leap off cliffs without smashing into the ground. A few brave souls had plunged from the Golden Gate Bridge in San Francisco in 1979, but the hobby had otherwise gone largely unnoticed. It was Checketts who designed the first dedicated, fixed bungee platform and took proper measures to make sure people were simulating their bridge suicides in a controlled setting. Gene immediately saw the ingenuity of Stan's idea. It took virtually all of the risk out of jumping while maintaining its heart-thudding thrill. If the worst thing happened and the cord snapped, guests would simply fall on top of the air bag Stan positioned at the foot of the tower.

My father brought Stan out for a site inspection. Normally, we never had to build any kind of freestanding structure—our attractions all used the natural slope of the mountain—but the bungee required a strictly vertical freefall with a permanent and stable launch site. They settled on an area near the Alpine Center. Catching the two of them in passing, I noticed Stan found the phrase "Class Action Park" very funny and seemed to be in tune with the frenetic pace of the property, marveling at everything in sight. He had been waiting for a place like this his entire career.

My father's idea of a business meeting with Stan was to indulge in his request for a pull-up contest. Despite pushing seventy years old, Stan was spry. He insisted he could beat Gene's kid in head-to-head competition. They pulled me out of a meeting to participate. I was in good shape but bigger than Stan. He assumed moving my larger frame would tire my arms out more quickly.

"This is what we'll do," my father said, and whispered to me. I nodded in agreement. When it was time for the contest, Stan appeared, his narrow shoulders ready to pump out rep after rep. Faking a shoulder injury like a points-shaving athlete, I stepped back and watched as Pete, my wiry older brother, stepped in. Stan had only specified he could beat Gene's son—he never called me out by name, and he had never met Pete. He stewed as Pete pumped out twenty-five pull-ups. Stan, motivated by the deception, managed twenty-six.

The agreement about the bungee tower took less than five minutes. The pull-up contest, betrayal, and resulting challenges for a rematch went on for over an hour.

"What kind of businessmen do this?" Pete said.

Stan and Gene were made for each other.

WITH WAVES OF FUNDING CAME DECISIONS ABOUT WHAT TO DO with the money. Sometimes, my father based decisions on what other parks were doing. While he would never emulate them directly, he wanted to be aware of trends in the industry. Recently, Great Adventure had introduced a stunt show based on the Batman film franchise. Costumed actors performed multiple shows daily, and since Warner Brothers owned both Six Flags and DC Comics, it was natural synergy.

My father had tried a live show with the Broadway Revue, but musical numbers were of little interest to our main demographic of wild-eyed teenagers. Whatever we did had to be participatory. If he were running Six Flags, people would get to jump on stage and punch Batman in the face.

One day, I came into his office to discuss an escrow issue with a condo and found him with his feet on his desk and his hands clasped behind his head. Normally, he'd be hovering over papers or barking into the phone. This was his relaxed posture, the one that said *problem solved*.

"You figure something out?" I said.

"Julie did," he said. He took his feet off the desk and leaned forward. "Gladiators!"

"What?" I said.

"The Roman Colosseum," he said. "Picture it: duels, jousts, and a champion among the people."

I pictured it: People from the Bronx on chariots pulled by miniature horses, whipping the Brooklynites. Rubber spears jabbed into eyes. Winners getting the hand of Miss Action Park. Litigation.

I was right on most counts.

Julie explained what they wanted to do was a take-off on *American Gladiators*, a TV show that had become popular in syndication. It was part obstacle course and part game show, with amateur athletes trying to best the show's resident heroes in physical contests such as scaling walls or dodging football-style tackles. The gladiators were a lineup of 'roided-out men and women in red-white-and-blue spandex and high-top sneakers who could swat mortals away like bugs.

Julie wanted to do the same show, only on park grounds. She had apparently gone to the Samuel Goldwyn Company, the show's producer, for permission to use the *American Gladiators* name and trademarks so we would have a recognizable brand to build on. They said no. She did not realize her mistake had been in asking anyone for permission. This was not my father's Ready-Fire-Aim mentality.

"We're gonna do the show anyway," he said. "We'll just change the uniforms and name."

He dubbed the Action Park version the New Gladiator Challenge Show. The heads of this flagrant trademark violation were Vinnie Mancuso, the former Wave Pool lifeguard and a longtime bodybuilder, and his brother, Mike. The two scouted local gyms for eight bodybuilders—seven men, one woman—who had "the look." The look, Vinnie explained, was veiny, with tanned tissue-paper skin and enough mass to toss around adults like children. He wound up with a small army of genetic and pharmaceutical freaks. Vinnie gave them sensational comic book names like Titan, Flash, Star, and Warrior. The names of the televised gladiators also happened to be Titan, Flash, Star, and Warrior.

The snowmakers built a series of obstacles on the hill, including a sloped treadmill, a twenty-four-foot vertical hand ladder, and a cargo-net climb. After a zip-line run, contestants would climb a ten-foot-tall wall on a rope, navigate a rotating cylinder, then jump into a ball pit and crawl under a low net to the finish line. At the end were twin platforms where contestants would stand and face the gladiators in a climactic jousting battle. The weapons were similar to the ones used on the television show, sticks with padding on both ends. They looked like Q-tips, albeit ones that could deliver a concussion. Because we put no limits on who could enter, these behemoths were often throttling men who might have stood five foot eight and weighed one hundred and fifty pounds. On platforms seven feet tall, one solid swipe from a Gladiator could send a contestant flying backward and onto a mat like they had just made contact with a high-voltage power line.

To prevent our cast from caving someone's face in, we fitted guests with lacrosse helmets. They were usually too big and often became dislodged, obscuring their vision and rendering them unable to see the trajectory of the giant staff smacking them in the face. Later, we gave them motorcycle helmets to wear. When the carnage grew too great, Vinnie would ask one of the gladiators to take a dive so the contestants could advance to another round and give the crowd something to cheer. When they were victorious, the civilians would raise their sticks and bask in the adulation.

While all of them were formidable, Titan was the most physically imposing. Vinnie enlisted a friend named Steve Liss for the role. Steve was two hundred and sixty pounds with 8 percent body fat. The ground trembled when he walked. He was an exceedingly nice guy, with a father who was a respected orthopedic surgeon in town, but he could transform into a convincing barbarian.

During one particularly violent encounter, Steve swung his jousting stick so hard it cracked. Rather than stand patiently waiting for a new stick, Steve theatrically broke it clean over his knee. The people erupted. Vinnie and Steve knew exactly what my father wanted out of this: a massive spectacle. For the big Fourth of July opening, Vinnie arranged for metal cannons with blank mortar shells to fire— *thwom, thwom, thwom*—to signal the start of combat. The pyrotechnics went off, sending hundreds of spectators into a frenzy. My father threw up his hands, embracing the energy of the crowd. He had finally found a live event that fit the park: A show where people beat the shit out of one another.

Within a few weeks, some of the gladiators reported that a man had approached them in the parking lot. He said he was recruiting gladiators for the television show and began to ask them about their training regimens, their real names, and who was responsible for the park attraction. Some answered dutifully, hoping to be picked for the syndicated series. Others, including Steve, told Vinnie that something was amiss. Within weeks, my father was served with a lawsuit from the Samuel Goldwyn Company alleging trademark infringement. The spy, a Goldwyn employee, had taken videotape of the show to play in court. On the video, contestants helpfully declared that the Action Park course was "very much like," "exactly like," and "identical" to the one they saw on the show.

There was really no defense to mount. Gene offered to put up a disclaimer saying there was no affiliation, but it was too late. The court granted the company's request for a temporary restraining order to block us from hosting the competition. The following year, my father revamped it as a Tarzan-themed fantasy show, in which people would compete against bodybuilders who were now dressed in leopard-print costumes. It was like challenging an army of buff Fred Flintstones. One of them even had a female escort who carried a boa constrictor, a practice that proved unwise when the snake began molting and bit her near her kidney.

The show was a success even with the more generic theme, but my father's insistence on hiring an emcee to incite the crowd like he had with the beauty pageants proved to be a fateful decision. The announcer was a sixteen-year-old kid named Danny. Dressed in African safari garb, with khaki shorts and a pith helmet, he fancied himself a little Don Rickles, heckling the audience and berating contestants. "Bet that hurt," he'd say, watching a man get bludgeoned with a stick.

The breaking point came on dollar-beer day, a promotion so

poorly thought out that no one ever took responsibility for coming up with it. (Ten-Cent Beer Night at a Cleveland Indians game in 1974, which ended in a riot, should have been a clue.) A very inebriated man was standing on the top of the hill overlooking the course and began to insult Danny, dressing him down about everything from his age to his lack of experience with women. Steve, who had taken a liking to Danny, tore the microphone from his hand and pointed at the heckler. His exact quote was not recorded for posterity, but it involved intimations that he, the onetime Titan, would soon arrive at the man's home to pleasure the man's wife.

Tossing aside his beer, the man and his comrades charged down the hill, screaming for the blood of the Tarzans. The heckler went straight for Danny, tackling him through a lattice fence. Steve came to his aid, and the Tarzans stood back-to-back, swinging at anyone who came within punching distance. Though they were mighty, they were outnumbered by drunken parkgoers, traditionally the winning team on park grounds. Vinnie waved them onto a golf cart, whisking them out of harm's way. Police from five different precincts came to round up the instigators and summoned a bus to transport all the arrestees into town. It was the first paddy wagon I had ever seen.

The show lasted one more season, this time with a military basic-training theme. Danny disappeared. So did the snake. And so did dollar-beer day.

LIVE SHOWS WOULD CLEARLY NEVER BE OUR STRONG SUIT. MY FA-ther continued to search for some sort of secret sauce for the park—a way to contemporize and finance it beyond the installation of yet another water ride.

"C'mere," he said to me one day in the office. "How are sales?"

"Sales are good," I said. I eyed the office for signs of a paintball gun.

"Did you know," he said, changing the subject, "that when Joe Louis retired, he went to work as a greeter for a casino?"

I didn't, but I knew my father enjoyed boxing. It might have been hereditary. Dockie had been an amateur boxer who accumulated a credible record. He used to have his grandkids pummel each other while wearing football helmets.

"No," I said. "Why?"

"Imagine," he said. "The resort as a training base for a bunch of boxers that I manage. They'll run around the place. Like an attraction."

"But you don't know anything about managing fighters," I said, forgetting that the phrase "but you don't know anything about" had no effect on him.

"I know real estate," he said. "And this will bring attention to the development and Great American stock. Plus, look at Don King and all the money he makes." At the time, Don King was the gold standard for making money in boxing without getting punched in the face. My father explained that Bob Brennan employed a guy named Jack Dell, who was losing his shirt on a stable of fighters. Dell wanted to sell part of his interest, but Bob wasn't biting. He had no taste for the sport. Gene, inspired by his own father's prowess, was intrigued by it. The fact that almost everyone not named Don King lost money in the ruthless world of boxing was not a consideration. Jack and Bob proposed a deal in which they would raise money for Gene and Great American Recreation if Gene agreed to handle the fighters. More money meant more capital, which meant a bigger park. My father agreed.

In short order, a number of fighters moved into the condo units and made the resort a training camp where they could disappear from the distractions of home and focus exclusively on their fitness. Gene set up a ring at the now completed Spa at Great Gorge so members could mill about and see the boxers spar. These weren't second-rate amateurs. They were big names, or soon-to-be big names in the fight game, including "Merciless" Ray Mercer, who had won an Olympic gold medal in 1988 and would one day win numerous heavyweight championship titles; Charles Murray, a spitfire light welterweight champion; and Al Cole, a wiry cruiserweight title holder. Other boxers floated through camps, including Roy Jones Jr., Oliver McCall, and Gerry Cooney, the "Great White Hope," who had accumulated an undefeated record before running into Larry Holmes.

Because Vernon was still as white as a bed sheet, the sudden materialization of a predominantly black squad of athletes—plus their sizable entourages—caused many double takes. Some people in Vernon had the temerity to make passing comments when they saw them around. Apparently, none of those people had seen these men beat their opponents unconscious on television. One local, a self-proclaimed Sussex County good old boy named Jack, seemed ornery around them until he got involved with the pick-up basketball games we played with the fighters and subsequently declared them "okay guys." That was about as close as anyone in Vernon was going to get to racial harmony.

Because Jack Dell retained a percentage on the fighters, he was a frequent presence at the camp. It was difficult to tell whether the fighters respected Jack the way they would a playful old uncle or whether he annoyed them.

I once invited Jack for a tour of the mountaintop cabin development. Suddenly he jumped off the path and into the woods. It startled me.

"Got him!" he cried. Emerging from the thicket, his expensive business suit covered in dirt, he held up a black snake and announced that he was going to stuff it in Ray Mercer's shorts. I questioned the wisdom of putting a snake in the pants of a man large enough to kill you with a backhanded slap, but Jack did exactly that, sneaking up on Ray and cramming the small snake in his trunks. Ray panicked, screaming at high volume and tearing his shorts off.

"Fucking Dell," he said.

Whenever one of the boxers had a fight at Madison Square Garden in New York or in Atlantic City, my father was completely in his element, basking in the carnival environment that was big-time prizefighting. When I went with Jimmy to a fight in Atlantic City between Ray Mercer and Tommy Morrison, who had played Rocky Balboa's protégé in *Rocky V,* a skirmish broke out between Jack Dell's entourage and Morrison's. Jimmy stood over our mother, shielding her from any wayward blows. When things settled down, we returned to our seats, where Katrina and a friend of hers named June were taking in the barbarism with a measure of disgust.

"I don't really like fighting," June said.

"It's more cerebral than it looks," I said as my father stood in the aisle wearing boxing trunks over his suit. "Give it a chance." As I spoke, blood sprayed over our seats. It was like being at SeaWorld. Katrina and June left early.

Mercer won that night, but in boxing, fortunes could change on a dime. The men dropped some pivotal bouts that could have set them up for higher-profile and more-lucrative matches down the road. Over time, Gene's boxing investment bled like Morrison's cuts. The whole enterprise became a money drain.

My father, who often prioritized fun over profits, stuck it out for a while. He liked having the boxers around. None of the men lived up to the stereotype of fighters being stupid. They were all quick, funny, and polite. But Al Cole was ever so slightly gullible, which my father picked up on immediately. He managed to convince Al that Native Americans lived in the woods by getting one of the snowmakers to dress in crude cigar-store Indian garb and run through the trees, sending Al into a panic. Another time, Al was speeding in the town of East Orange. Red lights lit up his rearview mirror. He pulled over. The cop saw the car was registered to Great American, and radioed the stop in to Mike Palardy, Gene's cousin and a cop himself. Mike called Gene. Cackling, Gene called the cell phone installed in the car. A very confused Al picked it up.

"Al," Gene boomed. "What did you do now, Al?"

For weeks, Al would tell anyone who would listen never to cross Gene Mulvihill. "He's got eyes in the sky, man," he said. "I'm telling you, Gene is everywhere."

AS FEARLESS AS THEY MAY HAVE BEEN IN THE RING, NONE OF THE fighters would go within a mile of the bungee tower, which had taken on a sordid reputation in the summer of 1992. A number of towers had popped up across the state, but many of them were only semi-permanent installations. Instead of a tower, operators used a crane to hoist people in cages to nose-bleed heights of up to one hundred and fifty feet. While much cheaper to operate, this was not particularly safe, as the cranes were not built to suspend humans above the ground. The Department of Labor began shutting the jump sites down.

The state was on an apparent spree of stifling risk, as they also tried to introduce a bill to prohibit the sale of alcohol in parks. My father, fearing for his Brauhaus, argued that they'd also have to shut down any liquor store or bar within one hundred miles of the Jersey Shore and its many rides.

The prohibition died, but the bungee stigma remained. It hit Stan Checketts hardest. Stan had erected several bungee sites in Florida, but state officials there were petrified of the towers and insisted he put up a morbid caution sign that consisted of three illustrations: a cord breaking, a person falling, and a wheelchair logo. Stan argued that airplanes and cars should come with the same warnings.

Amid this controversy, my father looked around and noticed something remarkable. Thanks to Stan's design and the precautionary air bag, Gene had one of the few bungee stations in New Jersey that was actually safe. His was the first to pass the state's mandated inspection checklist. The media profiled him as one of the most responsible bungee operators in the area. Jumping on the positive press, he denounced the use of cranes as risky—New Jersey banned bungee jumping from cranes that August—and hailed Action Park as one of the only places people could experience a structurally sound jump. He insisted that Stan utilize all the most stringent safety measures available, from using a new rope at regular intervals, to weighing guests, to making sure to use the right equipment. For the first and only time in his life, my father was being cited as a safety expert.

Once some of the hysteria died down, the jump proved to be a hit. Patrons paid five dollars—one of the few ride surcharges apart from the Aerodium   to ascend the 122 steps to the top of the platform, second-guessing themselves the entire time, and get buckled into a harness. Julie persuaded Snapple, then an upstart beverage company, to sponsor it. In exchange for renaming it the Snapple Snap-Up Whipper Snapper, the company gave Gene a lump sum that he turned around and gave to Stan to cover the costs, making the tower essentially free to lease that year.

Julie then persuaded Ben Farnsworth, a New York City–based newscaster from NBC's *Live at Five,* to perform a live jump on the news. Topher led him up to the seventy-foot platform and watched as the attendant fixed him into the harness. With a measure of disgust, Topher later described the scene to us.

"Farnsworth was a pussy," he said. "He kept saying he wasn't going to do it."

Farnsworth had been in a protracted argument with his producer in the news van, insisting they were arranging his premature death. Getting on the platform just made his apprehension worse. Topher was my father's son, reared on a diet of life-altering rides and calculated risk. This display of cowardice sickened him. Plus, a reporter chickening out would have made a lousy advertisement for the ride. As soon as the feed from the park went live, Topher pushed him off the platform. His entire broadcast amounted to, "I'm Ben Farnswoooooooooorth . . ." before he plummeted.

At the bottom of the descent, he dangled like a pendulum. "Let him hang," Topher said, like a mob boss trying to intimidate an eyewitness. The newscasters in the studio began laughing uncontrollably on air, slapping the table at the sight of their colleague swinging listlessly from side to side. It drew big crowds to the Snapple Snap-Up Whipper Snapper, happy to be spectators even if they didn't have it in them to try it themselves. If they did, we had complimentary "I Beat the Bungee" shirts waiting for them. A seventy-two-year-old man and former Army Ranger in World War II was challenged by his grandkids to do it. Compared to jumping out of airplanes, it was easy. He got the shirt.

Despite a septuagenarian setting a precedent, I had reservations about going up. The stairs felt like a slow walk to the gallows. At the top of the tower, the seventy feet felt like seven hundred. I put two clammy hands around the metal railing and looked down. Rather than cower, I suddenly realized the subject of all this controversy was not nearly as terrifying as the black maw of the Cannonball Loop. I stepped off, the whoosh of air screaming past my ears.

My father had only one complaint about the bungee. State restrictions prohibited anyone under the age of ten from jumping. He thought kids had every right to go on, assuming they had a parent or guardian's permission. He began seeking out the necessary approvals, and soon newspapers were awash in comments from pediatricians who warned that a child's fragile skeleton and developing cartilage should not experience the force of being jerked around on a bungee cord. Disappointed, he gave up on the idea of pushing children off the platform. I remained relieved that he never opened that nursery.

More than three hundred fifty thousand people would leap off the tower over the next five years. The worst injury sustained was a sprained ankle. Perceived as one of the most dangerous activities in the country, the bungee was actually the safest thing we had ever installed. Jim Bineau of the Brauhaus proved it. On a drunken dare, he jumped from the tower without a harness and landed safely on the air bag, laughing all the way down.

ALL OF IT—THE BUNGEE, THE BOXING, THE GLADIATORS—WAS AN attempt to keep my father's recreational business moving forward in the 1990s. Over time, the flickering lights and disconnected phones, which I had believed to be speed bumps, became endemic of larger issues. The boxing not only failed to bring in revenue but cost five million dollars, erasing much of the golf-course windfall. The mountaintop cabins developed in defiance of the land deal did not pay off, either. Since it was technically a camping site, we couldn't install permanent plumbing, and no one wanted to go "glamping" and poop in the woods.

It is here and now in the mid-1990s that I began to hear more about the toboggan accident, the scene from years prior that had largely faded from my memory. The men and women I saw being carted off that night had been staying in a condo owned by their uncle. Inside was a toboggan. Nearby was the Bunny Buster, an intermediate slope lit up by lights. The six of them congregated and decided that if the lights were on, the trail must be safe to use, even though it was close to midnight. They had no clue the lights were for the snowmakers. They jumped on the toboggan and rode down the Bunny Buster without incident. They could have stopped then and been fine, but they went down a second time, and then a third. That's when they lost control, flying into the air, through a fence, and over the edge of a twenty-foot embankment to the parking lot below. One had fallen off before the drop. The other five collided with the storage building and a utility pole, their bodies flung from the sled.

Though all of them survived, the injury list was agonizing: a broken leg, a broken back, collapsed lungs, a broken jaw. They sued, arguing the embankment was a man-made hazard that should have been removed or blocked off. My father and his lawyers believed the case was without merit. The lights had been on for the maintenance workers. The trail was closed. The tobogganists were technically trespassers. Above all else, there was the ski statute, the one that had kept Gene's recreational businesses alive for decades. The one that said to act only at your own risk.

The jury, seeing the wreckage of humanity, saw it differently. They awarded the plaintiffs $1.9 million. The court decided Great American Recreation was exactly 54 percent negligent, with the plaintiffs being 22 percent at fault and the condo owner 24 percent responsible. That meant the resort was liable for roughly a million dollars.

Like a Ray Mercer left hook followed by an uppercut, that decision was accompanied by another. A woman had caught her elbow in a section of a water tunnel, whipping back her body, and herniating a disc. Her doctor told her that, during her recovery period, she could paralyze herself with a cough. A jury sided with her, too, for $675,000.

My father appealed the decisions, sending the toboggan case all the way to the state Supreme Court. The Court upheld the initial ruling. Gene offered the victims the deed to thirty-four acres of land in lieu of money. He didn't have the cash, nor did he have a policy that would cover the amount.

Because, once again, he had no insurance.

Back in 1986, one of the biggest insurance companies for theme parks, Balboa Company, went out of business after their underwriter collapsed. It became harder for parks to get any kind of coverage at all. The famous Cyclone at Coney Island closed because New York demanded a five-million-dollar policy, which no company wanted to provide.

In response to this, New Jersey attorney general Michael Bokar approved a plan—with some lobbying from Gene—that allowed all operators to forgo the standard $100,000 in liability coverage per ride so they wouldn't get drained by exorbitant premiums. The old requirement would have meant maintaining $4 million in insurance for Action Park. The new rule said an operator could get away with a policy or bond as small as $250,000. My father opted for only a notch above the bare minimum, posting a $300,000 bond for the entire park. There was no coverage for the ski slope at all. Though most ski resorts had policies, the state didn't require it. To him, it seemed unimaginable that either Action Park or the resort would ever be liable for a massive sum. No judgment against either had ever exceeded the $100,000 paid to the Larsson family for their son's Alpine Slide accident.

Perpetually undercapitalized, Gene couldn't comfortably pay for those hefty policies, especially with our reputation. He still thought defending himself and paying settlements would ultimately be cheaper than premiums. Part of his reasoning was that the number of accidents had decreased overall in the late 1980s, dropping by a double-digit percentage across the state and plummeting at Action Park. It seemed like people were finally developing an understanding of the risks involved and adjusted their behavior accordingly. Also, we had gotten better at reducing the potential for problems, reinforcing safety instructions and tightening up rides by adding foam and hay in select areas. A steel divider had, at last, corralled the rogue drivers in Motor World, preventing them from taking free laps. We also brought in more capable engineers like Stan Checketts. The park's overall risk was finally ebbing. It had taken a rogue trip down a ski trail in the middle of the night for things to come undone.

The toboggan accident was only part of my father's troubles in those years. There was a crashing real estate market, which affected his investments. Attendance at the park was down by 22 percent; we lost over sixty-eight thousand visitors from 1994 to 1995. Bad weather. Stumbling boxers. It just kept piling up.

I watched as my father walked the tightrope, one that stretched back over two decades. I expected we would soon have word that an arrangement had been made, a deal brokered.

It never came.

In the spring of 1995, Action Park and Vernon Valley went into foreclosure due to $18 million in outstanding debt, owed to First Fidelity Bank, that had gone into default. In April 1996, Great American Recreation declared bankruptcy. More lawsuits were lost and judgments obtained. The total liability for personal injury claims climbed to $3.8 million, with forty-one cases pending. Not once but twice, federal marshals stormed the gates of the park, seizing admission revenue in order to pay someone who had won a lawsuit. If there is one certain sign of a business in distress, it is multiple police raids.

The bankruptcy case took up twenty horizontal feet of shelf space in the Newark bankruptcy court. Gene began searching for money to cover the park's overhead. Bob Brennan, the closest thing to a human ATM he had ever encountered, was under more duress than ever by the Securities and Exchange Commission and had just filed for Chapter 11 bankruptcy. He couldn't help. Bereft of emergency cash, my father tried liquidating businesses and looking for loans. He tried a transfer of assets from here to there, his trademark sleight of hand working overtime. He considered the bankruptcy another speed bump, a chance to reorganize and emerge from debt stronger than ever.

I had barely known a world in which the park did not exist. There was never any occasion to think it could ever be shut down. It had survived everything. So had he. Now the entire park had become a wound, and one he could not close.

Just before everything came crashing down, he had gone into business with Stan Checketts once more, opening a ride dubbed the Space Shot. The attraction used compressed air to shoot people two hundred feet in the air, making them weightless for two seconds before they descended in a controlled freefall in belted seats.

The Space Shot sat just near the Alpine, which was fitting symmetry. The Alpine was the first ride he had ever put in. The Space Shot would be the last.

Me, Michael Teschner, Jimmy, Gene.

River Ride 1 (a.k.a. The Toilet Bowl). Human clogs were not uncommon.

Chapter Fourteen

THE LOOP

"The new park, now called Mountain Creek, will open in June, with several changes and improvements from Action Park, which had a reputation for attracting troublemakers and being unsafe. The new owners are eliminating some of the more dangerous, adult attractions, and implementing more safety features."

Daily Record, April 26, 1998

When my siblings and I talk about what my father really wanted from Action Park, why he risked so much in pursuit of its fiberglass skyline, the answer is always the same. He wanted to feel at home.

When Gene was a child, his father, Dockie, transformed their basement from an uninteresting subterranean storage area to a covert wonderland. Over time, makeshift shooting ranges with guns and paper targets were interspersed with other novelties. A card table with a green felt top was joined by a pool table, a shuffleboard, and a bar. Bit by bit, Dockie built up a recreational hideaway, my father witnessing both its expansion and the joy it brought Dockie and his friends. Seeing games of every kind and hearing laughter drift up through the floorboards as he nodded off at night surely planted an idea in his head: To be host, to be responsible for fun and laughter, was the ultimate. Eventually, he would erect his own carnival, one with slides and loops instead of bar games. The park was his tribute to that rec room, a way of keeping his childhood alive. It's the same thing that all of us ultimately want.

When I think about Dockie and the basement, it's easier for me to understand why my father sometimes exhibited a fanatical desire to make sure it kept going. It was a determination that manifested in the insurance debacle, in the land deal, and in the 1990s, in a series of efforts to keep the lights on. It was why we let bodybuilders jab people in the face with a stick and pushed newscasters off ledges.

Then, after more than twenty years, there was nothing left that he could do.

People tried to keep the faith. Management remained on call, ready to be dispatched to the park at a moment's notice. A skeleton crew kept working, rationing things as insignificant as toilet paper in the event he was able to spin a threadbare budget. They watered the grass knowing that, if he did pull off a miracle, he'd be mad about the brown sod.

My father, who used to scream when rides weren't finished in time for Memorial Day, could not open the park by June. When the Fourth of July in 1996 came and went and the gate was still shuttered, I knew. Disappointed Vernon teens applied for jobs at the nearest fast-food restaurants, a defection that was once unimaginable. With balances owed to First Fidelity and other creditors, and refinancing unlikely, there were no more tricks, no more last-minute ideas, no more rabbits. There was only one remaining option. He would have to sell.

It was not the first time he had floated the idea. In 1989, he had openly spoken of selling Action Park to the International Broadcasting Corporation, or IBC, the then owners of the Harlem Globetrotters and Ice Capades. Like the pairing of P. T. Barnum and James Bailey, it seemed like a perfect marriage of sensibilities, and the IBC made an attractive offer. But just when a deal seemed imminent, it fell apart. Officially, the IBC said they wanted a more polished operation. Unofficially, it may have been my father who retreated, eager to be courted but wary of actually giving the park up.

Now there was no choice. In need of a quick bailout, my father entered intense discussions with a former NHL player turned investor who was prone to attending early-morning meetings, taking his fake front teeth out, and pulling a Budweiser from his briefcase. He was, in short, a perfect prospective buyer for Action Park. He was backed by Praedium, an investment group that flipped resorts like investors flip houses. (Coincidentally, Warner Brothers sold off Six Flags Great Adventure to a similar venture group, Premier Parks, around the same time.)

When Praedium seemed to be in a holding pattern, Gene brought in Intrawest, a massive ski resort conglomerate based in Canada. He pointed to the boundless opportunities the valley presented for the right owner. He had carried the baton this far. Now a behemoth could come in and continue to build on the foundation he had laid out. It was the sales pitch of his career, using skills of persuasion honed as far back as his barnstorming Kirby vacuum days. And it worked.

By early 1998, Intrawest was in full possession of the resort and park, putting in a $10 million credit bid and assuming responsibility for Great American Recreation's various outstanding loans. My father cleaned out his offices, took down the framed 1976 Alpine Slide advertisement from the wall, and walked away.

The dissolution of the park hit me in the gut as harshly as one of Bud Kelley's chickens. In my eyes, he had built Action Park from nothing, summoning rides and fun and thrills from the ground up. The park had been knitted into my adolescence, the backdrop for so many incomparable summers. There had been love and loss, fights and parties, all of it experienced through the prism of the park's unbelievable energy. It was like my life had been plugged into an amplifier. Now someone had ransacked my childhood closet, throwing out every toy, piece of sports gear, and memento I had ever accumulated. Instead of a video game system and an old hockey stick, someone had put an entire amusement park out on the curb.

Julie was equally dismayed, having spent so much of her life helping define the park's identity and putting out its many fires, both figurative and those that consumed giant water slides. We lamented that our friends were losing their jobs. Only my mother felt any sense of relief. The park had been my father's mistress for decades. It had finally lost its hold on him.

If my father felt sentimental, he didn't share it. There was no demonstration, no goodbye, no lament. His stoicism allowed for no external reaction to the loss of something he had spent two decades building and refining.

"There's so much other stuff to do," he said, and turned to the array of other businesses that demanded his attention, once again filling his time and his mind so he didn't have to think about it.

I believed him. For a while. And then I saw the stack of brochures on his desk, brought back from the trade shows in Florida. He was still attending, still inspecting rides he no longer had any use for.

WHILE I DIDN'T NECESSARILY EXPECT THE NEW OWNERS TO HAIL MY father as a visionary, I thought they might at least acknowledge the park as a pioneering effort in New Jersey recreation. Instead, they treated it like a condemned building that needed to be fumigated.

Action Park, a spokesperson said, would be revitalized, its "tacky midway atmosphere" and "carnival air" relegated to the past. They called the guests "testosterone-driven ruffians" who promoted injury and misadventure. "Thrill-seekers" would be banished. They claimed not even "third-world countries" would use equipment as decrepit as the creaking ski-lift chairs. I wanted to note that most third-world countries did not have ski lifts, but it seemed a moot point.

Vernon was predictably ecstatic over the sale. In its collective mind, the town was getting the best of both worlds. The park would remain, a rising tide that floated nearby businesses. (When it was closed, revenue for area storefronts like pizza places and gas stations plummeted.) And my father, their longtime nemesis, would no longer be in charge, finally unseated from his perch as a bulldozing developer. It was the deal they had been promised a decade prior, when the state had first sworn to evict him.

Even better, his replacement had a reputation for grand-scale development. Intrawest promised that their acquisition of Vernon Valley and Action Park was the first step into a greater future, one that would make Route 94 a full-fledged Main Street, with a shopping district and lodging all done in the style of a 1900s rustic village. Intrawest had a ton of money and no reservations about spending it. For their bucolic project, they needed a sewer solution, as the additional waste would exceed the sewer bandwidth already in place. Their idea was to send the sewage to a treatment plant five miles away and then five miles back to Vernon to be put in the ground. It was like a shit autobahn. Years earlier, my father had put in a similar length of piping for his sewer expansion. He spent $1 million. Intrawest somehow spent $20 million. It was a sign of indiscriminate spending to come.

Then they got to work on the park.

The opening salvo was the complete removal of Motor World, now considered an outmoded participation attraction that relied too much on the judgment of intoxicated drivers. Part of the area became a wetland sanctuary, a peace offering to the environmentalists who consistently opposed any kind of development. Next went the bungee tower and the newly opened Space Shot, their acceleration of the human form deemed too perilous. Scott Albershitter and his Aerodium were gone, too. (He never returned my boots.) Intrawest discarded all of it in an attempt to dwindle the testosterone-driven ruffian population. In order to persuade someone to spend $800,000 on one of their deluxe condos, Intrawest needed park guests to be as well behaved as possible. I was surprised they didn't demand visitors come in black tie.

Walking the revamped grounds, which now carried the generic name of Mountain Creek Waterpark to further divorce itself from its bloody past, came as a shock to my system in the summer of 1998. I looked for Surf Hill, where we had once launched ourselves into the air. The lanes remained, but they were roped off and dry to the touch. At Roaring Springs, the highest Cliff Dive jump had disappeared, leaving only the shorter platform. The brutal taunting of frightened jumpers had gone silent. The water quality was tested every two hours, the better to detect urine or feces from rogue swimmers. The steps snaking around the area now had non-skid coating. In a sure sign my father was no longer in charge, handrails were everywhere. (I wished we had them the time a hemophiliac visited the park and lost his footing. That was a dark day.)

Over at the Wave Pool, the depth had been reduced to just five and a half feet and the waves adjusted so that even a toddler could remain upright. There was still no single entrance, but the sides had been roped off so people couldn't just spill over like lemmings. Guests bobbed jovially in the nontreacherous current. A few actually seemed to be sleeping in their inner tubes.

Unable to resist, I peeked inside the pump room. There was no bed.

Approaching the Alpine Slide, I was relieved to see it was still standing. But as I walked closer, I noticed that patrons going down it were wearing helmets and knee pads. They seemed to be moving down the track at a relatively glacial pace. At the top, a video played on a monitor demonstrating proper use of the joystick and safety measures.

"Hello, and welcome to the Alpine Slide," a genial announcer on a fuzzy screen said. "Before you ride, we'd like to take a moment to ensure you have the safest experience possible. First, grab your helmet . . ."

The carts, I later learned, were modified to go at a more moderate speed, a far cry from the days when they had been hacked to tear down the lane until your cheeks billowed out. Even with all these safety measures, the attraction still made Intrawest nervous. In time, they would remove the Alpine entirely. With guests insulated from danger, overall park injuries would soon drop by two-thirds.

I instinctually kept looking around, bracing for a sprinting and thoughtless teenager about to plow into me in their rush to get to the next ride, but everyone was walking at a normal pace. I heard no squawking of radios, no static-filled screams for reinforcements, no team of medics sprinting through crowds with backboards to assist moaning patrons. The brewery, which had powered much of their poor judgment, was long gone. The park, which had once carried the chaotic sounds of a rock concert, now carried the quiet buzz of a community pool.

I searched for anything that looked familiar. The Kamikaze was renamed the Aqua Shot. It would soon be removed altogether, a victim of its inescapable ability to separate bodies and bathing suits. Rides with names like H2-OH-NO!, Vertigo, and Vortex dotted the landscape, promising to drop people from steep heights or through darkened tunnels and arrive at a leveled-out water slide. These were big, mass-produced things, corporate in concept from their bright colors to their lack of character. High Anxiety was a giant, yellow-and-red funnel that spirited people around its surface, a grotesque construction that stuck out like a sore thumb. Something called the Amazing Maize Maze used up four acres of a cornfield and let children collect "clues" to solve a puzzle. Without the snakes, though, there was little incentive to escape.

The feeling of something else being off nagged at me throughout the park. It was like walking into a familiar room and knowing something is out of place before you realize what it is.

Then I noticed it. Workers had taken down the Cannonball Loop. The site was now a blank space of uneven grass. It had stood right up until the end, my father never losing hope we would someday get it up and running.

I had come to see what had happened to Action Park, but it had not changed. It was simply no longer there at all.

I KNEW THAT CONFINING THE PROPERTY TO THE BOUNDARIES OF A standard water park, a generic and sterile place to take an expensive shower, was self-defeating. But it no longer carried the Mulvihill name. I could do nothing but watch.

Emulating my father's stoicism, I tried not to dwell on it. There was always plenty to do. My career in real estate development continued. With my father, I built Ballyowen, a golf course that became the top public course in the state, and which counted the pride of Ireland, Ann Murphy, among its operators. Falling in love with Vernon, she had made America her permanent home. The Crystal Springs development, consisting of a hotel, hundreds of residential homes, a golf course, and a spa, demanded all our focus. As president, I went to town meetings for approvals in place of my father. One day, I was approached by an employee from the Department of Environmental Protection, the people who had once tried to turn the town into Three Mile Island.

"Hey," he said. "You related to Gene Mulvihill?"

"He's my father," I said, and braced for a swing.

It never came. "Guy is a fucking legend here," he said. "The shit he pulled? Fucking legend."

I nodded, not sure if it was a compliment or a warning.

Over the course of the next decade, my father threw himself into other ventures that occupied practically every minute of his day. With Splinter and Topher, he pursued a robotic parking garage start-up. The wine cellar grew into one of the largest in the country, holding fifty thousand bottles. It was one of the main selling points of the widely acclaimed restaurant Latour that he opened at Crystal Springs. He also invested in a wine scanner that used magnetic resonance imaging to pick up levels of acetic acid and aldehyde, markers of deterioration. The machine could tell if the wine had gone bad without opening it, the better to value vintage bottles before they changed hands for considerable sums of money. It didn't quite take off, though. Facing resistance from the wine community for such progressive scrutiny, he said he would simply bide his time until they caught up to him. It was the story of his life.

He never completely abandoned the amusement trade, and his visits to the industry shows were fruitful—though now he was going as an exhibitor, not a buyer. Partnered with Stan Checketts, he built up a roller-coaster-and-amusement-ride firm, S&S Power, into one of the largest in the country, tapping into the single amusement genre that he had always avoided. Stan's ingenuity had drawn him in. For a while, S&S laid claim to having the world's fastest roller coaster—the Thrust Air 2000, which was installed in Japan and used compressed air to go from zero to 100 miles per hour in two seconds. The two also put a Space Shot–style ride dubbed the Big Shot on top of the Stratosphere Hotel in Las Vegas.

S&S forced its way into an industry dominated by only three coaster manufacturers, and when he and Stan sold the business, Gene made what might have been the single biggest windfall of his entire career. He had become Stan's Bob Brennan, funding his wildest notions.

Despite their success together, Stan never forgot the pull-up contest double cross. Once, Gene dispatched Topher to Utah to examine a ride idea that consisted of a chair lift that accelerated down a cliff. Stan instructed Topher to hop on and told him an automatic brake would kick in halfway down. As he careered down the cliff, the chair picking up speed, Topher was certain something had gone horribly wrong. He heard Stan yelling at him to pull the manual brake. There was no brake in sight. Topher screamed. He considered leaping from the seat and risking two broken legs to avoid a collision. Stan had not told him there were springs that would ease the chair to a slow stop at the bottom. Somewhere, *Live at Five*'s Ben Farnsworth was smiling.

As my father thrived, Intrawest, lacking his acumen in how to manage both the town of Vernon and its expectations, stumbled. Its major resort project, the Appalachian, opened a year late with units that were wildly overpriced. Its promises to renovate Route 94 into a Thomas Kinkade painting never materialized, which upset the people who had purchased condos based on assurances of such development. Lawsuits were launched, and property values dropped. The ski lodge burned down in an electrical-panel fire in 1999, forcing Intrawest to put up a temporary tent in its place. The owners promised to erect a bigger, better building within months. Instead, the tent remained for more than a decade as spilled beer soaked into its floor, creating a permanent stench.

As he had done with the Playboy Club, my father simply watched. And waited.

"NO," JULIE SAID. "NO. YOU'RE NOT DOING THIS. YOU CANNOT DO this."

It's 2010. My father has just told us he is buying back Action Park.

"No," Julie said, looking stunned, as though she just received a troubling medical diagnosis.

An even bigger conglomerate, the massive Fortress Investment Group, bought out Intrawest back in 2006, but Fortress was suffering from another real estate recession and missed a $524 million debt payment. Their ski investments were ailing from warm winters. Worst of all, no one in this gigantic operation had the first clue about how to run an amusement park.

Desperate to reinvigorate the property, Intrawest leased the water park to Palace Entertainment, hoping to benefit from its greater experience in managing amusements. When that failed to have any impact, Intrawest threw in the towel. They let it be known they were looking to sell, and sell cheap. My father swooped in, closing a deal in May 2010. He put in $700,000 and enlisted partners to fund the remaining $6.3 million. That was $7 million for a park and ski resort that had, conservatively speaking, $50 million worth of improvements over the past thirteen years. The screams of the NIMBYs could be heard from miles away.

"Don't worry," he said. "We'll get operators to run it."

"Oh, for God's sake," Julie said. "You know that's not going to work." Action Park was like a classic car that needed the delicate handling of a specialist mechanic, not a Jiffy Lube, and Julie knew it. "I'll run it," she told him.

"That's good, Julie," I said. I was happy for the two of them. I started to walk out the door.

"You're coming with me," she said.

I wanted to say no. I probably did say no many times. I was far removed from my park days and deep into a career as a developer. But I also had the same intrinsic reaction to someone else running the park that she had: It was bizarre and frustrating. The interim owners had remodeled the park based on a business plan instead of a sense of fun. It had lost its spontaneity. More important, it had lost us. It was like getting back a family heirloom.

"Okay," I said.

In classic Julie fashion, the first thing she did was tighten up the loose work ethic that had been allowed to flourish under the lackadaisical watch of Palace Entertainment, which remained through the summer of 2010. (We immediately got rid of them, and they immediately sued us for doing so, the first grand lawsuit of our comeback.) Charlie O'Brien had passed, and the ground troops at the resort lacked a terrifying authority to keep them in line. Like a crime-sniffing hound, Julie ferreted out party shacks on the mountain full of vodka bottles and rolling papers where workers would go to goof off during the day, a habit we thought had evaporated with the end of the 1980s.

The singed husk of the ski lodge was particularly grating to all of us, and it became a priority to restore it, as well as vastly improve upon its original 1960s design. Predictably, my father announced an impossible timetable of just eight months, so it would be ready for the

2011–12 ski season. Sensing an opportunity to leave my mark on the property, I strove to create a place where big-time operators from Aspen or Vail, Colorado, would come and feel like they needed to up their game. We opened a fine-dining restaurant called the Hawk's Nest, with a massive fireplace, giant windows, and chairs made from skis. Upstairs, a bar ran the length of a food court and dining area, where skiers would wait for a ceremonial ringing of a bell before warming up with shots, a new ski tradition that I dubbed the "shotski." All of it featured real wood walls and exposed beams.

The lodge, and everything in it, was one of my favorite projects, and I stood nervously as my father walked through it for the first time. He took it in like I had shown him a secret room of the Louvre. I let out an exhale as he wrapped an arm around me and told me he was proud.

ONE OF THE FIRST THINGS WE DID UPON REACQUIRING THE PROP-erty was reopen Surf Hill, long my favorite attraction in the park. It was also our first indication that things would be different. By 2011, the regulatory responsibility for theme parks had long since moved from the Department of Labor to the Department of Community Affairs. Compared to the ineffectual DOL, the DCA worked with military precision. They had doubled permit fees, instituted ride-design-approval fees, and performed many more inspections than their predecessors had. As the DCA required alterations to or simply shuttered riskier rides, the injury rate amounted to just one-third of what it had been at the height of the demented 1980s. Among the DCA's strict mandates was one that fundamentally transformed the park.

"We do not want anyone in the air," one of the officials said to me. "There can be no flying."

Propelling people off the ground and into the sky was something we did with considerable skill and efficiency. It was the landings that had been the problem. We still considered that kind of thrill part of our identity. The DCA would not budge on this point, and so we reintroduced Surf Hill to the world without the two expert lanes that provided extended hang time. (To the DCA's dismay, it still had the ability to strip people nearly naked.)

We also ran into problems with a ride I had found called the Drop Kick. The Drop Kick consisted of a massive inflatable slide that propelled visitors at high speed into an airbag. It was not an expensive ride, so we took out an option on it and began making plans to incorporate it into the layout. It felt like a perfect Action Park attraction for a new era, kinetic and safe, with a slight undercurrent of danger. A woman who worked in the personnel department thought it looked fun and agreed to a maiden voyage—no bribe needed. She landed on her head and got a concussion.

"Well, this is not going to fucking work," Julie said. The Drop Kick was sent back, deemed too perilous for modern parkgoers.

The DCA also had little patience for our subjective assessment of injury severity. We now had to report everything down to a stubbed toe, and even the most minor of bruises could get a ride shut down until an investigation was completed. If there was a serious accident, we had to immediately phone it in to a hotline.

We had to use that number only once. In the Gauley at Roaring Springs—we had decided against calling it the Toilet Bowl—the foam once again came up in the tunnel, and people got stuck underneath it, the water building up around them. Dr. DeLuca and his pioneering urgent-care center were long gone, so we sent the injured to the hospital to get checked out. Save for some bumps and abrasions, everyone was fine. The first time this happened, decades prior, we were able to unclog it like a drain line and have it open within minutes. This time the state investigated for weeks.

The change in atmosphere extended to the employees. Coming to the Tarzan Swing one day, I noticed a female patron plunging into the water. I felt a jolt of recognition as she paddled away, separated from her bathing suit top. I expected to hear catcalls, including from the attendant. Instead, he averted his eyes and, as she came toward him, stuck out a shirt for her to put on. He was a complete gentleman.

The park was suddenly alive around me again, humming with people and offering a sense of the familiar, but it wasn't quite the same. The spectators at the Cliff Dive didn't scream for people to wipe out. They cheered when the jumpers finally worked up the courage to make the leap. The frenetic pace had vanished, leaving only an assembly of responsible young adults and kids milling through. We were no longer a summer camp for raving teenagers, and that was fine, except those raving teenagers had once made up 80 percent of our attendance. In a concession to this new, placid mood, my father even elected to keep the handrails up.

The thing that had distinguished us—the underlying risk—was gone. And with it, so were the people who craved that risk.

I could tell my father missed that current of danger, that feeling that anything could happen. His thoughts returned to the time he had ordered the snowmakers to chop up a pair of wooden skis to give visitors a scare. Days into the ski season, he began roaming the grounds with a fake Taser someone had given to him. It was almost like a cattle prod, a long stick with twin probes at the end that lit up and made a buzzing noise at the press of a button. In anyone else's hands, it was a harmless toy. In his, it meant chaos.

He whispered conspiratorially to some of the staff, instructing them to get in line without a lift ticket. Suddenly, Gene materialized, driving the Taser into their bellies. The Taser lit up with a *zzzztt* sound, as though it were pulsing with voltage, and the employees fell to the ground in mock agony.

"Ya gonna try to get in line with no ticket, huh?" he said, jabbing their armpits. "Take that!"

He arranged for the Ski Patrol to come and haul the employees away, never letting on to the customers in line that it was a joke. He couldn't stop laughing about it for weeks. Julie was upset. Visitors posted on Facebook: "What kind of place is this?"

It was Gene's place.

A painting I commissioned for my father of everything he had built and the characters he had collected over the years.

My mother and my father.

EPILOGUE

Shortly after my father passed away, in October 2012, Hurricane Sandy bombarded New Jersey. It was one of the worst storms in the history of the state. High winds and torrential rain washed over the population like a biblical disaster. People lost power for weeks. Roads were closed, and gasoline was scarce. Yet the weather did not prevent scores of family and friends from ignoring the travel cautions and descending into town to pay their respects.

They were determined to come and bid a proper goodbye to Gene.

The pews at Christ the King Church in Harding Township were filled with rows of friends and family, knitted together, knee-to-knee, like revelers along the benches at Oktoberfest. Wacky Joe and the snowmakers came in suits, the first time I had seen them in anything other than flannel. Generations of Laziers mixed with Gene's country-club friends. John Steinbach sat quietly, six decades of friendship heavy in his heart.

Father Boland spoke for all of us. He recalled the bond that had started with Gene screaming about litter and deepened through a well of mutual generosity. He revealed a dimension to his friend's personality that was rarely detailed, telling us of the leaky roof Gene had sent his men to fix, and of all the times Gene listened when Father Boland brought him tales of parishioners who couldn't pay their mortgage or their hospital bills. Quietly—so quietly that few of us had ever heard such stories—my father would take care of those in need.

Other times he was not so subtle. Once, Father Boland recounted, he was looking to sell some church property that wasn't properly zoned. He was sure he would be taxed into oblivion as a result. Gene stood up at a town meeting, as he often did, but this time it was not to argue over the Aerodium or hamburgers. It was to defend his friend.

"Father Boland is a saint!" he railed at the board. "This is a church that gives back to our community! I can't believe how you're treating this poor priest!"

The town knew my father could keep this up for weeks. Father Boland got his commercial approvals that day.

There was the marine scholarship fund he had started, a nod to his own military service. The radioactive soil rallies. The golf tournaments for charities. The condos that acted as housing for people who needed a place to stay. The jobs he created when his friends needed to work. The wine he poured freely. When a childhood friend of his named Henry Porter became a prison chaplain, he received unsolicited checks every three months to underwrite his calling. When a friend named Billy Imgrund had serious eye surgery in New York City, Gene dispatched Vinnie Mancuso to drive his wife to and from the hospital. When Jimmy Sturr casually mentioned wanting to start a local variety television show, my father walked away, then reappeared with a check for ten thousand dollars.

Whatever Gene was fortunate enough to have, he shared. He kept nothing to himself, including the park, where kids of modest means, accompanied by Father Boland, were ushered in and fed for free.

The church filled with memories of his time among us. He was loyal to his friends. He stood behind everything he sold, whether it was a ride or a vacuum cleaner. He trusted his troops, including his own children, to march alongside him. He went to church weekly. He was, in all ways, a believer: in a higher power, in people, and in himself. Someone spoke of the fact he had squeezed in one last New Jersey Oktoberfest a few months before he passed, and we all agreed that was good.

After the service, I remained in the front pew with my siblings. Pete had arrived from New Hampshire. Jimmy came in from Colorado. Someone brought up the old family station wagon, which he would cram with six kids, our mother, and luggage for eight. Down the highway my father would go, toward the Glen, toward a ski trip in Aspen, the speedometer nudging up to seventy miles per hour. We did not always know our final destination, but we trusted that he did, and that he would get us there.

It was like that now, the feeling of all of us squeezed into a small space, accelerating down the road. But now, he had disappeared from behind the steering wheel. Suddenly, we didn't know where we were going, and no one was driving the car.

I SAW HIM TWO NIGHTS BEFORE HE PASSED. HE INVITED ME OVER for dinner. That was not unusual, but he insisted on making me a drink, which was different. Often, I would just grab a beer from the refrigerator. This time he brought the glass to me and smiled. It was not like him to be so doting.

"This is for you," he said.

More strange occurrences followed. The day he died, I walked out of my parents' house to see five rainbows appearing in unison. A day or two later, when Hurricane Sandy smacked into the Jersey Shore, it knocked over a roller coaster at one of the ocean-side pier parks. It was as though he was taking one last swipe at the competition.

There had been no time to prepare his affairs. Until his last moments, when his salt-rich diet likely contributed to a suspected heart attack, my father was in fine health and good spirits. If he thought at all about the winter of his life, it was to make passing mention of taking a few of the resort rooms and combining them to make an assisted-living area for himself if the need arose. When Julie asked what else he had considered, or if he had made out a will, he looked at her strangely.

"What if you hit your head or something?" she asked. "Who's going to figure all this out?"

He shrugged. He could not process what she was asking. He never thought he would run out of time. Even slowing down seemed impossible.

My father's business interests had been innumerable and ongoing. Puzzling through them was overwhelming. His habit of writing contracts on napkins, or not at all, made our heads spin. Scores of business associates came out of the woodwork, insisting Gene had promised them this, hadn't delivered that, or owed them money to cover a deal that was never completed. Most seemed sincere. Some were just opportunists hoping to capitalize on his haphazard bookkeeping. It took years to make sense of his complicated portfolio.

At the forefront of it all was the park, which had been run in his absence once already. We were determined not to let it fall into mediocrity again.

Not having him around for the final word, Julie and I made our best guess as to what he would have done. The rides were uniformly expensive and required what seemed like endless analysis of their potential for success. The full weight of his approach hit us between the eyes. It took a tremendous appetite for risk to buy an attraction costing hundreds of thousands—or even millions—of dollars without a firm idea of whether it would be popular enough to turn a profit.

Looking for a port in the storm, I called Stan Checketts. He began pitching me on an attraction that had been gestating for years. Gene had been high on it, he said.

The idea was similar to the Space Shot, using compressed air to launch people into the air. This time they would not be strapped to anything. It was like the human cannonball in the circus. After sailing through the sky for one hundred yards or so, they would land in nets. Or maybe they would land in water. Stan wasn't totally sure of that just yet. He figured it would take six months or a year of testing to prove it was safe. He would install it on the Las Vegas Strip, and then, if all went well, bring a version of it to the park.

I listened. If it worked, it would be unbelievable. And Stan, unlike some of the engineers who crossed my father's desk, was recognized by his peers as a genius in the industry.

I told Stan we would talk more about it, then hung up. I thought of all the times my father had been pitched something almost as crazy. Rides that sent people down asbestos chutes and flayed them alive. Race cars powerful enough to evade police on highways. A giant ball that rolled down a mountain and shot across a busy highway. Each time, he said yes. There was no hesitation. He needed no context and no justification beyond asking himself if it was something that would thrill people and give them an experience they would talk about for years to come.

In the end, I never called Stan back about the human cannonball. I could never take the risk. I was not my father.

IN THE SUMMER OF 2014, WE REVERTED TO THE ACTION PARK NAME, ditching the Mountain Creek label. Some of the investors fretted, worried the connotation would dredge up stories of maimed visitors and apocalyptic landscapes.

"Don't worry," I said. But they were proven right.

Internet commenters began to detail injuries sustained long ago that read like case studies in a medical textbook. The national news media picked up on our throwback ad campaign and began running articles about our heyday. BuzzFeed published a laundry list of anecdotes people sent in about their brushes with disaster at the park. (Despite this testimony, I was sure no one had ever contracted hepatitis from the water, and that no one called the town ambulances the "Action Park Express." Everything else was pretty much true.) The ever-expanding Wikipedia page read like a workplace safety report. People traded stories about scars earned or mishaps narrowly avoided. The park had become a symbol for a generation that didn't need warning labels on its hair dryers.

The investors demanded a slogan to clarify that the new Action Park would not be the same liability wonderland. We came up with "All of the thrills and none of the spills."

All of this attention paid to my father's creation was oddly heartwarming. So much of it led with the bombastic wipeout tales, but they were inevitably followed by comments about how much people remembered and loved the park. Time and again, they said it was the most fun they had ever had. Rather than being "architects of their own doom," as one colorful newspaper article put it, they were the authors of their own happy memories. Enough years had passed that people could look beyond some of the more sensational headlines and see it for the innovative creation it truly was.

People were finally acknowledging Gene's pioneering spirit, too, a credit I felt was long overdue. In the late 1970s, a water park was an anomaly. Today, virtually every theme park has a "wet" component, promising to soak guests in increasingly elaborate ways. Interactivity has become a permanent fixture. Universal and Disney spent billions to immerse people in fantasy worlds like Harry Potter, where they can move freely and engage with the attractions at their own pace. After opening *Star Wars*: Galaxy's Edge in Disney World, Disney Parks chairman Bob Chapek said his goal was to make guests "active participants in their own stories." A swinging cart ride in development by an amusement manufacturer measured how loud guests in two separate compartments screamed and waved their hands. The ride sprayed the less enthusiastic group with water. Other designs in the pipeline aimed to give riders control over the direction or speed of rides so no two experiences were ever the same. My father didn't have the budget of these places, but his philosophy of leaving people in control predated them by decades.

The public appreciation of Action Park's past made me enthusiastic about moving forward. With Bill Benneyan, the park's president and chief operating officer, I traveled to the International Association of Amusement Parks and Attractions Expo, the amusement convention where my father was a celebrity. Strolling around the exhibition, I came to a dead stop in front of a booth. On the display was a photograph of a tube that ended in a three-hundred-and-sixty-degree circle.

It was a modern-day version of the Cannonball Loop.

I hurried to find Bill. "You need to see this," I said.

We talked to the men behind the booth, who were from Ohio. They explained that patrons would be strapped into small pods and loaded into the ride. Because they were basically immobile inside of the pod, which was in constant contact with all sides of the tube, they would clear the loop without running the risk of slamming their face into the slide. They had made it tragedy-proof.

"This is like the Loop at Action Park," I said.

"Oh, yeah, we've seen that," one of them said. "But this is kind of the perfected version of it."

I disclosed the entire story, from my hockey-equipment-encased test jump to our repeated efforts to keep the Loop open and free of catastrophic injury. I could think of no better way to come full circle than to finally give people the experience my father had long pursued. With no time to lose before the next season, Bill and I flew to Ohio to see it in person as soon as we could. It happened to be December.

The company had built the prototype and set it up outdoors. The temperature outside was barely ten degrees. To keep the water inside the tube from freezing, they ran ethylene glycol through a heating element rigged to a huge furnace. It kept the water flowing, creating a fine mist that rose up like stage smoke at a concert. These were my father's kind of people.

Far removed from my daredevil days, I was not about to go in first. Erin, the salesman, volunteered instead, stripping down to his underwear and strapping himself into the cage that would propel him down the slide and through the loop. With a thumbs-up, he descended into the chute and disappeared. We waited for him to emerge. We waited some more.

"He's fucking stuck," Bill whispered.

Or worse. I remembered the endless trials of the Loop and the way it mercilessly devoured flesh and teeth before expelling riders, as though it were teaching a lesson. It was possible no version of it could ever be safe.

After an extended moment of panic—the water continued to flush through the tube, providing ideal drowning conditions—they pulled Erin out through the hatch. He was conscious and unbloodied and explained that the water was still frozen in some spots. He had almost made it through.

"It'll be good to go now," he said. He smiled. I was relieved to see all his teeth intact.

I looked over at Bill, who had developed an appetite for building out the park with bigger and more ambitious attractions. I suggested he make the voyage. He was shaking like a leaf.

Mr. Mulvihill, I don't think—

You'll be fine, Bill.

He squeezed into a wet suit, promptly had a panic attack because it was too tight around his neck, and finally settled down enough to go through with it. The ride ejected him intact. It was perfect. They had eliminated the unpredictability of the Loop.

My excitement was short-lived. Crunching the numbers based on our projected attendance was sobering. Julie insisted it was more money than we could afford, and I had to agree. Doodling something and then tasking a ragtag crew of snowmakers to build it, I learned, was economically feasible in a way that cutting-edge ride technology was not.

After much deliberation, we decided not to take the risk. It was a sentiment that extended to the park itself.

The amusement business was more volatile than ever. Roller coasters ruled the day. The major parks all had branding from movies and intellectual properties. The one thing that made us distinct—the freedom—was being regulated out of existence. The park had been stripped of its novelty. When Julie and I looked to expand or add an attraction, we had to present the idea to the board of directors who had invested with Gene back in 2010. While civil, they made it clear they had agreed to do business with Gene, not Gene's kids. They trusted his judgment. Ours was another story.

Julie and I decided it was time. We sold the park to one of the investment partners, the Koffman family, in 2015. Almost as soon as it was out of our hands, the state decided to close the Tarzan Swing and the Cannonball tubes, the two remaining fixtures from the early days. A third party had come in and done biometric testing on the swing, outfitting a volunteer with a motion capture suit. Its determination was that the potential for injury began as soon as someone grabbed the rope. An activity that had been allowed for close to forty years was suddenly too hazardous. The new owners didn't have my father's temerity to fight back. They were content to be just another water park.

The Action Park entrance sign came down. This time it was for good.

THREE YEARS AFTER WE LET THE PARK GO, I INVITED MEMBERS OF the Wave Patrol over to my home for dinner. Smoke, who now sells elevators, was there. So were Bob Krahulik and Chuck Kilby. Artie Williams of Motor World came. I also invited Mac Harris, though he never soiled his hands in the park.

"Captain—" I said.

"Heineken," Mac said. "Yeah, yeah."

Smoke brought his original Wave Patrol jacket, which stretched around his shoulders, the cuffs stopping just above his wrists. The letters on the back were breaking free of the stitching and folding in half. He strutted like a prizefighter who had slipped on his old ring robe.

We spoke about the days long since gone, the summers spent corralling lunatic teenagers while we turned the color of wood varnish. I told them I had recently spoken to a veteran Vernon newspaper reporter who floated the old rumors that my father had been involved with organized crime.

"Just because your dad's best friend's father was the biggest mobster in New Jersey doesn't make him one," a slightly tipsy Bob Krahulik said, railing at the slander.

"This is not helping," I said.

Smoke reminded us that he tested many of the rides, including Surf Hill and the Aqua Skoot, in exchange for a case of beer, which he found just as desirable as the hundred-dollar bill. Smoke later used some of these liquid rewards to throw an employee party at his house while his parents were away. He thought he had cleaned up enough afterward to keep it a secret, but when they came home, they immediately confronted him about it. He had forgotten he had spray-painted ACTION PARK PARTY on his driveway with an arrow pointing to his house.

Artie, the lone veteran of the greasy Motor World crew, remembered the engine jockeys being ostracized from the park's social hierarchy, a rejection that sometimes led to criminal behavior. A mechanic who worked with Mike Kramer decided to swap out one of the Lola engines with the one in his beater car, a substantial upgrade in power. When he was found out, employees lured him back on the promise that he wouldn't be turned in. Kramer then locked the gate and called the cops. No one knew what became of Kramer, who left sometime in the 1980s. We all agreed he was probably still smashing a wrench into something.

We talked about the mountaintop parties, where Smoke insisted someone had caught fire. I didn't recall that level of idiocy, but we were prone to leaping across bonfires, so it was possible. Chuck Kilby reminded us the park once hosted the New Jersey State Lifeguard Championships, held in the Wave Pool. Doug Rounds won the first year, Smoke the second. A finer lifeguarding force you could not find.

"The bathing suits gave me jock itch," Smoke said.

"STDs have the same effect," someone said, and Smoke grew quiet.

Some of the guys who sanded down paint on the rides or were exposed to toxic fumes in the tubing expressed relief that they hadn't developed cancer. Chuck Kilby, one of the most dependable of all my friends and a man who seemingly feared nothing, admitted he never once considered going down the Cannonball Loop. He was too afraid he would get stuck and drown.

Someone brought up Blizzard Beach, a Disney water park that opened in 1995 and centered around an invented backstory that it was a ski resort that had "melted," with warm-weather attractions springing up in its place. It was either some kind of acknowledgment of my father from the Disney people, a rip-off, or the most bizarre confluence of events possible. He had longed to be the Disney of the northeast. Disney had co-opted him instead. It felt fitting.

We spoke of the now neutered Vernon property, where Mountain Creek attracted a modest number of visitors annually and was struggling financially, and of what it once was—the park we knew. People were crazed, yes, and we were part of the crew of misfits who ran it. But the chaotic atmosphere sometimes obscured the fact that my father had constructed a monument to exhilaration, a place to step outside the boundaries of everyday life. In its own unique way, the park was a fiberglass metaphor for adversity. Here was a place to navigate danger, to test your constitution and sharpen your judgment. Life doesn't follow a preset path. It doesn't roll along a track as you sit comfortably behind a safety bar. It throws obstacles in your way. It flings you into uncharted territory and threatens to knock you down. It hits you in the testicles with a tennis ball at violent speeds. You have to be tough. You have to hang on. You have to learn how to steer, bank, and navigate the curves.

Inevitably, some people will forever think of my father as a berserk

Willy Wonka, an eccentric purveyor of amusements who thrived in an era of limited regulatory oversight, a man who bent the rules until he heard them crack. In truth, his goal was to make sure everyone had the time of their lives, and we all did. The evenings he spent sketching rides, the time and effort that went into securing money, the juggling he did to keep it open summer after summer was never anything he had to do. He had plenty of success in other businesses. He did not need to enter a world as volatile as the theme-park industry, one man against corporate giants. He did it because that was his nature, because fun outweighed virtually every other consideration. He never wavered from his philosophy that life was for living and that risk was part of it. There will never be another Action Park because there will never be another Gene Mulvihill.

"Who the fuck builds a water park on a mountain?" Chuck said. "Who does that? But it worked out."

As the night wound down, and people began heading out the door, Smoke handed me his cell phone. On the screen was a picture of the Wave Patrol in our prime, a collection of young people who were tasked with more responsibility than they realized. I looked at the kids in the photo and wondered if they knew it would be the greatest job any of them would ever have. I wondered if they knew how good they had it then, and if they knew the reason why.

When I was thirteen years old, my father decided to open an amusement park.

The Wave Patrol. Top row, from left to right: Nancy Hallam, Robby Pelez, Scott King. Second row: Me, Glen Smocovich. Third row: Timmy Barber, Vinnie Mancuso, John Sweeney, Tim Olson, Tommy Smith. Bottom row: Jonathan Holl, unknown, Denise DeSimon, Augie Toth, unknown, Sue Mitchell

Acknowledgments

The mythology surrounding Action Park presented the authors with the narrative equivalent of a trip down the Alpine Slide. Go too fast and you risk getting caught up in the mania and heightened recollections of those who were there. Too slow and you can't capture the frenetic pace that defined the era. Separating fact from fiction was a priority; we did not intend to veer into the realm of the exaggerated, suffering the bumps and bruises of printing the legend when the fact is plenty insane on its own.

To supplement Andy's recollections, we spoke with more than seventy people. Some were and remain his closest friends. Others knew Gene well. All offered invaluable insight into a place that, by all rights, should never have existed, helping us understand the peculiar series of circumstances that kept the park alive and thriving for nearly two decades. All gave freely of their time and memories to help fill these pages with details of days long gone but never forgotten.

Stig Albertsson, Scott Albuschkat, Kurt Bailey, Rob Bixon, Rick Bolger, Chuck Dickinson, Glen Friedman, Rick Hunter, Bruce Kawut, Tom Merrell, Tim Nagle, Gus Picariello, Michael Redpath,

Steve Richer, Evan Schuman, Bob Wolek, and Gary Zuercher all gave us much-needed perspective on the park's operational side.

Father John Boland, Bob Brennan, Bunny Cacula, Suzy Chaffee, Stan Checketts, Al DeCotiis, Bud DiFluri, Tommy DiMaggio, Bill Dusche, Carmen Imgrund, Mark Imgrund, "Wacky" Joe Mazier, Vic Marotta, Sam McNulty, Jessi Paladini, Mike Palardy, Tony Pecoraro, Chaplain Henry Porter, Adam Ringler, Roy Scovill, John Steinbach, Jimmy Sturr, Marshall Swartwood, and Debra Evers Tierney helped pull back the curtain on Gene.

Phil Altinger, Benji Bressler, Bill Benneyan, Jim Bineau, Dave "Brownie" Brown, Andy Buckley, Kevin Curley, Mac Harris, Dale Kelley, Chuck Kilby, Bob Krahulik, Mike Mancuso, Vinnie Mancuso, Vernon "Kip" Merritt, Nicole Molina, Ann Murphy, Steve Sokil, Kevin Steinbach, Rich Szuch, Jeff Taylor, Adam Tracy, Charles "Chaz" Wagnor, Rob West, Artie Williams, and Laurie Zickler rewound their friendship with Andy to jog memories and add details. A special thanks to Glen "Smoke" Smocovich, the true heart of Action Park.

Jim DeSaye, Chris Ish, Steve Liss, Frank Sherwood, and Corrine Zimmerman wore a path around the grounds of Action Park and recalled their time with fondness.

Steve Langenthal took us through one of the darkest days in the park. We thank him for it.

Several other former park citizens contributed but thought it best to have their names withheld from print as they are now respectable members of society. Where requested, names were changed to protect the extremely guilty, and some of the more rampant excesses were omitted owing to matters of good taste. If you see one of the authors in person, they'll be happy to share a few tales.

Many people who helped define the park are no longer with us. We're certain they're building rides or chasing trouble up in heaven with Gene. Otto Binding, Jim Conlin, Tom Conlin, Dick Croul, Sam DeGonge, Ron Dyno, Pat Galgano, Phil Gerard, Stanley Holuba, Bud Kelley, Jack Kurlander, John Lehman, Charlie O'Brien, Al "Indian" Paugh, Amos Phillips, and Bobby Piercy will never be forgotten.

We're forever grateful to Jon Fine for seeing a spark of potential in the story of Action Park, and to Rick Kot at Penguin Random House for listening to his friend Jon Fine. Sam Raim at Penguin picked up the baton and saw us through the challenging prospect of telling three stories in one—Andy's, Gene's, and the park itself. He smoothed the rough edges and got us back on track when we were lost in the woods. Cliff Corcoran examined the manuscript with a diligence not normally associated with Action Park and we're better for it. Alec Shane at Writers House believed in the story from its earliest incarnation, which was scarcely more than a loose assembly of ideas, and walked us through the nuances of the publishing business with support and welcome optimism. Finally, Matt Klise saw us to the finish line. This book owes its existence to them.

It was a serious responsibility to the Mulvihill family to do justice to their father's story. Splinter, Pete, Jimmy, and Christopher all labored to realize their father's vision, even when they didn't know what exactly that vision was. Julie was and continues to be Andy's partner in the resort business and the best operator around. Their mother, Gail, stood by Gene and the family through the best and worst of times. Ellen Mulvihill and her sister, Erin, came along for the ride, too. The park belongs to all of them.

Andy wishes to thank his wife, Katrina, who urged him to set the record straight on Action Park for their daughter, Alex, a next-generation Mulvihill carrying on the same thirst for fun, adventure, and the pursuit of greatness.

Jake wishes to thank his father, Tim, his sisters Lisa, Dawn, and Susie, and his brother, Brandon, for their unwavering support; Jenn

ACKNOWLEDGMENTS

Wood, for keeping him sane; Professor Aja Martinez, for pushing him; Anne, for always inspiring him even in absentia; and S.H., just because.

And thank you, Gene. For everything.

Except the Cannonball Loop.